GRUNTS

GRUNTS

The American Combat Soldier in Vietnam

—

Kyle Longley

Routledge
Taylor & Francis Group

LONDON AND NEW YORK

First published 2008 by M.E. Sharpe

Published 2015 by Routledge
2 Park Square, Milton Park, Abingdon, Oxon OX14 4RN
711 Third Avenue, New York, NY 10017, USA

Routledge is an imprint of the Taylor & Francis Group, an informa business

Library of Congress Cataloging-in-Publication Data

Longley, Kyle.
Grunts : the American combat soldier in Vietnam / Kyle Longley.
    p. cm.
Includes bibliographical references and index.
ISBN 978-0-7656-2285-3 (cloth: alk. paper)—ISBN 978-0-7656-2286-0 (pbk.: alk. paper)
    1. Vietnam War, 1961–1975—United States. 2. Soldiers—United States—History—
20th century. 3. Vietnam War, 1961–1975—Psychological aspects. I. Title.

DS558.L655 2008
959.704′3373—dc22   2008005110

ISBN 13: 9780765622860 (pbk)
ISBN 13: 9780765622853 (hbk)

Printed in Canada

Contents

Preface and Acknowledgments   *vii*
Introduction   *xiii*

Chapter 1   Johnny Get Your Gun: Decisions to Enter the
U.S. Military During the Vietnam War   3

Chapter 2   Building GI Joe: Induction and Recruit Training
During the Vietnam Era   38

Chapter 3   The First Wave: The American Infantryman in
Vietnam, 1961–1968   69

Chapter 4   The Winter of Their Discontent: After Tet Until the
Withdrawal and Fall of Saigon, 1968–1975   115

Chapter 5   Coming Home: Reintegrating Into Society and
Memory of the American Infantryman in Vietnam   158

Epilogue   *191*
Notes   *195*
Bibliography   *221*
Index   *235*
About the Author   *245*

Preface and Acknowledgments

In the spring of 1981 Novice Kniffen walked into our classroom with a slide projector. The tennis coach at Andrews High School in far West Texas, on this particular day he brought some personal slides to share with his young, impressionable students, most of us not far from our eighteenth birthday and registering for the Selective Service System newly implemented by hawkish President Ronald Reagan who many feared wanted to commit U.S. soldiers to a war in the jungles of Nicaragua and El Salvador.

That day, I learned more about the Vietnam War than from any textbook to that point. His slides showed a thin young man from the small town of Clyde, Texas, in the rice paddies and jungles of Southeast Asia, primarily in a forward fire base not far from the Cambodian border. He told us of stories of boredom and of one day firing with some comrades on a water buffalo; some Americans becoming so angry after hitting it countless times and it refusing to stay down that they ultimately finished it off by tossing a grenade and blowing it up. I sat transfixed at how he retold the story of the base being overrun by the enemy and how he jumped in a foxhole and just fired at anything, ultimately being one of a few hundred who walked away unscathed.

The presentation by Coach Kniffen firmly embedded in me an interest in the Vietnam War, one punctuated by walking past a triangular U.S. flag that stood at the front of the principal's office at Andrews High School with the picture of a young Marine, a casualty of the Vietnam War. I never realized, however, that some day I would embark on the path of writing a book about the experiences of American combat soldiers in Vietnam.

Yet, the pull always existed. When I started on the path toward a PhD in U.S. foreign relations, I ultimately chose the University of Kentucky, where I studied with George Herring, one of the deans of the historians of the Vietnam War. In graduate school, I focused on the United States and Central America, but most of my closest colleagues concentrated on the Vietnam War. I resisted the urge until I began a biography of prominent antiwar senator Albert Gore Sr., which returned me to the topic. Then, one day, I read a powerful story about a group of nine young Marines from Morenci, Arizona, and their experiences in the Vietnam War. At that juncture, I decided to work on two simultaneous projects on grunts, going back full circle to that day when I first became nterested in the topic in Coach Kniffen's class. The ultimate result has been this book and a forthcoming one on the Morenci Marines.

There are so many people to thank for their support and assistance during this process. First, Marilyn Young, George Herring, Mark Von Hagen, and Carol Reardon read the manuscript, as well as Lieutenant Colonel John Shaw who read several chapters. Each took time out of their busy schedules, and meticulously reviewed the pages and made recommendations on how to improve them. In addition, my great friend Bob Brigham always provided support and suggestions on materials to reference, building on his own work on the Army of the Republic of Vietnam (ARVN). Since graduate school, he has remained a close friend and confidant, and along with his wife, Monica, provided me encouragement in many endeavors.

Others along the way, particularly people working at numerous archives throughout the country, have been very helpful. Jim Ginther at the Marine Corps Archives in Quantico, Virginia, deserves special recognition for helping me on both projects. In addition, various archives, including those of the Texas Tech Vietnam Center and the University of Kentucky, have been especially good sources of materials, providing hard copies as well as creating wonderful Web sites that made available very useful oral histories. Their staffs have made the research on this book much easier.

A special thanks goes to my close friend and mentor Shirley Eoff, Professor of History at Angelo State University. She provided wonderful editorial support, reading and correcting every grammatical misstep. This proved an especially hard duty as her brother, Eddie Eoff, served as a tunnel rat in Vietnam. Severely wounded, he ultimately died at an early age of cancer related to exposure to Agent Orange. I know she relived a lot of her experience dealing with her brother's severe wounds and early death, and I truly appreciate her assistance in the past, present, and I am sure the future.

I also wish to recognize several colleagues and friends who have been especially helpful. At Arizona State University, I have the great pleasure of working with wonderful colleagues who have challenged me intellectually in the classroom, numerous doctoral and master's committees, and private conversations, including Ed Escobar, Art Rosales, Kent Calder, Catherine Kaplan, Steve Batalden, Linda Woods, Gayle Gullett, Phil Vandermeer, Peter Iverson, Don Fixico, Steve MacKinnon, and James Rush, as well as my Learning Community friends, Keith Miller, Roxanne Doty, and James Foard. I also must recognize my wonderful friend and intellectual mentor Vicki Ruiz, who remains one of my closest confidants. Finally, many in my field have been supportive of me, such as David Anderson, Andy Fry, Mike Schaller, Robert Schulzinger, Robert McMahon, Nick Sarantakes, Mitch Lerner, Seth Jacobs, Fred Logevall, Mark Lawrence, Thomas Schwartz, Walter LaFeber, Emily Rosenberg, Darlene Rivas, Mark Gilderhus, Jurgen Buchenau, Jason Colby, Lorena Oropeza, Jeffery Wasserstrom, Brad Coleman, Jim Siekmeier, Mike Parrish, Chip Dawson, and many, many others.

I have many family and friends to thank for their encouragement and support along the way, including my parents, Joe and Chan, who have nurtured me over the past forty-four years. They made many sacrifices so I could pursue my passion for history and teaching, and my father especially provided for me a great role model of what an educator should and could be. The same goes for my best friend, Dwayne Goetzel. He and his wife, Dawn, have been wonderful comrades and great supporters, always ready to listen to me and provide words of encouragement. Also, a special thanks goes to Dick and Alice "Dinky" Snell, who have supported my work with a generous fund with which to do research and attend conferences. I owe them a lot for being such good benefactors.

Finally, I want to thank a series of friends whom I have made over the past five years as I worked in our President's Community Enrichment Program. They include Irving and Barbara Rousso, Migs Woodside, Peter and Regina Bidstrup, Merv and Lorraine Lakin, Dick and Olga Seiler, Ken Veit, Bernard and Carolyn Garrett, Carol and Shel Sobel,

Shirley Baker, Phyllis Shycon, Mikki and Stanley Weithorn, Barbara Gallagher, Bob and Rona Rosenthal, Jay Simon, Glenna Shapiro, Fred Salmon, Bernie Goldman, Alan and Joan Cohen, Jean and Jim Meenaghan, Janis Lyon, Kathy Simon, and Harriett Friedland. In particular, I am going to miss Harvey and Steve. These along with many others have been good friends and given me some of the best teaching experiences ever. I only wish all my classrooms had such enthusiastic, intelligent, and supportive students.

This book is dedicated to some wonderful people who have played a significant role in my life. First, George Herring has been my intellectual mentor as well as good friend for nearly twenty years. I remember my first meeting with him at Billy's Barbeque in Lexington, Kentucky, when I faced a decision regarding schools for doctoral studies. I knew immediately that he would be the best choice for me. As many of his students can attest, George provided a wonderful experience to anyone willing to listen and learn from one of the most approachable and intelligent mentors available to younger scholars. I spent many hours in his classroom amazed at the breadth and depth of his knowledge. We also spent many hours outside of the classroom playing softball, attending department and private functions, and just hanging out where I watched and learned from a true master of the field and, just as important, found out how to be a good mentor and colleague. I try to tell him often how much he has meant to me in my personal and intellectual development, but I fear the words will never fully express my true gratitude for the time and energy he has devoted to me.

In a different way, I want to recognize two important people who helped me during and after graduate school. Dottie Leathers and Darlene Calvert proved that the most important people in graduate school often remain the administrative assistants who help graduate students like myself wade through the often seemingly insurmountable bureaucracy. They also proved loyal and supportive friends who went above and beyond the call of duty with invitations to their homes for dinner and other socials and contributed daily emotional support in a process that often proved difficult. As in so many other departments, administrative staff like Dottie and Darlene holds a department together and makes life easier and more enjoyable for both faculty and graduate students. I thank both of them, and only wish Darlene had lived long enough to see this book in print and my recognition of her. Nonetheless, I sincerely appreciate all they did and dedicate this book to them as well as George.

Finally, I thank the people closest to me for their support during the past four years. My wife, Maria, provided me more than she could ever know or I could ever verbally acknowledge. The daughter of an academic, she knew the drill when we married, but the wife carries much more burden than the child in terms of endless hours of the disappearance of a spouse to research and write a monograph. She endured my always talking about the project with friends and colleagues during dinner conversations and at parties. In addition, she provided constant encouragement and pushed me to finish it and quit obsessing about every little detail that she recognized did not really matter.

Maria also provided coverage for me as I had to take time away from our two sons, Sean, who is eight, and Drew, who is three. Both are the truest joys of my life, and they watched me sit for hours at the computer working away, Sean constantly asking me questions about why I had so many books on the Vietnam War and what was it (a question that remains as elusive as ever for explaining the conflict to an eight year old). I tried often to stop and listen about his day when he came bounding through the door, but too often, deep in thought, I reminded him that daddy had to work. I hated it, but someday when he reads this book, I hope he and Drew understand why I seemed so preoccupied with something that occurred forty years ago when I was their age. In the end, this was a group project with Maria providing the emotional support and the boys affording the needed distractions away from heavy topics. I truly love and appreciate them for it.

Finally, I must thank the wonderful people at M.E. Sharpe who took and molded this book into the final product. A special thanks goes to my editor, Steve Drummond, who shepherded this project through from its earliest origins. He is a great editor and just equally as good of a person. I look forward to working with him in the future as well as others, including Pat Kolb, Editorial Director, who recognized the potential and supported the project. Katie Corasaniti provided significant assistance in preparing the manuscript for production, and Henrietta Toth took it through copyediting and production with a great deal of energy. Others played an important role, including Jesse Sanchez, the designer, and Richard Gunde, the copyeditor. It has been a pleasure to work with each.

Introduction

On July 4, 1966, a brilliant, scorching sun beat down on a large crowd gathered at the bus stop at Foster Sims's Texaco station in the small copper mining camp of Morenci, Arizona. In the shadow of the red clay hills, nine young men, the oldest twenty and the youngest seventeen, waited with their friends and families to board the small white bus for the trip to Phoenix and then to San Diego.

Significant contrasts existed among them. Red-haired, fair-skinned Stan King, for example, stood six-foot-five and weighed 230 pounds, towering above Leroy Cisneros who was five-foot-five and 150 pounds with dark hair, eyes, and complexion. Despite the physical differences, they shared many things. Their fathers toiled for the Phelps Dodge Company (PD) in shifts of twenty-six days on, two days off, either in the deep open-pit copper mine or under the twin smokestacks of the always fuming smelter that pumped billows of white smoke into the clear blue sky. Each lived in segregated housing since PD put Mexican Americans in several parts of the town while Joe Sorrelman, the star quarterback and Navajo Indian whose parents spoke no English, headed each evening to Tent City in the shadows of the smokestacks and Bunker Hill Cemetery.

Overall, the group represented a cross-section of the mining camp, the children of working-class miners who had few options other than going straight into the mine or seeking their adventure elsewhere in organizations such as the U.S. Marine Corps. As one of the group, Mike Cranford, observed: "We were small-town people. We still believed in mom and apple pie. It was part of my duty as a man, growing up, to join the service. They didn't have to draft us. It was a part of what we were supposed to do."[1]

The journey had actually started several months before in March 1966. Sergeant Earl Peterson, in his Marine dress blues, had jumped in his black Cadillac and traveled more than 100 miles from another mining town, Globe. That day, several of these young men sat in Mrs. Helen Arnold's English class when she announced a pop quiz. None had prepared and each breathed a sigh of relief when suddenly the principal arrived and announced that anyone meeting with the Marine recruiter could skip the quiz. Immediately, volunteers ran toward the door, almost trampling each other in an inadvertent rush toward their future.[2]

Once in place, Peterson mesmerized the young men with stories of the world's toughest military branch, building on perceptions already strongly ingrained by John Wayne movies and the experiences of their male relatives in World War II and Korea. Soon, others arrived at the popular local restaurant, the Copper Kettle, where Peterson continued to regale them with tales of Marine lore. Despite the protests of several coaches and teachers, star football player Bobby Draper had joined them as had several others including King, who had been off at the University of Arizona but had returned home to heal a broken heart after his girlfriend rejected his marriage proposal. By the end of the day, Peterson ferried nine recruits around town in his big Cadillac with several of them hanging out the windows to proudly announce their decision.[3]

Since eight of the nine had to complete high school, they deferred their enlistment until the summer. When the nine finally arrived for boot camp in San Diego on July 5, 1966, Marine drill instructors (DIs) wearing their Smokey the Bear hats and pressed khakis awaited them. Physically intimidating and fitting every stereotype of a DI, they immediately pounced on the recruits, yelling obscenities, questioning the young men's manhood, and ordering them to line up on the yellow footsteps painted on the ground, heels together and toes pointed out with barely any room in front or behind. Dazed and disoriented, the Morenci boys reacted without question. Soon, they marched off to leave behind all vestiges of civilian life, losing their clothes, hair, and even watches as they lived now only on Marine time. They put on the green fatigues and headed to their Quonset huts to start the most grueling, exhausting trial—at least to this point—of their young lives.[4]

Unlike many others, the nine stayed together during boot camp in

Platoon 1055. They endured the demanding physical and psychological requirements of the most rigorous basic training of all U.S. armed forces. Friends provided encouragement to the heavier-set Bobby Dale, who sometimes fell behind on long, tortuous runs under the baking Southern California summer sun, his nose and lips caked in white zinc to protect his light complexion. In another case, Van Whitmer made a mistake in crossing through another platoon lined up for dinner. A melee ensued, and the other eight jumped in and saved Whitmer from a vicious beating. Being together surely paid dividends that others who entered without friends never received. In September 1966, on graduation day, they proudly posed together for numerous pictures in their dress khaki uniforms, mingling with a few parents and friends who had made the long trip from Morenci.[5]

After boot camp, only a small group stayed together, receiving the designation of MOS (Military Occupational Specialty) 0311 infantry, sometimes affectionately referred to by other Marines as MOS "Bulletstoppers." Others headed to advanced training as military police or mechanics. Within a short time, all finished the additional instruction and by December 1966, Cisneros, Draper, Sorrelman, and Larry West boarded a troop ship, the U.S.S. *General Gaffey*, bound for the Republic of Vietnam while the others headed for different destinations, including Hawaii and Guam.[6]

During the long trip over, the four stuck together, sharing memories of home as they endured living in the bowels of the overcrowded ship. Finally, after weeks at sea, they anchored in Da Nang, each rushing to the edge of the ship to finally see dry land. Cisneros remembered landing during a rocket attack and immediately understanding that they had left the safety of home. The putrid stench of urine and feces and rotting trash combined with the heavy smell of diesel and explosives filled their nostrils. The heat and humidity almost knocked them to the ground as their memories flashed back to standing in front of the huge blast furnaces under the twin smokestacks where several of their fathers toiled. For thirteen months, they would not stop sweating in the harsh, wet climate of South Vietnam, the green and lush environment that stood in stark contrast to their beloved home in the red clay canyons of Greenlee County.

Over the next two years, each of the Morenci Nine ended up in Vietnam. Miraculous stories developed. Cisneros survived more than forty missions as a point man in the very dangerous duty of Marine reconnaissance. Several times he barely missed being blown apart by enemy grenades and mines and watched several comrades die. Sorrel-man initially received a relatively safe duty of guarding an airfield, but requested a transfer to the fighting, which the Marines granted. Only a small miracle kept him from death as one day a Marine chaplain found him and told him to pack his bags due to a family medical emergency. The next day, he jumped precariously on a supply helicopter's landing skid as it bounced off the ground during a heavy enemy barrage. Once back at Camp Pendleton after attending his older brother's funeral, he learned that the day after he left, his platoon had been wiped out with the exception of one man.[7]

Not everyone was as lucky as Sorrelman and Cisneros, or West, who survived their first tour. In August 1967, while on patrol, Draper's squad walked into an ambush. Before a rapid deployment force could respond, the enemy killed everyone, reportedly putting a bullet in the head of each for good measure. A couple of months later, King died from a gunshot wound after only being in the country for six days. Thousands of miles away, at the same moment, his mother, Penny, awoke in a cold sweat. She leaned over and told her husband that Stan had been killed. A Marine officer arrived a couple of days later to deliver President Lyndon Johnson's condolences, confirming her horrible dream.[8] These early deaths struck the community especially hard as both had been star athletes, visible leaders in the small town already reeling from a lockout by PD. Elsewhere, the remaining family members of the Morenci Nine worried that the next knock on their door would be that of the Marine officer carrying the dreaded telegram from President Johnson.

Unfortunately, the Marines kept coming with bad news over the next few months. In the bloody aftermath of the Tet Offensive, Whitmer died in April 1968, followed soon after by West in mid-May, less than a month after he began his second tour of duty after having trouble readjusting to garrison life in California. Finally, Robert Moncayo had left a very easy duty in Hawaii where he had been a wrangler for horses for Marine officers and their families who took beach rides. Right before, his wealthy girlfriend's family had hosted a party on a yacht for him. He died on June 18, 1968, on a hill just outside of Khe Sanh, less than three weeks after arriving in the country.[9]

From June 1968 to November 1969, the Marine officers carrying telegrams from the president stopped their visits to the families of the Morenci Nine. Sorrelman, Cisneros, and ultimately Cranford mustered out of the Marines and returned home to work for PD. That left only Clive

Garcia Jr. in the military, although many others from Morenci remained in Vietnam. Garcia originally had received assignments in Hawaii and Guam. He impressed his commanders so much so that the Marines sent him to Army Ranger training, which he finished and proudly donned his black beret whenever possible. Restless, he kept requesting duty in Vietnam, despite the misgivings of his worried mother, Julia, whom he had told upon returning with the body of Moncayo that: "Your eyes are swollen. You've cried too much, Mama. Life itself really isn't that bad. We only have a few sad minutes, and all we can do is accept and live with reality."[10] He argued that his friends had served, telling his brother that "I must go do my part" or "I might just as well spit on the graves" of his fallen comrades.[11]

Finally, the Marines honored his request despite his recent engagement to a beautiful Californian, Susie Hibbard. In late November 1969, he and his radioman tripped a booby trap and both died. A dispute arose over the event as the "official" story reported that he was near his base camp, and he died immediately.[12] Yet, a comrade with Garcia when he died later told the family that he had been in Laos running a secret mission when the explosive detonated. Instead of dying instantly, he suffered since commanders denied repeated requests for his extraction, as according to official policy there were no Americans operating in Laos at the time.[13]

Garcia's death triggered national interest in the story of the Morenci Nine. The *Los Angeles Times*, *Arizona Republic*, *Time*, and ABC News dispatched people to cover his funeral. They found a community reeling from the deaths, but not surrendering to the grief of the loss of six of their young men in such a short time. Coach Vern Friedli stressed, "This is too tough a community to be broken. Bent, perhaps, even stretched out of shape. But not broken."[14]

Garcia's funeral took place on a dreary, overcast day with grey skies barely hanging above the small town on Tuesday, December 9. The Catholic church that had hosted funerals for others who died in Vietnam again opened its doors to one of its own. However, this time, it was in the process of being torn down as PD expanded the mine and buried the old town under tons of rocks. As a result, people covered the windows with plastic to prevent the cold wind from rushing in.[15]

Despite the weather, hundreds crowded into the building to pay respects and view the flag-draped coffin in the shadows of the large crucifix flanked by statues of Mary and Joseph. Three Irish priests led the service, as Clive's six-year-old sister, Kathy, walked hand in hand with one of her older brothers to the front of the church to stand alongside their grieving parents.[16]

After a heartrending Mass, a caravan traveled to the cemetery situated in the shadows of the fuming smokestacks where only eighteen months earlier Garcia had stood and helped bury Moncayo. After the honor guard fired the twenty-one gun salute, one that jolted family members, Julia rose from her metal chair under the cold drizzle and leaned over the coffin as they prepared to lower it and said: "Thank you for being my son, my son. Oh, my dear boy, thank you so much." Soon, the last of the dead of the original nine took his final resting place in the red clay of their home.[17]

Afterward, the story of the Morenci Nine quickly faded from the consciousness of most of the country. Some efforts unfolded to write a book and one Hollywood producer approached the families to develop a movie, but the family and friends and, to a large degree, the community resisted. They preferred to handle their pain and anguish individually.[18]

Cisneros, Sorrelman, and Cranford especially dealt with the problems of "survivors' guilt," questioning why they had returned and their friends had not. Cisneros appeared to handle it the best, maintaining the memory of his friends while moving on with his life although he battled various demons.[19] Sorrelman experienced flashbacks and admitted to drinking too much and fighting often in an effort to displace his anger.[20]

Cranford in particular struggled as he remained in the area, while the others left after the disastrous 1983 Strike. Wracked by guilt as he worked with West's father and burdened by undiagnosed post–traumatic stress disorder (PTSD), he fought the demons with alcohol and self-destructive behavior. At one point, he had crosses with the names and dates of death of each of his six friends tattooed on his left arm, running from his wrist to his shoulder. Ultimately, in 2004, he finally received treatment and a monetary settlement for what doctors in the VA hospital in Tucson characterized as a severe case of PTSD.[21] He recently died at the age of fifty-eight.

Time ultimately helped heal some of the wounds and allowed for some efforts to remember the group, although they continued to remain local. Cisneros has emphasized the importance of remembering his fallen comrades: "I don't want them to be forgotten because they sacrificed their lives. Those guys have been dead for 30 years but not in my mind. I want my kids to at least know that Bobby Draper, their dad's best friend, died in Vietnam for a good reason."[22] On July 4, 1997, a committee erected a memorial to the nine at Morenci High School. Located just outside the main entrance and beside the flagpole, it recognizes the individuals of the Morenci Nine. Daily, it serves as a reminder to the young people of their sacrifices and is part of local political culture that continues to serve as a major conduit for the armed services.

Later, Vietnam veterans built a memorial on the bluffs overlooking Clifton, Morenci's sister city only a few miles down the mountain. Again, the Morenci Nine figure prominently as their dog tags hang along a wire with those of other Greenlee County veterans from all the country's wars, running underneath the flags of all the branches of the military that stand behind a large American flag. Underneath is a box containing a Bible and a plaque on the front quoting John 15:13: "Greater love has no one than this, that he lay down his life for his friends." On the windswept bluff above the red canyons cut by the San Francisco River, the lives and the deaths of many, including the Morenci Nine, remain immortalized for future generations.

Throughout the country, in small farming and mining communities, in urban ethnic enclaves and suburbs, sometimes even in affluent neighborhoods, millions of young men followed the path of the Morenci Nine. They often joined for the same reasons, partly driven by the specter of the draft, sometimes by the opportunity for adventure, and often because they wanted to prove themselves to their elder male role models. Imbued with a sense of mission of defending their country against the Communist hordes, they boarded buses and planes destined for training camps throughout the country and ultimately Vietnam.

Once in Vietnam, the young men often encountered the same hardships as soldiers who preceded them in most American wars, although as the war lingered, those arriving found themselves fighting an increasingly unpopular war. They battled boredom, sometimes punctuated by intense fighting in an extremely hostile environment complete with cobras, leeches, and pesky mosquitoes. American soldiers faced a tough enemy and fought alongside, in the eyes of many grunts, an unreliable ally among an ambivalent and apparently ungrateful South Vietnamese populace.

Like three of the Morenci Nine who survived the ordeal, the typically very young American soldier returned to a country that demonstrated little appreciation for their sacrifices, especially as the war continued. They battled negative stereotypes and some struggled to overcome physical and psychological damage, although many adjusted comparatively quickly, like many of their fathers who fought in World War II. Their families, wives, parents, and children, along with friends and some comrades persevered in helping their loved ones overcome the trauma of Vietnam, although some never surmounted their experiences.

This book focuses primarily on the young men who became the combat soldiers in Vietnam, mainly Army and Marine infantrymen; as one veteran emphasized, "Nothing was more wretched than being a grunt—nothing."[23] While concentrating primarily on average soldiers, the work also presents the views of their junior officers, especially the first and second lieutenants who led them into the field. In addition, this book includes stories of others, outside of the traditional grunt label, who experienced significant combat and danger, such as the helicopter crews, Special Forces, corpsmen, and those who fought on the swift boats on the rivers of South Vietnam.

While stressing the similarities of the experience of the combat soldier in Vietnam, this work acknowledges as well the differences from time and location. A Medal of Honor recipient, Bob Kerrey, emphasized that in 1969 when he arrived:

> An army soldier with the Ninth Division saw a different war than one with the First Air Cavalry. A marine with the First Division would not have recognized the war fought by navy SEALs. Pilots faced a different set of risks, as did navy Seabees or army engineers or for that matter any of the so-called support personnel who often found themselves at greater risk than a combat grunt.[24]

Nonetheless, there were significant similarities. While each American had a different perspective, depending on where he served, when he served, and the type of duties that he performed, the plethora of sources stress far more commonalities than variations. This book seeks to re-create significant elements of the long struggle that American infantrymen experienced during their tour of duty in South Vietnam, including the homesickness, the boredom, the terror of combat, the heroism, the brutality, the guilt of surviving, the return home, and the adjustments. It also underscores the impact of the service on the family members— wives, sons and daughters, mothers and fathers, and siblings—as well as friends.

There are many challenges in the use of materials employed in this study. Oral histories and memoirs, even letters written at the time, reflect a distance of time from an event that can lead to errors. The rapidness of the events and the effects of personal perspective must be considered. Bias always enters into the process, especially after the fact, when people rarely seek to portray themselves in a negative light. Despite these challenges, the materials provide insights into the experience, usually corroborated time and time again by other veterans relating to joining, recruit training, combat, or the return home. Ultimately, significant continuities have developed from the readings of the materials in the various sources, as well as from the many others consulted that never directly reached the text.

The organizing principles of the book include important factors, such as masculinity, race, and class. Building on the works of authors such as Christian Appy and James Ebert, it incorporates more of a national approach than some predecessors.[25] The study ranges from the experiences of those from big cities such as New York and Seattle, to suburbs such as Massapequa, New York, and to smaller towns such as Morenci, Arizona, and Cookeville, Tennessee, and many other locales and regions. It also includes the experiences of African Americans, Native Americans, Asian Americans, and Latinos. While noting differences, it stresses similarities in experiences built around social constructions of masculinity and race, both at the local and national levels. These constructions help create more continuity among the stories and unify experiences.

For many younger readers Vietnam has begun to fade in historical consciousness, as a generation born after 1960 has virtually no real memories of America's longest war; instead movies and distortions through the lens of political partisanship have shaped perspectives. This book challenges the stereotypes of popular culture by using the letters, diaries, and oral histories of the Vietnam combat soldiers to highlight their significant sacrifices in Southeast Asia and to address some of the myths circling around the people who bore the brunt of the fighting and dying on the front lines in the jungles, rice paddies, and mountains of South Vietnam.

Nonetheless, some warnings are necessary. As an observer noted in relation to telling the story of the Vietnam combat soldiers: "You have to watch out for exaggerating what you did. But no matter how you try to talk about it, it still sounds bigger, worse, more deadly, and more romantic than it actually was."[26] Also, the problem of the limitations of empathy continues. One veteran emphasized that he only talked with his buddies about Vietnam. On a couple of occasions, he tried to talk to his wife about it, "but like most people, she can't visualize Vietnam in its entirety and impact. I guess you just had to be there and see it to understand it."[27]

Ultimately, a major goal of this book is to spark more research about many of the topics, as a substantial number remain underdeveloped in the existing literature. Time is a precious commodity in the process as the Vietnam veteran generation ages quickly. Too many have already died, some victims of the war years beyond when they last stepped on Vietnamese soil. Their memories, from the humblest private to the most senior leader, deserve preservation and incorporation into the social fabric of America. If this book provokes others to examine these topics further, then I will consider it a success.

GRUNTS

1

Johnny Get Your Gun

Decisions to Enter the U.S. Military
During the Vietnam War

Living most of his life on the plains of Minnesota, Vietnam veteran Tim O'Brien internalized Middle America's view of being an American. Although he earned a degree in political science at Macalester College and became an antiwar protestor, when his draft notice arrived after graduation, he answered the call to fight the Communists. He explained this apparent anomaly by stressing that "piled on top of this was the town, my family, my teachers, a whole history of the prairie. Like magnets, these things pulled in one direction or the other, almost physical forces weighting the problem, so that, in the end, it was less reason and more gravity that was the final influence."[1]

Millions of other young Americans joined O'Brien in the U.S. military, hundreds of thousands ending up on the front lines fighting the Viet Cong and North Vietnamese thousands of miles away from their homes. Like O'Brien, they faced numerous pressures to answer the call of duty, even as the war became extremely unpopular. Many national, regional, and local forces that made up the social fabric of America in the Cold War conditioned young men about their obligation to serve the nation in a time of peril. Ultimately, millions left the comparative safety of small farming communities, and mining towns, urban ethnic enclaves, and suburbs of the United States for the dangers of Vietnam. While most, like O'Brien, survived, more than 58,000 died. Those that returned often bore emotional and physical scars from the brutal conflict.

The Road to Vietnam for the Combat Soldier

Many paths to Vietnam evolved for the combat soldier. As in previous conflicts, many volunteered for service, especially in the early stages of the war, driven by patriotism, economic opportunity, and sometimes a choice of jail or the military. More than 53.1 million people comprised the Vietnam generation, with approximately 8.7 million men and 250,000 women joining and with 2.3 million serving before the war intensified in 1965. More than 15.9 million men never served, receiving deferments or never being called.[2]

In addition, many of the people who volunteered took positions in the U.S. Air Force, Navy (outside the Marines), and Coast Guard. Many chose those branches to reduce their chances of combat and because the Navy and Air Force often offered significantly more marketable skills for serviceman reintegrating into civilian society. They truly never faced the real danger of ever serving in Vietnam outside of people such as Navy corpsmen.

Ultimately, only a small fraction of the Vietnam generation, approximately 2.5 million Americans, went to Vietnam. Of those, most remained in the rear areas, and the hard fighting fell to around 300,000–500,000 young American men, the majority infantrymen, although combat engineers, artillerymen, and helicopter pilots and crews saw significant combat. Fighting the battles more than 10,000 miles from home in a place most Americans could not locate on the map before 1965, therefore, fell on a relatively small minority of the Vietnam generation.

While only a small percentage of the draft age men actually served in Vietnam, the specter of the conflict affected everyone. How to deal with military service, either through volunteering or being drafted, concerned everyone, including wives and children, girlfriends, mothers and fathers, and brothers and sisters. The war defined a generation at an early age, and continued even in its aftermath to have a substantial impact on many lives.

The Draft

The draft constituted an important factor for young men during the Vietnam War, including many who volunteered. While it had been used in periods of emergency in the United States, it was not until the post–World War II era that a peacetime draft became an ever-present reality. Yet, for most Americans today, it is a distant memory. With the movement to an all-volunteer army in 1973, a significant number of American men, those born after 1955, have no direct experience with conscription.

The draft had a significant influence in determining who fought in Vietnam. Draftees comprised many of the fighting men in Vietnam that took the field of battle, especially after 1967. By 1969, they were only 16 percent of the entire military, yet were more than 88 percent of the infantry in Vietnam. Draftees constituted 28 percent of the Army deaths in 1965 and by 1967 rose to 57 percent, with numbers increasing by 1969.[3] The system produced a steady stream of combat soldiers, both through direct and indirect coercion, for the front lines of Vietnam.

Little Groups of Neighbors

The structure of the Selective Service System had been in place with few interruptions since 1940. Older citizens, typically prominent community leaders, dominated local draft boards in counties or municipalities throughout the country in what one author characterizes as "Little Groups of Neighbors." According to the Selective Service System, each board consisted of "friends and neighbors of the registrant it classifies." Members of the board had the "responsibility to determine who is to serve the nation in the Armed Forces and who is to serve in industry, agriculture, and other deferred classifications."[4]

The national Selective Service System, headed by long-time administrator Lewis Hershey, oversaw the system that established quotas for state boards that then mandated individual board requirements determined by needs and volunteerism from the individual areas. By 1966, 4,087 local boards existed, with at least three members and typically five on each board. Usually, one paid staff member handled the paperwork and others, including medical advisers and appeal agents, helped the board. The local boards ranged in size from one in Colorado that administered twenty-seven registrants to another in Los Angeles with more than 54,000 potential draftees.[5]

The home board reviewed the files of each person and classified the young man according to his occupation, student and marital status, and medical condition. Local factors often affected this process, as some agricultural communities gave high priority to farmers, arguing that crop production affected national security. In some cases, boards generously granted exemptions to teachers. In all cases, an appeals process existed for those seeking reclassification away from the dreaded 1-A, although successes often depended on various political factors.[6]

The Letter

For many young men, the arrival of a letter from President Lyndon Johnson (and later President Richard Nixon) announcing their induction into the U.S. military constituted their worst fear. One veteran recalled, "I went home one afternoon, walked up to my bedroom and saw a letter on the bed. My father yelled, 'Jon, you got a letter. I think it's from the President.' I remember picking up that letter, looking at it and just sitting down, not believing it. I had to report in seven days to Whitehall Street [in New York City]."[7]

For many draftees, receiving the letter sparked a feeling of dread and thoughts of evasion. One veteran considered leaving for Canada but hesitated. "I had been drafted so now if I took off I was running! And I didn't want to do that." He feared being branded a felon, exiled from his country, isolated from friends and family, and forced to carry the stigma of being a coward. Plus, "at that time you didn't know [that] [President Jimmy] Carter was going to tell them, 'That's okay, come on home.'"[8]

Despite such apprehensions, the majority reported for duty, although the numbers of those failing to report increased as the war progressed. By 1967, out of the draft call of 298,559, only 7,234 failed to show up, with 1,314 prosecuted by the government for their action.[9] Several highly publicized incidents evolved such as the resistance of World Champion boxer Muhammad Ali (formerly Cassius Clay), but those occurred infrequently in the general scheme of the bureaucracy that cycled millions of Americans into the military during the war.[10]

In the end, the vast majority of young men fulfilled their duty. While many middle- and upper middle-class men actively avoided the military through a variety of maneuvers, most young men marched into the induction centers determined to complete their service, serve their country, and move on with their lives. One veteran summed up the feeling of most: "I guess I just accepted it and figured, hey, let's go give it a shot—make the best of it."[11]

Twists of Fate

The draft notice often arrived very quickly when a person lost his deferment after flunking out of school, being dismissed for disciplinary reasons, or taking off some time to earn money. In one case, a student at Johns Hopkins Medical School took an arm off a cadaver and drove the Beltway between Baltimore and Washington, DC. At one of the tollbooths, "I stuck the frozen arm out of the window with some money in the hand and left the toll attendant with the arm." Soon after, the university's president, Milton Eisenhower, whom he described as "a real fucking hawk," decided that the student needed a leave of absence. "A week later I had my draft notice. They turned me right in to the Board."[12]

In another case, local politics affected outcomes. Thomas Brown had taken more than 100 hours at Texas Tech when he decided to take some time off to work as a machinist. He thought he might avoid the call as he was twenty-four and married, but he was wrong. "I think there's a little bit of political problems on the draft board in Plainview. My father had been involved in a lawsuit with one of the guys on the draft board and I honestly think that he decided, 'Ah . . . I'll get back at him. I'll pull his son, I'll put him in the Army.'"[13] Soon after, he received his draft notice.

Many stories reflect such twists of fate. The draft often proved to be arbitrary, driven by factors such as class, race, religion, and political connections. While most Americans in the early 1960s supported the draft, by the end of the decade, opposition mounted. Calls for reform increased, leading to the elimination of most deferments and ultimately culminating in the decision to go to an all-volunteer army in 1973.

Project 100,000

Social experimentation during the "Great Society" of the Johnson administration added another dimension to joining the military and reflected on the class dimensions of the system. The establishment of "Project 100,000" at the urging of people such as Senator Daniel Patrick Moynihan (D-NY) created a very controversial program. When Moynihan discovered that more than half of those failing the Armed Forces Qualification Test came from large families with incomes under $4,000, he characterized it as "de facto job discrimination" for "the least mobile, least educated young men." In particular, he focused on African Americans, arguing that "given the strains of disorganized and matrifocal family life in which so many Negro youth come of age, the armed forces are a dramatic and desperately needed change; a world away from women, a world run by strong men and unquestioned authority."[14] In response, Secretary of Defense Robert McNamara led the charge in implementing a program, "Project 100,000," that provided more assistance to those that failed, a second chance with on-the-job training. He pronounced that "the poor of America have not had the opportunity to earn their fair share of this Nation's abundance, but they can be given an opportunity to serve in their country's defense and they can be given an opportunity to return to civilian life with skills and aptitudes which . . . will reverse the downward spiral of human decay."[15] McNamara established a goal to give at least 100,000 recruits the extra assistance necessary to enter the military.

Negative reactions characterized the overall reception of these men that became known as the "Moron Corps." One Army officer recalled that "a lot of these youngsters then began flunking out of basic and then they were recycled and they would be recycled and they would be recycled and it was tough on them." He talked about how those who failed for physical reasons received extra training, while the Army gave extra tutoring to those that could not pass written tests because they lacked basic reading and math skills. He acknowledged, "We got most of them out and through the system. Of course, they all went in the infantry units, most of them, and went overseas."[16]

In another case, a Marine lieutenant commented that his platoon had a forty-year-old machine gunner who had been a product of the "ill-conceived" Project 100,000. The other younger Marines had to take care of "Pappy." He concluded, "I had a hard time figuring out how his skills with a machine gun were going to help him earn a living after the Marine Corps."[17]

Defenders pointed out that 84 percent of the Project 100,000 men finished training only eight points below a control group of regular volunteers and draftees. Many completed their service honorably and gained some educational and job skills along the line.[18] Still, the overall program appeared poorly imagined and funneled large numbers of people from the lower socioeconomic strata and often minorities into the military where they encountered discrimination and hardships. Also, a substantial number ended up on the front lines in Vietnam.

Draft Inequities

As the Project 100,000 program highlights, the burden of the most brutal fighting in Vietnam often fell on a lower strata of American society.
Unlike the millions of draftees and volunteers during World War II who
came from all classes, many combat soldiers in Vietnam were working-
class and lower middle-class teenagers (the median age was nineteen,
as opposed to twenty-five in World War II), although there were many
exceptions. The availability of deferments for college students, people
in trades deemed of national interest, and physical and mental handicaps
reduced the draft pool significantly and created substantial inequities.

The unfairness sprang from many sources, but the availability of educational deferments for graduate students through 1967 and undergraduates
until 1969 constituted the most common. Originally designed to ensure
that the country maintained sufficient numbers of students in math and
science, the draft allowed young middle- and upper-class youths to use
educational opportunities to avoid putting themselves into the same draft
pool as most lower middle- and working-class men. When exemptions
for graduate school disappeared in 1967, the quantity of college-educated
recruits increased, although their numbers remained small in comparison
to working- and lower middle-class recruits, who had a much higher
chance of serving not only in Vietnam, but in combat units.

Many other young Americans, more than 3.5 million, avoided military
service through a medical exemption. Young men lucky enough to find
a sympathetic physician to write a document outlining a disqualifying
condition received preferential treatment. In most cases, understaffed
induction centers deferred to a private doctor's opinion, allowing exemptions for everything from bad knees (submitted by a NFL quarterback
who continued to play), to spinal conditions and psoriasis, to a pilonidal
cyst on the ass. In one Seattle area center, an observer noted that the
draftees arrived and separated into two groups, "those who had letters
from doctors or psychiatrists, and those who did not. Everyone with a
letter received an exemption, regardless of what the letter said."[19]

Racial discrimination also played a role in inequalities. African
Americans constituted 11 percent of the American population, but only
1.3 percent of the draft board members. Four southern states with significant African American populations had no African Americans on local
boards. Until 1966, Jack Helms, the Grand Dragon of Louisiana's Ku
Klux Klan, headed the largest draft board in Louisiana.[20] In the North,

problems also persisted. In New York City, African Americans constituted 14 percent of the population but only 3.3 percent of the board members.[21] The same problems confronted Latinos and Asian Americans, primarily in the West, where their numbers far exceeded their representation on local draft boards.

The National Guard and Reserves provided another form of avoidance of military service, an option heavily favored by those with political connections. More than 1 million men served in the Guard or Reserves during the Vietnam War, with only 37,000 activated and 15,000 venturing to Vietnam. President Johnson strongly resisted calls for mobilization, fearful of upsetting Middle America. Guard and Reserve appointments became prized placements. By 1968, the Guard had a waiting list of more than 100,000, which turned into a deficit by the early 1970s as the war wound down. Typically, only those with political connections, especially at the state level for the Guard, had any real chance of securing this duty that greatly reduced the chance of going to Vietnam.[22]

The sons of politicians, the wealthy, and professional athletes jammed the doors of the Guard and Reserves. As an example, Major General George Gelson Jr. of the Maryland National Guard graced the pages of *Life* in 1966 wearing a Baltimore Colts jersey and announcing: "We have an arrangement with the Colts. When they have a player with a military problem, they send him to us." In another case, the Detroit Lions traded fifty-yard–line tickets to a reserve unit for places for a star halfback and tight end. In Texas, the Dallas Cowboys had ten players in one Guard unit.[23] When combined with the scions of the wealthy, such as future vice president Dan Quayle and future president George W. Bush, the Guard and Reserve unit often appeared more like a Who's Who in America than the traditional units before and after the war.

The Guard and Reserve offered numerous advantages for the lucky ones able to find a slot. The units typically required a six-month active duty obligation for basic training and then annual summer exercises and monthly meetings. Many guardsmen and reservists found most units had a very lax attendance policy, more voluntary than mandatory. In theory, missing required meetings should have led to the person being classified as Absent Without Leave (AWOL) [Unauthorized Leave (UA) if in the Marine Corps] and required immediate activation to regular duty, although this rarely occurred. Most reservists and guardsmen simply waited out the war in the relative comfort of their homes and jobs.[24]

Numerous critics of such inequities arose. Lawrence Baskir and William Strauss wrote that "the draft was not, however, an arbitrary and omnipotent force, imposing itself like blind fate upon men who were powerless to resist." "Instead," they argued, "it worked as an instrument of Darwinian social policy. The 'fittest'—those with background, wit, or money—managed to escape. Through an elaborate structure of deferments, exemptions, legal technicalities, and noncombat military alternatives, the draft rewarded those who manipulated the system to their advantage."[25]

A two-tour veteran of Vietnam, Colin Powell, also bitterly denounced the system: "I can never forgive a leadership that said, in effect: These young men—poorer, less educated, less privileged—are expendable . . . but the rest are too good to risk. I am angry that so many sons of the powerful and well-placed and so many professional athletes . . . managed to wrangle slots in the Reserve and National Guard units." "Of the many tragedies of Vietnam," he wrote, "this raw class discrimination strikes me as the most damaging to the ideal that all Americans are created equal and owe equal allegiance to their country."[26]

Despite the critics, the majority of Americans supported the system through the early 1970s. The draft created a steady stream of American soldiers during the 1960s, both through the conscription and its ever-present coercion of many others. The system clearly discriminated against those unwilling or unable to manipulate it. While many men volunteered out of a sense of duty, for economic opportunity, or for the promises of adventure, a significant number found the push and pull of the draft an irresistible force that swallowed them into the U.S. military.

Draft Induced

The specter of the draft often played a substantial role in many young men volunteering. This became especially true as the draft calls increased after 1965 and slots in the Guard and Reserve grew scarce. An inevitably of service developed, especially for those not going to college or lacking connections to ensure medical exemptions or access to the Guard and Reserves. Unwilling to put their lives on hold, they volunteered in large numbers in an attempt to end the uncertainty and to give them some sense of control on the branch and location of their service.

Numerous surveys demonstrated the power of the draft. In 1964, 40 percent of all volunteers admitted that the fear of the draft motivated their enlistment, while the number increased to 50 percent after 1965.[27]

In Senate Armed Services Committee hearings in 1967, the annual report by the Selective Service System found that 1,090,000 enlisted men joined the service. Of that number, the military drafted 345,000 and another 380,700 joined voluntarily after receiving pre-induction notices. The overall numbers fail to include others who sought better military assignments in the Air Force or Navy to reduce the chances of service in Vietnam. Nevertheless, more than two-thirds were either draftees or subsequently draft-induced as the Vietnam War intensified.[28]

Many examples of this phenomenon can be documented. One South Dakotan complained that he completed college with a teacher certification. In many areas, teachers received preferential treatment, but he emphasized that his "draft board didn't honor that deferment." As he interviewed for jobs, the school districts always checked his status. When they found out it was 1-A, they refused to hire him. "After six or seven of these occasions, my wife and I sat down and had a long talk about going to the service and getting it over with, because we felt that all the doors were being closed on us." He ended up a rifleman in Vietnam in 1969.[29]

The draft could also affect the type of service selected by coerced volunteers. The Navy and the Air Force typically ensured significantly less dangers than the Marines or Army, unless placed in special duties like the SEALS or a Navy corpsman. They also provided substantially more opportunities to learn a useful trade and more comforts on the ships or airbases than were accorded the grunt. Many young men flocked to them during the war, and they rarely had any problem filling their quotas.

On the other extreme, people volunteered for challenging duty along with people who most likely fought on the front lines because of the draft. An example was Phil Ball, who wrote that "I figured that the Army was going to draft me anyway, so I might as well join the Marines; at least that way, I would have something to be proud of. The Army was looked upon as the worst bunch of misfits, but the Marines were tough misfits, and they had the elite reputation of being the best in the world."[30] Another admitted that he joined the Marines because "I'd rather be over there with motivated people, people who've got their shit together, as opposed to being in a paddy with a bunch of zeroes who don't even want to be there."[31] As a result of such attitudes, throughout most of the war, the Marines remained almost entirely a volunteer force.

Many of the draft-induced volunteers as well as draftees shared the frustration and bitterness of an Arizona Marine. He noted, "Vietnam was a lower middle-class war. If you had money, you went to college. I didn't go (to war) because I wanted to. I went because I was too stupid to know better."[32] Many others would echo such thoughts after they found themselves on the front lines of Vietnam. Yet, many others proudly noted their accomplishments of serving in the most dangerous duties and underscored how it shaped them for the future.

The Culture of Service

Whether a volunteer, draft induced, or a draftee, the young men of the Vietnam era had choices about avoiding the military. Yet, most fulfilled their duty. Such large numbers of volunteers, especially during the first half of the major fighting, require some explanations of how the nation and its leaders conditioned young men toward military service. Obviously, the draft always played a role, but other forces pushed young men to fulfill their duties. Comprehending the impact of Cold War America on the young men, most of whom rarely questioned the assumptions on which their service rested, provides understanding how the military filled its needs.

Understanding the national political culture of the time ensures a good starting point for understanding the pressures placed on young American men to join the military. As author Loren Baritz underscores, "our national political culture is a product of thousands of small and not-so-small ideas. They exist in the collective wisdom of the agencies and departments of government, of the players in the political parties, of the press, the president. . . . This political culture is built slowly, bit by bit, so that future decisions have precedent, probably several."[33]

Baritz's viewpoint reflects a very national perspective and often downplays local realities and class differences as well as racial and religious ones. Still, his analysis is perceptive. Veterans across the country shared many experiences that coalesced into unifying themes that help explain how a generation of people dealt with the challenges of service during the Vietnam era. Powerful forces such as patriotism and the sense of duty ensured a steady stream of people into the military.

The socialization process helps explain some of the differences between those that joined and those that more actively sought deferments. Smaller towns in rural areas or the ethnic enclaves in large urban or suburban communities added layers to the complexity, ones exacerbated by class issues of money and influence. Anonymity in larger cities or living in like-minded communities that opposed the war, typically more middle and upper middle class, helps explain variations also. Yet, the commonalities of social constructions of masculinity, which include factors such as the importance of family and community and the shaping of perceptions by political and entertainment role models, all affected decisions of the millions of young men who came of draft age during the Vietnam War.

The Cult of True Manhood

One of the most important factors shaping the decision to volunteer or meet the requirements of the draft outside of economic pressures was the social construction of manhood in America, one with an added layer of complexity created by the Cold War.[34] The question of masculinity as often defined in a broader national political context, but with strong local factors shaping individual responses, proved fundamental to the experience. While issues of class and race clearly affected the process, the young man's perception of masculinity in relation to military service crossed those lines and helps explain differences in people's responses to the draft and decisions relating to volunteering outside of obvious ones such as economic need.

Author Graham Dawson argues that "masculinities are lived out in the flesh, but fashioned in the imagination," which creates a "range of possible selves" that individuals then choose to construct their lives around the narratives of their experiences.[35] In America during the 1950s and early 1960s, the social construction revolved around families (particularly males), the community, and a strong set of national standards perpetuated in the educational system and media that established primarily masculine values of military service. The closer the young man to the source of modeling (i.e., father or uncles), the more likely some reality corresponded to perceptions, but the further away in areas such as the movies or political folklore, the more probable that the construction lacked grounding in real events and time. This led to more of the life being "fashioned in the imagination" than reality and later contributed to significant questioning of these masculine myths by some combat veterans.

In many cases, young men who represented the largest number of combat troops in Vietnam came from local cultures, especially in working class, lower middle class, and agricultural communities, that measured young men by their physical rather than intellectual skills. Physically demanding sports provided important arenas to demonstrate masculinity, as did the type of work that a person performed, whether in the fields or factories or other labor-intensive jobs. Muscle and stamina marked the measure of the man, not his ability to add numbers or write essays. In such communities, physical prowess signified a good potential breadwinner and differentiated males.

For many young men from such communities, masculine differentiation even influenced the choice of the branch of military. The Marine Corps ranked at the highest in terms of toughness and challenges with the Navy and Air Force viewed at the other end. The Army fell in between in terms of the preference of service with the infantryman at the highest echelon, with additional levels attributed to those choosing specialized training such as Special Forces or SEALS. Jobs such as desk duty or supply (depending on the nature) existed at the lower end. Many sought to demonstrate courage and hardiness in the face of extreme danger and to continue the grand traditions of their national heroes and forefathers.

Many levels to the masculine conception appealed to many young men during the time, even those with reservations about the war. They included the influence of fathers and other male family members, the impact of other male role models in the community and at the national level, the imprint of institutions such as the Boy Scouts, and the effect of media such as movies, television, books, and music. All these reinforced masculine beliefs regarding service, especially in the face of the Communist threat, and helped push many young men into the military.

Fathers and Sons

An important factor in the decision of many young men to join the armed forces was the fact that their fathers, as well as other male family members, had been in the military and established a tradition of service. Many of the Vietnam-era soldiers were sons of veterans of World War II (the "good war") and Korea. Large numbers of other family members also had served, commonly in the "good war," Korea, or as a result of the peacetime draft during the Cold War. In all cases, families boasted more veterans as a result of World War II and the Cold War than at any other point in American history outside of the Revolution and Civil War.

The baby boomers born in the immediate aftermath of the war only learned about the "good war" and tangentially Korea in the context of the Cold War. While their family members often warned about the horrors of war, they also regaled them with the stories of the struggles from the "good war," which reinforced the impressionable young men's thoughts about bravery and heroism. Many shared the attitude of an Army veteran who had talked to men from the World War II generation who had missed fighting because of being in college or receiving other deferments. He believed that they often regretted missing the seminal event of their generation. "I was the perfect age to participate in Vietnam and I didn't want to miss it, good or bad. I wanted to be part of it, to understand what it was."[36]

As a result, young men of the Vietnam generation had multiple military role models that often added pressure to follow in their father's footsteps. E. Anthony Rotundo has observed that in American history "veterans compared the younger generation's easy life with the heroic sacrifice and hardship of the war generation. Could the sons be equal to the fathers? Would they have a like opportunity to test their manly worth in the fires of war?" While he focused on the Civil War generation and its relationship to that of the 1890s, in the 1950s and 1960s such a feeling gripped young men who witnessed their fathers and others remembering their experiences and participating in commemorative, shared experiences on national holidays such as the Fourth of July or Veteran's Day.[37]

Examples from different parts of the country support this notion of familial conditioning. John Brown from Pennsylvania grew up hearing stories of his ancestors' service dating back to the Revolutionary War and continuing through World War II when even one of his uncles, a Quaker, had served in the Aleutian campaign. He recalled, "As for me, I was raised in the tradition of service to the country if the call came."[38] Another veteran remembered, "One way or another in every generation when there was a war, some male in the family on my father's side went to it. It [military service] had never had it drilled into me, but there was a lot of attention paid to the past, a lot of not-so-subtle 'this is what a man does with his life.'"[39]

Others expressed similar feelings. An Arizona veteran, Steve Guzzo, summed them up well. He noted that his forefathers had gone into the military and he believed that "I can do anything that anyone can do." Upon returning home, he wanted to be "able to look anyone in the eye because I had served my country."[40] Guzzo's colleague from southeastern Arizona, Oscar Urrea, added that his family had ancestors who had fought for Mexico dating back to the Texas Revolution and continuing through the Mexican Revolution. His parents reminded him of the family heritage of service, both to Mexico and the United States. It created a powerful push factor when it came time for him and his brothers to make a decision on serving.[41]

The pressure could be extremely intense and some had daily reminders of the power of the father. This appeared especially true for sons of career military men. One Army veteran stressed, "I grew up in a military family. My father was a colonel in the infantry and had been a highly decorated battalion commander in World War II. I had always been impressed by him and what he accomplished." He added that living in Europe in the 1950s and moving throughout the region "I saw the big role the U.S. had in rebuilding and reshaping Europe. So I grew up with this sense of purpose and responsibility."[42]

An extreme case of the pull of the father was that of Lewis B. Puller Jr., the son of the highly decorated Marine Lewis "Chesty" Puller. The senior Puller fought heroically in Haiti and Nicaragua in the 1920s, Guadalcanal, and Pelieu during World War II, and the famous Marine breakout from the Chosin Reservoir during the Korean conflict, where he declared after being surrounded by the Chinese: "Those poor bastards. They've got us right where we want them. We can fire in any direction now!"[43] For his bravery, he received numerous decorations and became a true legend in the Marine Corps.

The introduction began early as the younger Puller remembered as a five year old entering to wake his sleeping father. But before he did, he began tracing his fingers around the tattoo on his father's bicep, the emblem of the Marine Corps. He knew its importance as a symbol on his mother's prized gold and silver pin that also bore the shape of his father's tattoo.[44]

Other memories reinforced the younger Puller's place in the world. When his father received a gold star in lieu of a fifth Navy Cross for his heroics in Korea, Puller recalled his father walking across the field following the ceremony in his dress uniform full of medals. He claimed "the memory of that frozen instant more than three decades ago is as fresh and firmly fixed in my mind today as any of my most vivid boyhood recollections." Although only six and truly unable to understand its full meaning, Puller observed that on "that now distant drill field beneath the glare of a Southern California sun, I had first begun to grasp the concept of battlefield glory and with it sensed commitment to a calling over which I would be powerless."[45]

Over time, the intensity of the shadow of his father became greater.

He watched people visit his father and meet him in public and each shared a common thread of exalting the famous Marine. "I decided early on that I wanted men to feel toward me the way they felt toward my father, as throughout my youth I witnessed examples of hero worship toward him that would have befitted the denizens of Mount Olympus."[46]

Ultimately, he followed in his father's footsteps in the fall of 1967. After graduating from the College of William and Mary, he traced his father's path fifty years earlier and traveled to the Marine recruiting station in Richmond to enlist.[47] Once the Corps granted a waiver for his poor eyesight, he endured the Basic School and became a lieutenant on the front lines in Vietnam. A few months into his tour, he tripped a mine and lost his legs and most of his fingers. As in many other cases, following in his father's footsteps extracted a severe toll.[48]

Other Male Role Models

Few adolescents relied only on their fathers or male family members to shape their perceptions of masculinity, especially at the community level. In particular, teachers and coaches as well as prominent local leaders such as scoutmasters and religious leaders had a significant impact, especially for young men with limited male influences at home.

Teachers exerted an enormous influence over many young men. In an era when teachers commanded respect and society reinforced their value within an established hierarchy, they often had a powerful hold over their charges. This proved especially true in junior and senior high school, where male faculty members became more common. Like the fathers of the young men, many had fought in World War II or Korea. Also, like most fathers, the sense of the mission of the Cold War of protecting the country from the Communist threat permeated them.

Coaches also significantly shaped these young men. While teachers saw the students once a day, coaches often interacted with them for three to four hours on the practice field and on long trips for games. The sheer nature of sports, especially the extremely physical ones such as football, basketball, and wrestling, embodied concepts bearing a striking resemblance to military life. These included endurance, team cohesion, obedience, and toughness. Even the language of the games like football took on military metaphors of ramming through the line, containing the opposition, and many others as presidents Lyndon

Johnson and Richard Nixon often employed them when describing the war in Vietnam.[49]

The educational system itself reflected the Cold War consensus. Few educators anywhere would have even discussed, much less looked at in depth, the culture of dissent as represented by scholars such as Charles Beard, William Appleman Williams, Howard Zinn, and Noam Chomsky. Teachers typically taught consensus history that rarely questioned American intentions or actions, especially those of its leaders, and painted the world in black and white, with the Soviets and their allies as the villains. As one veteran noted, "Our teachers told us that we were fighting communism and that was the thing we had to do. So all through high school I was in favor of the war."[50] Another added that he attended Catholic school where "we were inculcated with a strong anti-communist bias by the nuns and priests who taught our daily lessons. . . . By the time I was nine or ten, I firmly believed that Joseph Stalin was the incarnation of evil and that the United States was locked in a death struggle with the Soviet Union that would decide the fate of the free world."[51]

It would not be until the middle of the 1960s that changes occurred, and they often only trickled down to major settings in the large urban areas of San Francisco, New York City, and university towns such as Berkeley and Madison. The vast majority of Americans, especially those in the small towns and farms and cities of the heartland of America, sustained the long-held principles and traditions of this nation.[52] These focused on God and country, the latter implying the need to defend democracy and capitalism from the Communist threat no matter where in the world it was found.

Examples of educators shaping decisions about military service abound. In one case, John Ketwig found himself at a football game a year after graduating from high school. While receiving scholarships to several universities, including Syracuse and Cornell, he had decided to stay home and work at a car shop. That night, one of his teachers, a Mr. Gott, approached him and asked him about his draft status. When he responded, "I'm One-A," Gott responded, "Enlist. You can get some education. Training. How to fix cars, if that's what you want. Guaranteed. They send the draftees to Vietnam. You'll probably go to Germany. Even if you do go to Vietnam, you won't be infantry." He added, "Enlist. I did. It'll make you a man, do you a lot of good. Teach you some responsibility; get you out from under momma's apron. You can get out after three years, with benefits. You'll never regret it. Best years of my life were in the army."[53]

In another case, an Oklahoma veteran remembered, "While I was at Will Rogers High School, my football coach was my main role model. As a high school graduate he had joined the marines and fought in the major battles of the Pacific." "His name was Chuck Boyles," the veteran recalled, and "he often spoke with feeling about his experiences. He would speak to us before a game, and often would relate the concepts of duty, dedication, teamwork, fellowship, and united effort to his war experience."[54]

The teachers and coaches reinforced what young men saw as a rite of passage in many communities: mainly military service. The rituals of life that surrounded the commemoration of military service made the task much easier. Several times a year, on holidays such as Memorial Day, Fourth of July, and Veterans Day, most communities held special ceremonies. Towns and cities erected numerous statutes and memorials, capped by parades that featured the veterans, often wearing their uniforms and medals. In small, albeit powerful symbolic ways, these activities reminded young men of their duty and the recognition that came with it.

As young men constructed a path for themselves, the latter proved especially important. They saw the tangible benefits of service. Most acknowledged that once they served, they would return to a powerful fraternity as an equal, one that continued until their deaths. Membership in organizations such as the Veterans of Foreign War (VFW) and the American Legion ensured comradeship and opportunity enjoyed by many of their fathers and recognition by the community for their sacrifices and often bravery in the defense of their country.[55] For many young men, especially those planning to return to their hometowns after service, this proved a significant push factor.

Making Boys Into Men

Communities reinforced American values of service to the country in many ways, among them organizations with religious roots such as the Boy Scouts. Founded in 1912 to accomplish, as one observer notes, the introduction of "coddled boys to the wilderness, to competition, to hardy play and strenuous virtue," the Boy Scouts indoctrinated young men with all-American values. Responding to fears that increased urbanization had undermined masculine constructs, the Boy Scouts believed that "men were intervening to provide 'boyish' experiences so that boys would not lose touch with the sources of manhood."[56] Designed to reinforce principles of respect for God and country and create a generation of men skilled in the outdoors and unified by common principles of duty, honor, and loyalty, the Boy Scouts grew quickly throughout the country. As an historian observes, "They were founded and run by adults with adult concerns in mind, and they placed a heavy emphasis on subordination of the boy to his larger group."[57]

During the 1950s, the number of Cub Scouts and Boy Scouts increased astronomically as the baby boomers matured. In 1950, just over 2 million participated, rising to 3.7 million in 1960 and 4.6 million in 1970.[58] Looking at the oath of the highest order, the Explorer Scout, provides some insight into the group. It stressed: "I believe that America's strength lies in her trust in God and the courage and strength of her people. I will, therefore, be faithful in my religious duties and will maintain a sense of personal honor in my own life. I will treasure my American heritage and will do all I can to preserve and enrich it." It concluded, "I will recognize the dignity and worth of my fellowmen and will use fair play and goodwill in dealing with them. I will acquire the Exploring attitude that seeks the truth in all things and adventure on the frontiers of our changing world."[59]

The Explorer oath demonstrates how the scouting movement helped reinforce elements of the national political culture. The emphasis on duty and service to God and country played out in many rituals such as learning how to properly display the flag. Meetings concentrated on traditional American history, often relating to idealized versions of the Native Americans. Competition for promotions through merit badges and leadership positions characterized the local troops, and in many ways paralleled military structures.

The Boy Scouts also concentrated on preparing young men for the physical rigors associated with military service. Scouts earned merit badges for sports and by learning how to hunt, fish, and camp. Summer retreats often provided instruction in the use of rifles and other weapons such as bows, a first for many of the young men. They emphasized a physical regimen that often included obstacle courses and skills such as rappelling. Such activities aimed to create young men not weakened by the urban lifestyle, but imbued with the virtues of the Americans who fought and died to settle and protect the country. Adult males, many veterans, dominated leadership and tried to pass on a view of a strong America to a new generation of Cold Warriors who could be called upon to defend America.[60]

The impact of the scouts on young men who fought in Vietnam permeates many veterans' stories. One recalled his experiences as a scout and how they paralleled military service. His group of eleven and twelve year olds had campouts where they separated into platoons and played army. Often, they marched ten miles along the creeks and through the mountains of southeastern Arizona. During the summers, they took off to camp where they hiked, fished, and practiced firing small rifles, something that they often did at home in an old abandoned building under the supervision of scout leaders. The parallels to the military training appeared obvious to him when he entered the 101st Airborne in 1969.[61]

Likewise, a helicopter pilot who became an Eagle Scout before entering the service in the early 1960s characterized the Boy Scouts as a "paramilitary organization," and remembered being taught how to put on the uniform properly, to stand at attention and salute, and to march. His troop took special trips to Army and Air Force bases such as Williams Field in the Phoenix area, where they played on the simulators. When he reached Eagle Scout status at sixteen, he received a prize of a two-week cruise aboard a Navy ship in the Pacific, which included a port call in Acapulco, Mexico. For him, there were strong similarities between the Boy Scouts and the military.[62]

Millions of young men received similar indoctrination through the Boy Scouts during the 1950s and 1960s. The organization focused on making American males stronger in the face of internal threats of becoming emasculated by urban lifestyles and the affluence of the 1950s and external threats that challenged the values of God and country. It became a rite of passage for many young boys, many not even teenagers. It reinforced concepts of duty and service, making it easier for armed service recruiters and the draft system to move young men into the military, even during the more tumultuous period of the late 1960s.

In John Kennedy's Service

While numerous male role models at the local level existed, important ones developed at the national level for young men growing up in the 1950s and 1960s. President John F. Kennedy exuded the most self-confidence, virility, and patriotic fervor.[63] His life sparked numerous books and the popular movie *PT-109* in 1963, and Catholicism added another layer of allure for many young Americans who shared his faith. The vibrancy radiated by Kennedy, despite behind-the-scenes battles with health problems and addictions, shaped a generation of Americans who responded to his inaugural address in January 1961: "Let every nation know, whether it wishes us well or ill, that we shall pay any price, bear any burden, meet any hardship, support any friend, oppose any foe, in order to assure the survival and the success of liberty," and concluding with the immortal words: "Ask not what your country can do for you—ask what you can do for your country."[64]

Many examples of the Kennedy mystique shaping volunteers and draftees alike appear in the veterans' recollections. One remembered that he joined the Army with an eye toward Special Forces because of the operation and "that fact that you've got a Catholic guy that's going to be president. He's ex-military. It just seemed like everything was jelling. I had been thinking seriously about enlisting. It was not too long after that, that I just decided that now's the time."[65] Another veteran, Philip Caputo, wrote that "War is always attractive to young men who know nothing about it, but we had also been seduced into uniform by Kennedy's challenge to 'ask what you can do for your country' and by the missionary idealism he had awakened in us."[66]

Kennedy's appeal crossed cultural lines. A Native American veteran from South Dakota who did three tours in Vietnam declared, "A lot of Vietnam people are from the Kennedy generation, the Camelot generation. We had a president we all loved and were enthralled with as one of the real heroes, the PT 109 thing, and 'Ask not what your country can do for you, but what you can do for your country.'" "Later he spoke about the 'torch is passed' to you," he recalled. "For a lot of us thirteen, fourteen year olds at that time, it meant us. We took it as meaning us, and when he was killed, it was like that torch was passed to us."[67]

For several, Kennedy's example even affected the type of service that they selected. One Navy veteran remarked, "Swift boats were like fulfilling a childhood fantasy. They was [sic] neat—JFK, PT-109, the whole nine yards of 'ask not what you country can do for you, but what you can do for your country.'"[68] For the offspring of a prominent Massachusetts family, John Kerry, a fascination with following Kennedy's path proved powerful. After meeting the president and sailing with him as a high school senior in what he characterized as a "memorable" event, he traveled to Yale and immediately joined the Navy after graduation in 1966. While skeptical of the war, he ultimately volunteered for service on the small Swift boats that traversed the dangerous rivers and canals of Vietnam, much like Kennedy had done in the South Pacific on the PT boats.[69]

President Kennedy helped shape a generation of Americans with the call for service to defend America and improve the world. While equal numbers of women responded in areas such as the Peace Corps, many young men looked to the vibrant president with envy, a man of learning and power with a beautiful wife and admiring masses. His youth, virility, strength, charisma, and war record reinforced many long-standing principles of masculinity for an entire generation coming of age as Vietnam became the centerpiece of the American effort to protect democracy.

Being John Wayne

Movies also played a part in building the national political culture that shaped many people, especially in relation to gender roles. In nearly every community in America through the 1950s and 1960s, theaters served as central sources of entertainment, even with the advent of television. An entire generation shared a love of movies and the break that they provided from the monotony of everyday life. Like every generation since the development of this medium, one that grew in importance with the mass distribution through the television, film emerged as a major source of entertainment, as well as social conditioning.

Many young men flocked to movies such as *To Hell and Back* (1955), the life story of Audie Murphy who, like many of them, had come from modest beginnings. Unlike most, he had risen through the ranks to become the most decorated U.S. soldier in World War II. From there, he became a movie star and everyone knew his story, although most did not know about his battles with alcohol and nightmares caused by the war. A Marine veteran remembered that he never forgot about Murphy in *To Hell and Back* and the final scene where he jumped on a burning tank and sprayed the Germans with machine gun fire. He called it the "greatest movie I ever saw in my life."[70]

While Murphy provided the real everyday hero, the one most often glorified in war films of the period (as well as Westerns) remained John Wayne.[71] For many of the Vietnam generation, he represented the ultimate example of masculinity, a man of imposing stature, swagger, and outspokenness. This transferred into a commanding on-screen presence that combined bravado with misogyny and the willingness to bravely challenge all odds. For many young men of the period, Wayne became their imagined ideal of manhood, especially in relation to military service through films such as the *Sands of Iwo Jima, The Flying Tigers, The Lon-*

gest Day, *In Harm's Way*, and *The Green Berets*. This occurred despite the fact that he avoided service during World War II and his sons who came of age during Vietnam never volunteered or served.[72]

Besides Murphy and Wayne films, many other movies made during the postwar era glorified the noble sacrifices of American citizens, even those from the humblest origins. In movies such as *Halls of Montezuma* (1950), *Battle Cry* (1955), *Pork Chop Hill* (1959), *The Great Escape* (1963), and *The Battle of the Bulge* (1965), the remembrance of World War II and to a lesser degree Korea became central to many young men's views of war. Prominent actors such as Gregory Peck, Richard Widmark, and Van Heflin, and many more appeared in the films, adding to their credibility.[73] The movies lacked the vivid portrayal of death, blood, lost limbs, and atrocities that became more standard after the Vietnam War in films such as *Platoon* (1986), *Full Metal Jacket* (1987), and *Saving Private Ryan* (1998).

Television, the emerging media in the 1950s and 1960s, added another layer to the creation of a wartime ethos among young men. First, it broadcast many of the war movies, including the old ones that came out before many of the young men could view them. In addition, new shows appeared; the best example is the ABC series *Combat* that debuted in 1962. It covered World War II from the viewpoint of the infantryman crossing France in 1944 and 1945. Starring Vic Morrow as Sergeant Chip Saunders, the series hosted numerous emerging stars including Lee Marvin and Robert Duvall in guest appearances. It and other television shows such as *12 O'Clock High* (1964–67) and the *Rat Patrol* (1966–68) reinforced the perception of many young men about the "good war" and their responsibility to defend America.[74]

Evidence of movies and television shaping perceptions of war appears frequently among veterans' memoirs. In Massapequa, New York, a Marine recruit, Ron Kovic, remembered going to the movies and being influenced by them. In *Sands of Iwo Jima*, he watched John Wayne's Sergeant Stryker charge up the hill, only to be killed right before he reached the top. Then, the film cut to the famous raising of the flag with the Marine Corps hymn playing. He wrote, "I loved the song so much, and every time I heard it I would think of John Wayne and the brave men who raised the flag on Iwo Jima that day. I would think of them and cry."[75]

Many others remembered how movies influenced them. A Tennessean recalled, "In my mind, it was part of the same thing that John Wayne and Audie Murphy and all those other guys [did]. We were serving our country and we were making the world safe for democracy."[76] Another veteran remembered "films like *Back to Bataan*, *Sands of Iwo Jima*, and *Flying Leathernecks* left strong impressions on our young minds." He noted that as early as age six, "we dreamed and fantasized of the day when we would take up arms and defend our country's honor in some remote tropical jungle, returning home with a chest full of medals."[77] Another recruit, a Marine, stressed, "Frankly, I had never talked with anybody about combat experiences. I simply went by what I'd seen in John Wayne movies. I believed it all."[78]

These patriotic movies and television shows underscored themes of service, sacrifice, and heroism that undoubtedly shaped an entire generation of Americans. However, one Marine later noted that combat lacked the music and the drama and romance that were often part of Hollywood war movies.[79] Another veteran stressed, "I was very naïve. I got my idea of war from movies where the good guys don't get killed."[80] One more noted, "War ain't like you see in John Wayne. You'll be there and you're dead and I'm still talking to you. Somebody you know one minute and then he's dead the next and he's gone."[81] These ideas ultimately developed after the personal experience of combat, but sometimes too late trying to live out the ideal.

Other Media Influences

While movies and television probably exerted the greatest influence, other forms of media including books, magazines, and comics also stirred imaginations and shaped the perceptions of young men. As in many generations, young men read books on popular heroes of American history such as George Washington, Abraham Lincoln, Robert E. Lee, and Theodore Roosevelt, as well as those of contemporary leaders such as Dwight D. Eisenhower and John F. Kennedy. In each case, the leader's military career received prominent attention. In addition, young men of the 1940s and 1950s found military role models and heroes in other sources, including a favorite of the period, comic books. These included *GI Joe* (as well as action figures with field manuals), *Sergeant Rock*, *Sergeant Fury*, and other comic books such as *Captain America* and *Superman*, which preached the virtue of truth, justice, and the American way.[82]

In addition, for most of the war, country and western music proved an avid supporter of the effort in Southeast Asia. Popular songs received significant air time such as Stonewall Jackson's "The Minutemen Are Turning In Their Graves" (1966), Autry Inman's "The Ballad of the Two Brothers" (1968), and Tom T. Hall's top charting "Hello Vietnam" (1965) in which he highlighted a young man who went to war because "we must save freedom in that foreign land or freedom will be slipping thru our hands." Others joined the chorus such as Merle Haggard in his hit song, "Okie from Muskogee" (1970) when he declared: "We don't burn our draft cards down on main street, but we like living right and being free."[83] Such songs had a substantial following in Middle America, particularly in areas where support for the war continued such as the South and the Mountain West.

In the earliest stages of Vietnam, a genre of literature and music even developed around the conflict and glorified primarily one group, Special Forces. Books, including Robin Moore's *The Green Berets* (1965) and Barry Sadler's *I'm a Lucky One* (1967), became the basis for the John Wayne movie, and Sadler produced a huge hit in 1966 with his song, "The Ballad of the Green Beret." The books and the movie exalted the ability of the elite forces to serve not only as soldiers, but also as diplomats with the ability to win the "hearts and minds" of the Vietnamese. The works also highlighted the value of the non-com and the grunt, and produced a slew of comic books and action toys complete with different uniforms and field manuals.[84]

Such literature and music obviously impacted future soldiers' perceptions. One remembered, "My reading material started with G.I. Joe comic books and ended with military histories, as I filled my mind with a martial heritage I was determined to make my own. Great generals and Medal of Honor recipients were my heroes, not quarterbacks or home run sluggers; tanks turned my head about the time my peers were drawn to sportscars."[85] Another recalled, "I read Marine Corps history when I was little. I read all the books on the Marines. I did. And I always wanted to be a Marine. So I joined after I got drafted out of college."[86]

Building the Military Man

There were many levels to the masculine conception relating to war that appealed to young men during the Vietnam War, even those with reservations about the conflict. They included the influence of fathers and other male role models at the community and national levels, the imprint of institutions such as the Boy Scouts, and the effect of the media. While undoubtedly more existed, such as the construction of the Christian soldier in defense of the faith, all these reinforced masculine beliefs regarding military service, especially in the face of the Communist threat, and helped thrust many young men into the armed services.[87] In many ways, American culture produced for many an imagined masculine self that promoted military service as a rite of passage into manhood.

The Racial Dynamic

While masculinity remained an important part of how soldiers constructed themselves, for many Americans race also played a significant role and added to the complexity of the choice to volunteer or respond to the draft. Often minority decisions regarding military service revealed significant commonalities, especially the economic push factors. Minorities typically populated the poor, working class, and lower middle class in America. Also, among many minority groups there persisted a strong sense that they had to prove their patriotism and their equality with whites. Others had strong warrior traditions of military service dating back for centuries. For African Americans, Latinos, Native Americans, and Asian Americans, the Vietnam War created some significant challenges, as well as opportunities for those who chose to serve.

African Americans

During the Vietnam War, African Americans constituted the largest minority group in the military, especially in front-line combat units. They built on a long legacy of service in the U.S. armed services dating back to the Revolutionary War, which significantly increased after slavery ended in 1865. During the major wars of the nineteenth and twentieth centuries, they had served in segregated units until 1948 when President Truman ended the practice. During Korea, African Americans finally began integrating into different units, although significant resistance continued. Thus, the Vietnam War constituted the first time that fully integrated American units, both in the Army and Marines, went into the field.[88]

Despite the integration, African Americans faced significant challenges in the military due to the racial discrimination prevalent in American society. While often more color blind than many of it civilian counterparts, the military had more than its fair share of people who brought their prejudices with them. Nevertheless, African Americans joined in large numbers during the 1950s and 1960s and reenlisted at a rate twice that of whites during the initial stages of the war.[89]

Like many poor and working-class men, African American men, especially in the South and inner cities, saw the military as offering an escape from stifling unemployment and lack of opportunity. They also lacked effective methods of draft avoidance through college and the Guard and Reserves.[90] Military service also provided African Americans with a chance to prove their equality in a typically white institution and, like many of their fathers, to demand equal rights for those called on to fight and die for their country.

From the beginning, African Americans often faced discrimination in recruiting, although this could vary by region. In one case, a captain told a sergeant recruiting for the Green Berets: "Don't send me any niggers." He encouraged the sergeant to avoid open discrimination for fear of hurting the organization's reputation, but stressed it would be easy to reject them because "most will be too dumb to pass the written test. If they luck out on that and get by the physical testing, you'll find they have some sort of police record. . . . You don't have to give anybody a reason for not accepting him."[91]

Despite such challenges, African Americans volunteered in large numbers. A Louisiana Marine recalled that when he finished high school in 1963, the first in his family to do so, he weighed only 117 pounds, and "nobody's gonna hire me to work for them. So the only thing left to do was to go into the service." He thought about each branch, but decided on the Marines because they "was bad. The Marines Corps built men. Plus just before I went in, they had all these John Wayne movies on every night."[92] Another African American veteran emphasized, "I thought we were going to help free the Vietnamese from Communist aggression. I volunteered. I believed in it. My family was proud of me." He admitted, "The African American community was very divided about the war . . . but there was also still a belief that we should go into the military to show the nation that African Americans could make an equal contribution to the cause of freedom and equality."[93]

The African American community became more hostile toward the war over time; nevertheless, African Americans served and died in large numbers in Vietnam. Many volunteered for elite groups such as airborne, one explaining that "we joined because of pride and the $55 extra a month. It's a challenge. The brother likes the challenge. We're tough and we want everybody to know it."[94] Such attitudes, combined with the tendency of the Army to place its less-educated men in the front lines, created significant casualties. The death rates of African Americans in 1966 were disproportionally large when compared to their 12 percent share of the population. This led to a concerted effort by the military to reduce African American deaths, which leveled off by the end of the war at 13.1 percent.[95] Overall, African Americans made a significant contribution to the U.S. effort.

Latinos

Like African Americans, Latinos served in large numbers in combat units in Vietnam. The number of Latinos in Vietnam is difficult to determine exactly as after 1949 (and until 1979) the U.S. military began listing Latinos as Caucasian at the request of several Latino civil rights organizations. Nevertheless, while difficult to quantify precisely, Latinos played a substantial role in the Vietnam War, building on significant contributions made during World War II and the Korean War. As evidence, one of the most common names on the Vietnam Memorial is Rodríguez.[96] One study indicated that 20 percent of the Latinos that served in Vietnam died and 23 percent suffered wounds, while another study found that of the 470,000 veterans suffering from PTSD, 27 percent were Latinos.[97] As with most groups, as Victor Martínez observes, they "fought for reasons that were ill-defined, often confusing, but for the most part devoid of any cogent understanding of the political and economic forces at play which took them from" the United States to Indochina.[98]

While Mexican Americans composed the largest portion of Latinos, others also fought. Puerto Rico provided more than 48,000 troops, many of whom only spoke limited English, losing 345 in Vietnam. This does not take into consideration those Puerto Ricans born in the commonwealth who moved to the United States or those whose parents emigrated to the United States.[99] This gave Puerto Rico, which ranked twenty-sixth in population when compared with U.S. states, the distinction of having ranked fourteenth in casualties and fourth in per capita combat deaths.[100]

The Puerto Ricans faced a significant obstacle, that of having Spanish as their native language. In the 1950s, the Defense Department established a special English immersion course for Puerto Ricans entering the army. Once completed, the recruits transferred to basic training. During the Vietnam War, the language course became a casualty of war as the need for recruits intensified and lower standards, partly established under Project 100,000, pushed more Puerto Ricans into the service without proper language skills. Finally, in 1970, a Puerto Rican recruit, Carlos Rivera-Toledo, won a case that found that the Army had not provided adequate training, specifically English language skills. The federal judge ordered him released from duty.[101]

The Puerto Ricans often distinguished themselves in combat despite some obvious obstacles. Most veterans who fought with them characterized them as being extremely tough and hard-nosed. One recalled, "The Puerto Ricans were made to fight. Those guys are tight. If you get on their wrong side, you're in trouble; but if you get on their good side, they will stand by you. They are good people."[102]

Other Latinos, including Cubans (many recently settled in the United States following Fidel Castro's victory), Dominicans, and some foreign nationals from Latin America who volunteered fought alongside the Puerto Ricans. However, Mexican Americans constituted the largest Latino population in the United States and the principal minority group in the U.S. military outside of African Americans.

While difficult to determine exactly, a substantial number of Mexican Americans made a significant contribution to the war effort. A good estimate is that Mexican Americans from the states of Arizona, Colorado, California, New Mexico, and Texas at the time comprised 10 percent of the population but ultimately 20 percent of the casualties in Vietnam.[103]

The draft often ensnared Mexican Americans. Many lacked economic opportunities, which created few choices for going to college or securing placements in the National Guard or Reserves. Few ever contemplated running away as the community had high standards of loyalty to the group and especially the family. Some dissent developed as the war intensified, but it paled in comparison to that of the African American community.[104] Because many Latinos comprised significant portions of the lower socioeconomic strata, economics often played a substantial role in their decisions to join. A Mexican American from Texas, Manuel Valdez, had enrolled at the University of Texas-Arlington in 1965, but when his family moved to Corpus Christi, he remembered, "My family didn't have enough money for me to stay in college, and that's when I started thinking seriously about joining the Marines. I knew I didn't want to be drafted. I wanted to make my own decision."[105]

The large number of World War II and Korean veterans in the Mexican

American community who had distinguished themselves and established a legacy of service also affected decisions. Many young Mexican Americans remained intensely patriotic and wanted to prove themselves to their Anglo counterparts, much like African Americans. One Mexican American veteran from Bakersfield, California, emphasized, "I enlisted a couple of years after high school. At the time I was young and innocent and I was under the impression that enlisting was the All-American thing to do."[106] Another Mexican American veteran noted, "I was gonna get drafted so I went ahead and volunteered. It was part of trying to be an American and patriotic and the whole romantic notion of war. When we got to Vietnam, we wanted to prove that we really were Americans. Even now I think we Chicano guys want to prove how patriotic we were."[107]

Another variation on the theme arose from another California veteran who admitted to being an illegal alien brought over at the age of one and then becoming a permanent resident. "I felt that it was a good trade for being allowed to live here [U.S.] and go to school. By serving this country, I felt it was a way of paying off."[108] While not everyone shared his beliefs, many Mexican Americans remained supporters of the war throughout most of the conflict, and the community provided a steady stream of infantrymen into Vietnam.

Native Americans

Native Americans also volunteered in large numbers in comparison to their proportion of the population, suffered significant casualties, and received recognition for their valor in Vietnam. Young men from many tribes including the Iroquois, Sioux, Comanche, Cherokee, Navajo, Hopi, Apache, Seminole, Utes, and Cheyenne fought in the jungles of Vietnam. Each carried their cultural traditions, although the depth of that commitment depended on the individuals and their ties to tribal traditions.

Native Americans encountered significant obstacles in gaining recognition of their contributions. One observer notes that as a result of the historical evolution in the United States "Native Americans are viewed as having disappeared or as 'remnants' of a vanishing race." Another adds, "The deep impression made upon American minds by the Indian struggle against the white man in the last century has made the contemporary Indian somewhat invisible compared to their ancestors."[109] Geographic problems also existed. Most Native Americans lived in sparsely populated areas of the American West or in many cases blended into the large urban areas where ethnic identities became confused with other groups including Latinos. Surnames also made it difficult to identify individuals and problems existed of classification as some Native tribes did not receive official government recognition.

As a result, Native Americans expressed their frustrations at the lack of acknowledgment, but underscored their presence in the military. One veteran observed, "Everywhere I went over there [Vietnam], I saw skins. But nobody ever put us in the papers like they did the blacks." Another added that "all the white guys that I know who were in 'Nam said that they were buddies with an Indian. Unless they're lying, man, there were more Indians over there than anybody knows about."[110]

Native Americans joined the military during the Vietnam War for many reasons. Historian Tom Holm argues postwar surveys indicate that for many, "military service was part of an honorable family and/or tribal tradition. They wanted to be warriors—to protect their land and their people. And, in the tribal tradition of reciprocity, they wanted to gain respect from other Native Americans."[111]

As with other minority communities, economics and a lack of educational opportunity also played a role in many decisions to join the armed forces. One Native American veteran from South Dakota emphasized "there wasn't anything on the reservation for me to do. That was a way to start doing something. I started in the military and figured later on I would go to college, use my GI Bill."[112] A Navajo veteran stressed that "there wasn't anything else, man; no jobs, I was too young to sit down and learn things in the old way. I was done with school. I just went in and signed up."[113]

Beyond economic motives, many of the Native American communities also had cultures that recognized the martial spirit and celebrated it in oral histories and ceremonies. Stories of the resistance to the westward movement of the whites dominated tales of the bravery of Tecumseh, Sitting Bull, Quanah Parker, Geronimo, and Cochise. The bravery of Native Americans during World War I, World War II, and Korea, particularly during the struggle in the Pacific where stories of the Navajo Code Talkers became well known over time, added levels of historical memory of military service and honor. Other elements of Native American culture and that imposed on it by the outside further encouraged a spirit of patriotism. The Bureau of Indian Affairs (BIA) forced many young Native Americans into boarding schools that promoted a version of American history that indoctrinated young Native Americans with values of service and devotion to the United States.[114]

Many examples developed of the impact of these various influences. One Native American veteran noted, "A lot of us Indians were living with our tribal archetypes as being warriors. We had a purpose. Some tribes actually declared war on the Vietnamese by tribal resolutions. Tribes are sovereign states and can do that, whereas the U.S. didn't."[115] Like other groups, male role models in Native American society reinforced the concept of service. One Cherokee Vietnam veteran who won a Distinguished Service Cross recalled that "most of my relatives have fought in wars . . . there have always been warriors in my family. I have a . . . cousin, in World War II, his name is Jack Montgomery, he won the Medal of Honor in Italy. And I always looked at that picture of him . . . that was a really great honor."[116] The allure of military honors and other reasons attracted many Native Americans and ensured a steady supply of volunteers and draftees throughout the war.

Asian Americans

Asian Americans, most of whom have received little recognition, also fought valiantly. The primary groups consisted of Chinese Americans, Japanese Americans, and the Korean Americans, but included others who hailed from the Philippines, Guam, and the islands of Micronesia. Each cluster carried its own cultural symbols and traditions, although at the center were honor and respect dictated by religious and ethical teachings. Anti-communism ran especially deep in the Chinese American and Korean American communities, largely due to the events following World War II on the mainland of Asia. However, there remains a dearth of knowledge regarding Asian Americans as few sources exist on their service.

Like many of their counterparts, Japanese Americans carried a strong tie to World War II that shaped their views of service. Some were born in concentration camps constructed by the U.S. government to house the Japanese Americans during World War II. More important, many had older family members who had served in the U.S. military, including the famous 442nd Regimental Combat Team during World War II, which had been immortalized in the movie *Go for Broke* in 1951.[117]

One Japanese American veteran who won the Distinguished Service Cross for heroism in Vietnam and who had two older brothers serve in the 442nd remembered, "My whole life I grew up on the tradition of the 442nd. I was convinced that one of the reasons we were allowed to get out of the camps and accepted in American society to the degree that we were, was the blood shed by the 442nd. So growing up," he added, "I thought military service was an inevitable rite of passage. All six of my older brothers served in the military. I could hardly wait for my turn."[118]

Many Asian Americans would follow the example of their fathers, driven by economic reasons, a sense of duty to family and country, the draft, and other factors shared with many other Americans.[119] Yet, their contribution has received the least attention among the groups and remains underappreciated, especially when contrasted with that of World War II. Like other minorities, race played a role in their decisions to join the armed services and ultimately affected the type of service they entered.

The Masculine Female?

While men composed the majority of those who served in Vietnam, a small, albeit significant number of women volunteered. Their motives provide a good comparison and contrast to male recruits for understanding the reasons for enlisting. Women worked as nurses, clerks, air traffic controllers, and intelligence agents, as well as in the Red Cross and other non–governmental organizations such as Catholic Relief Services. The Defense Department estimated 7,500 served on active duty from 1962 to 1973, while the Veteran's Administration put the number at 11,000. Overall, more than 30,000 military and civilian women served in the Vietnam War.[120]

In some ways, women who volunteered for service in Vietnam gave the same reasons as their male counterparts, including the impact of family service or patriotism, demonstrating that gender lines often blurred. One noted that "my mom had been a Navy nurse during World War II, and I think that had a lot of impact on my decision" to join.[121] Others highlighted the service of their mothers, not typically their fathers, as nurses, Donut Dollies, and others during World War II, which underscored a gender-specific notion about volunteering. Another added that she went to nursing school because "it was a chance to contribute, it was very patriotic, it was an American thing to do. I couldn't do it as a soldier, but I could do it as a nurse."[122]

Like many of their male counterparts, women also volunteered out of a sense of adventure and the opportunity to prove themselves. One veteran nurse remembered, "While I was in basic training, I heard all these people just back from Nam talking about how exciting it was. Professionally, it was the chance of a lifetime. I have two brothers and I grew up in a neighborhood where I was the only girl my age. I used to play guns with the boys all the time. I figured I could manage in Vietnam."[123] A Virginia volunteer noted that she had attended Virginia Tech, a school with a heavy military influence. "Although I'd never had any contact with anybody in the military, I was really drawn to it. Besides, you grow up with Audie Murphy and John Wayne movies, and—even if you're a girl—you know you're going to go and be a hero somewhere."[124]

In many ways, the young women who went to Vietnam shared many of the rationalizations of their male counterparts, including idealistic ones. One nurse wrote: "I also was a John F. Kennedy person and I just felt it was one way of honoring him."[125] Another, Lynda Van Devanter, a devout Catholic from Arlington, Virginia, and passionate admirer of Kennedy, wrote that she chose nursing as a way to "make my contribution to society. I was part of a generation of Americans who were 'chosen' to change the world. We were sure of that. It was only a matter of waiting until we all grew up."[126]

While these rationalizations for service in Vietnam paralleled those of their male counterparts, the dominant paradigm of explaining volunteering for Vietnam, especially among nurses and non–governmental workers, was the opportunity to be a caregiver, a gender specific and acceptable duty within the context of the times. One writer explains that this led to the perception of "their invisibility and silence" for many years. "By and large, women in Vietnam were caretakers and helpmates. They had been trained to take care of people—wounded people, sick people, children. And they 'did' for men because, in the military and elsewhere, that's what women did."[127]

Numerous examples exist of this mindset. One nurse joined because "American men were being shot and killed in a foreign country and I honestly felt American women should be there to take care of them. I guess it came from being raised with a very strong sense of family and duty. I looked at my younger brothers and thought, 'My God, if they go to Vietnam and get shot, who would take care of them? If I don't go, would it be right for some other nurse to go in my place to take care of them?'"[128]

Another expanded that line of thought, but in relation to her opposition to the conflict. "I wanted to go to Vietnam to help people who didn't belong there. I objected to the war and I got the idea into my head of going there to bring people back. I started thinking about it in 1966 and knew that I would eventually go when I felt I was prepared enough," which ended up being November 1970.[129] Yet another added that when her younger brother enlisted in the Marines, she overcame her opposition to the war and volunteered for the Red Cross's Supplemental Recreational Activities Overseas (SRAO) program. "I couldn't get away from feeling that there were guys over there like my brother—guys who grew up with apple pie and country. . . . I didn't want to support the war, but I wanted to support those guys."[130]

Women in various positions traveled to Vietnam. While limited in their exposure to direct combat, much like many American support staff during the conflict, they played a small, albeit important role. They shared many of their male counterparts' reasons for joining, but typically with an added motivation of fulfilling the established gender role of care provider. While countries such as the Soviet Union and Israel had actively incorporated women into the armed services, the United States lagged behind. It would take another three decades before the widespread use of women in combat zones in military functions would occur and only after the imposition of the all-volunteer service.

The Last Days of Freedom

The majority of young men and women entering the military, whether draftees or volunteers, often took the last few days before their induction to party with friends, visit family, and in some cases marry before shipping out. Most accepted their fate. Some looked forward to the challenge, while others sought simply to make the best of the situation. They comprised part of a generation asked to fight a war against Communism and to protect democracy from the godless hoards owing their allegiance to Moscow. Along the way, they became embroiled in one of the most controversial conflicts in American history, but for many the politics mattered much less in the immediate threat of dealing with the anxiety of facing the drill instructors in boot camp or basic training.

Each of these individuals made choices during the Vietnam War. A series of often-complex factors molded by their local communities, the national political culture, their socioeconomic background, and their race and gender shaped how they dealt with volunteering or the draft. No one factor affected every person; rather multiple threads often dictated the decisions made and how individuals followed up on them. For many young people in the generation, it constituted the seminal decision of their young life.

2

Building GI Joe

Induction and Recruit Training During the Vietnam Era

Young men heading into recruit training were in for a rude awakening. In one case, a Marine remembered exiting the plane and meeting instructors, with the Navy ones telling their charges, "All you guys going in the Navy, your bus is over here." In contrast, the Marine said, "All you sons of bitches that are thinking you're going to be Marines, get on that fucking bus and shut your mouth!" As they boarded the bus and took seats, he yelled: "Keep your feet flat on the floor, your hands under your knees, your faces straight ahead, and shut up." When an African American from Chicago retorted, "Yeah, who are you?" the Marine promptly beat him up, leading another recruit to think: "Whoa, I think I'll just keep my mouth shut here and see what's going on."[1] In another case, a Marine recalled arriving at San Diego at night: "I think that is so your [sic] down there and you're disoriented and you don't know where it is so you couldn't run out the gate if you wanted to because you don't know where the gate is."[2]

Millions of young Americans experienced the trials and tribulations of training (basic training for the Army and boot camp for the Marines) during the Vietnam War. Few ever admitted to enjoying the weeks of grueling psychological and physical punishment designed to weed out undesirables. Nonetheless, they learned how to operate weapons, how to handle basic combat operations, and most important, how to follow commands and endure physical hardships. While the training was intense, most of the recruits survived and moved on to Advanced Infantry Training (AIT), where they learned more, all the while believing that they were likely one step closer to boarding a ship or plane destined for the Republic of Vietnam. In fact, as the war escalated, many headed there as soon as they completed their AIT and received a short leave. They immediately put their training to use, although many would lament that it never actually prepared them for the battles in Vietnam.

You Are in the Military Now: The First Step

The first step before recruit training involved reporting to the induction center for physical and intelligence testing. Lines of young men, some tightly gripping doctors' excuses that would be their exit ticket, snaked through induction centers across the country. For most, it was an introduction to waiting in long lines, the humiliation of being stripped naked and poked and prodded, and the endless, mind-numbing testing that was the military. While only typically a day-long exercise, it was a sign of things to come for many who passed and found themselves classified as 1-A and given orders to return within a short period for a trip to training.

In one case, William Merritt remembered going to the induction center on Valentine's Day in 1968. Protestors stood outside "out to stop a war that might grab at them, out to stop the war by bullying me." Once inside, he characterized it as "bleak as a jail" decorated by signs that read: "INDUCTEES, FOLLOW THE RED LINE TO PROCESSING AREA." The lack of color was noteworthy as the "ceiling was gray. The floor was brown. The walls were dirty green." As he marched down the hallway, another sign appeared: "DRAFT DODGERS, FOLLOW YELLOW STRIPE TO EXIT." Marching on, he encountered several lines painted on the floor. One read: "DRAFT AVOIDERS (TEACHERS, MARRIEDS) FOLLOW THE DULL GRAY LINE." Another read: "CANDIDATES FOR HARDSHIP, PSYCHIATRIC, OR SECTION 13 DISCHARGES FOLLOW THE DIRTY PINK LINE."[3]

The day was long and tedious, characterized by endless physical exams and filling out papers. "Of all the pieces of paper, only one made much difference, the one for choosing a combat arm. And that one made a great deal of difference indeed," he stressed, not understanding the realities that this "wish list" usually had no real effect. Choices included armor, artillery, infantry, and signal. Each, he rationalized, had significant drawbacks. Finally, Merritt settled on the Corps of Engineers because they built things, and "whatever they did in Vietnam had to be better than what the other combat arms did. So I went to war as an Engineer. Close enough to watch, but far enough away to put it all behind me at night." With the decision made and all the forms completed, "at the end of the day, I followed the red line back to the door. Outside it was dark. The demonstrators had moved on."[4]

Merritt's experience paralleled that of many recruits. However, on at least one occasion, there was some comic relief. In June 1966, Gillian Koupman arrived at the Las Vegas induction center carrying a draft notice. The appearance created quite a stir. "Wearing short shorts, the 5-foot-6 Las Vegas showgirl, whose measurements are 36-24-36, convinced board members rather easily that it was a mistake," reported the *Los Angeles Times*.[5]

Despite the occasional mishap, the machinery usually worked quite efficiently. Once the recruit passed the requisite exams, he received his assignment and typically a short period to prepare to leave. Apprehensions abounded as World War II and Korean-era veterans told their stories of the hardships of training and the military. Some recruits looked forward to the challenge and a change in scenery. Most contemplated their futures and a few toyed with the idea of fleeing to Canada, but the vast majority simply accepted their fate and prepared to make the best of it.

The Hard Goodbyes

For many young men, the goodbyes as they left for training were very hard, although they paled in comparison to later ones for those leaving for Vietnam. Many had never left their families for more than a few days and most had not traveled far out of the region where they had been raised. While some had few ties, most faced the difficult task of leaving their families, girlfriends, and childhood friends for at least two months, with little contact outside of letters and occasional phone calls.

Leaving was particularly hard on those with wives and children. While those fighting in Vietnam were limited at first to career soldiers, as the troop shortfalls increased, more married men faced the draft and often left behind fledgling families. People at bus stops and airports throughout the country witnessed tears falling and long embraces followed by apprehensive looks by parents and spouses as the young men parted, especially as the casualty counts increased and more people realized that this could be a step toward Vietnam. It was a pattern repeated millions of times across the country during the Vietnam War.

Cultural differences sometimes separated experiences, especially in the Native American community with its historical traditions and ceremonies for new warriors. In one case, a Lakota Sioux from South Dakota prepared to leave when his grandfather entered and began singing a traditional song that said "be strong, you're a man now." The elder added that the young man needed to be seeking his black face, as young warriors should hide their faces as killing was not what God wanted. The older man concluded: "Be strong, you're representing the people now, your grandfather (the President) has you to go, walk with pride, reveal the Lakota braveness."[6]

There could also be short good-byes. In one case, a recruit showed up at the induction center for some tests a day before his departure date. As he prepared to leave, a sergeant bellowed that the group would leave in thirty minutes. Astounded, the young recruit begged for some time to return the company car and to see his wife. They gave him an hour and the only person he saw was his mother who had to drive him back. As he spent his first "miserable night" at Fort Benning, he complained, "The army wouldn't even let me make a phone call. I wasn't in the army; I was in prison."[7]

The Great Challenge: Surviving Training

Few people looked forward to training, including potential officers who built on their preparation in ROTC programs or the military academies and headed to Branch Officer Basic Course in the Army or The Basic School (TBS) in the Marines. Family members and friends had told recruits many stories about their own experiences of being forced to run all day to the point of exhaustion, drawing kitchen patrol (KP) and latrine duty, and enduring the physical abuse heaped on all recruits by the drill instructors (DIs). While often exaggerated, the stories created a sense of dread as well as excitement of being able to prove to their fathers and brothers that they could take it. It was the next stage in the rite of passage for millions of young men, marking to a degree the transition of a boy into a man for millions of young Americans.[8]

First Impressions

The indoctrination often began even before arriving at the training center. The military's goal was to totally disorient the recruit and begin breaking him down and ridding him of his individualism and any questioning of authority. Instead, the Army and Marines wanted young men who responded quickly to a command and were physically and psychologically fit to endure intensive stress. As a result, one author underscores, the "recruits found themselves in a very competitive and masculine environment in which much of the impetus for the training came through peer pressure, negative reinforcement, and carefully applied increments of stress." It was "a process that is not without accompanying pain," he concluded.[9]

For the Marines, instructors began the process as the recruit left the plane or bus. They rounded up everyone and began quickly herding them onto a bus for the ride to the depot at either San Diego or Parris Island, all the while heaping upon them verbal and sometimes physical abuse. When the bus arrived, everyone rushed off the bus and stood on the yellow footprints painted on the ground, leading one recruit to observe that "the footprints were painted so close together that my face and body were smashed up tight against the guy in front of me; the guy behind me was smashed up tight against me; . . . a formation we would soon come to know as 'asshole to bellybutton.'"[10] Drill instructors would start in on the group, cussing and grabbing the recruits, driving them toward the barber's shop where everyone was sheared bald, leading one person to note that "that's the first dehumanizing thing, so you all look alike." Running them all over, at first in their underwear and socks, the drill instructors continued the assault on their new recruits, stripping them of any outside goods including watches as the Marine Corps now told the man the time of day.[11]

After recruits received their uniforms and footlockers, the drill instructors marched them to a Quonset hut and told them to take a bunk. After momentarily settling in, the lights came on and an instructor started yelling: "You ladies have gotten into the wrong, these are the wrong Quonsets." This continued until 5 A.M. when the regular instructors arrived and began yelling for everyone to get out of the bunks, overturning those whose occupants failed to respond quickly enough. One noted that by this time, many were asking: "God, what the hell is this?" Another worried that "I ain't going to make it to Vietnam, I'm going to die right here in San Diego."[12]

The Army experience often was no better. One veteran from Pittsburgh remembered arriving at Fort Polk, Louisiana, believing that it would be much warmer than home, but lamented: "I got there and it was so damn cold." He and the others stood around for two days in a parking lot, taking tests with occasional breaks for some apples and the bathroom. "You could see the gate. . . . I kept looking at the gate. I kept saying, 'If I could run home. Boy, did I screw up.'" The only thing that helped was a guy who had already done a stint in the Marines. He told the others that "it's not going to be a picnic, but believe me things are going to get better. They're going to get us uniforms and a barrack and you're going to get something hot [to eat]. This will not last forever."[13]

Sometimes the transition was less severe. An Army recruit, Jerry Morton, arrived at Fort Dix, New Jersey, in August 1966. Leaving the bus, he entered a building, received his uniform and other necessities, and an assignment to living quarters. Then, for ten days he wandered around waiting for basic to start, in what they called Zero Week. Occasionally, he received a job such as picking up trash or washing pots and pans in the mess hall. Daily, he wrote letters to his wife, although he could not receive any because he had no assigned mailbox. It was a frustrating week, a wasted one as no one received credit toward fulfilling the two-year commitment. However, ultimately a bus arrived to take them to where basic training began with the shouting, the running around, and the seemingly never-ending stream of orders. It was another rude awakening, like the one faced when a recruit left the plane or bus to become part of the U.S. military.[14]

Not everyone could handle training. One veteran recalled that as they boarded the bus to head to Fort Jackson, a sergeant had singled out one of the young men as a group leader because "he looks like the soldier type." However, when they arrived at the base, the first night, he collapsed under the strain. He disappeared, but a few days later, he returned to the group bruised and with welts on his face. The drill instructors kept him in quarantine, constantly under guard. But soon after, he split again only to be caught once more. The last the men heard of him, he was in the psychiatric ward.[15]

While such cases occurred, the vast majority learned quickly to respond to the commands of the drill instructor. He tolerated no debate and punished those who failed to respond quickly. The idea was to shock the system and begin the transformation of the recruit from individualistic civilian into a soldier, one willing to obey commands and sacrifice for the group. The Army and Marines had less than eight weeks to accomplish the goal, and the instructors made the maximum use of it, including the first day where they set the tone for the next few weeks.

Settling Into a Routine

The first few weeks of training were the hardest for most recruits, especially those who lacked endurance and stamina. The typical day started before sunrise and continued until around 9 P.M. when instructors declared lights out. The Army and the Marine Corps regulated almost everything during the day including times to clean up, dress, eat, go to the bathroom, and even the occasional few minutes for a smoke break. This ensured regimentation and conformity, two of the major goals of training. One recruit observed that he felt like there was an "invisible noose around my neck which doesn't tighten or isn't noticed unless I try to move."[16]

Physical training, often marching and running in the heat of the day, occupied a significant part of the early stages of training. Yells of "close it up, keep your interval, close it up," echoed on the roads as the soldiers carried their packs and labored under the weight of heavy steel helmets. One commented: "I do not know which was worse, the monotony or the effort—the monotony of putting one foot in front of the other hour after hour or the effort of keeping five paces distance from the man in front 'so's one round don't get you all.'" Only commands of "close it up, damnit, people, keep it closed up," and the relief of the five-minute break before the order of "off your ass and on your feet. Saddle up, move out!" broke the routine. He concluded after such marches that the "sense of the Marine Corps experience . . . was pain."[17]

Recruits also attended classes where they learned rudimentary skills and received basic information. In training, one recruit wrote that there was a lot of studying in numerous classes about tactics, weapons, and history of the military, which required significant study time. "They work us harder than the average college student. But there's a reason. We are learning how to kill, while the college student is learning how to live."[18]

The Army often utilized the time to further indoctrinate the young men in their purpose. The Defense Department produced films such as *The Anatomy of Aggression* and *The Red Menace* showing the Communists on the march after World War II, and images of the hammer and sickle spreading across the world burned in the recruit's mind the naked aggression and threat to their families and way of life.[19] In another, the *Night of the Dragon*, Charlton Heston narrated the official Vietnam story of the U.S. intervention to stop the "terrorist agents" and "murder squads" from taking over South Vietnam. The film highlighted the United States and its allies providing aid to the "valiant South Vietnamese people" against the evil aggressors from Hanoi. It depicted positive images of the South Vietnamese trying to build a democracy in the face of the enemy, and concluded with the scene of brave ARVN soldiers dropping out of helicopters into battle to turn back the Communists.[20]

The physical training, constant psychological strain, and monotonous class time left the young men physically exhausted. In one case, a recruit noted that he lost thirty pounds during basic. "I got plenty of food," he explained and that while the food was typically good it was hard to eat after running through a physical drill. He added, "I was so exhausted, I couldn't put a morsel of food in my mouth. A lot of times I'd just . . . skip supper and go right to bed, and then sleep for about 4 or 5 hours, wake up and organize my clothes for the next day, polish my boots" and then go back to sleep.[21]

The DI

The fundamental power relationship in training was between the recruit and the drill instructor, who established the tone for the two-month period. The DI became surrogate father, mother, and teacher with the goal of turning the men into soldiers who could survive in combat, whether in Vietnam or Western Europe. By the end, many recruits shared the feeling of one who observed of his DI that on "Mother's Day I should send him a card, he was a real mother."[22]

The basic training experience could be uneven, depending on the drill instructor. At one extreme were the sadistic, sometimes corrupt DIs. A young seventeen-year-old Mexican American recruit from Colorado, Gonzalo Baltazar, followed in the footsteps of his six brothers and joined the Army with thirteen others from his small hometown. He characterized his basic training as particularly "negative" since "they ran us to the ground all the time, to exhaustion. We were beat; we were beaten up." Baltazar bore a scar from an incident when a drill sergeant complained about his care of his M-14, "so he hit me between the eyes with the butt of my weapon." "Us not realizing that this was wrong," he remembered, "we never reported it, because if we would have reported it to the inspector general, they would have gotten into trouble."[23]

Baltazar even reported financial extortion. His drill sergeants entered the barracks on payday demanding money to pay fines supposedly levied by their commanding officer because of their recruits' poor performance. Noting that these gross forms of abuse did not happen in other groups, Baltazar emphasized: "To this day, if I ever had to go through it again and I knew about this, then I'd report these guys. But we were scared. I was 17, I was scared half to death once I got in there and so were the others."[24]

A Marine veteran noted similar experiences at Parris Island, where "the drill instructors would hit us in the stomach or punch us in the kidneys, but I saw one get so mad at a recruit that he broke his dress sword across the guy's head. He knocked the guy out. Then he marched the whole platoon off and left the guy laying there." Yet, he rationalized that "evidently the recruit was a total screwup. This was in the fifth or sixth week of training, and he should have knowed [sic] his left from his right by then."[25] In another case, a recruit found himself in trouble so the DI put him in a wall locker and six other instructors began "banging on it and telling me I was going to die in Vietnam."[26]

Many DIs, however, were professional and genuinely concerned with the progress of the recruits. They relied more on verbal rather than physical abuse, utilizing punishments such as extra push-ups and running as well as threats of KP duty to ensure compliance. A South Carolina volunteer stressed, "I didn't have much trouble with boot camp except for some of the psychological games the DIs liked to play. I never felt anybody was badgering me, though, nor did I ever see a DI hit anybody."[27] A Mississippi volunteer added, "The drill instructors yelled at us a lot, but I never saw one hit anybody."[28] Finally, one Marine wrote his family: "All the brutality that you hear about in Boot camp is 90% false, and the other 10% is just a lot of hard work."[29]

For many recruits, especially as the Vietnam War intensified, the drill instructor became more valuable. By 1967, most DIs were Vietnam veterans, some with more than one tour. Their practical experience in fighting the enemy impacted the perceptions of the men. One Army recruit expressed pride that many of his DIs had earned Purple Hearts and every one of them had a Combat Infantry Badge (CIB). "All of a sudden you knew you were probably going to end up there, so maybe you should listen to these guys. Maybe they could tell you something that would help you survive. And they would tell it the way it was."[30] Another veteran remembered that the DIs rarely talked about their own experiences in Vietnam, but that they would consistently bark, "That'll kill you over there! That'll kill you over there! . . . They just would refer back to Vietnam when you made a mistake, that that would cost you your life." Motivated by the desire to survive, most recruits heeded the warnings.[31]

Like most elements of the military, most young men learned to adapt to the circumstances enveloping them. Early on, most learned coping mechanism for dealing with the DIs. John Ketwig observed that almost immediately he believed that the secret to surviving the assault by the drill instructors was "to act intimidated when confronted personally, and blend into the background whenever possible."[32] Another Army recruit added that he would merely respond to the commands as "'Yes, Sergeant,' and all this. 'Sure I'll give you 20 push-ups,' it's no big deal, you know, don't get excited about it . . . I'd just talk under my breath, say, 'Yes, sir,' and do it. It's over with. It's done." Yet, he noted, "A lot of young kids just couldn't cope with that. They didn't have the discipline to cope with it."[33]

Breaking Down the Recruit

The fundamental goal of the first part of training was to break down the recruit, removing well-indoctrinated elements of individualism and self-expression and replacing them with conformity and obedience. One of the functions of basic training and boot camp was to create a man who could respond to commands, do it efficiently and confidently, and not endanger the group. It seemed contradictory that the first part of basic required often physical and psychological abuse, but the drill instructors had less than sixty days to complete the process and then rebuild the recruit into a professional soldier.

Initial actions attempted to remove the individualism from the recruit. DIs banned all first-person references. As one veteran noted, you "speak to the drill instructor in the third person only: 'Sir, Private Flaherty requests permission to speak to the drill instructor, sir.'" This tactic signified that there were no individuals, only team members, and initiated the psychological distancing of the recruit from civilian life where the individual defined the person.[34]

Sexuality also played a significant role in the process. The drill instructors relied heavily on reinforcing conformist behavior on underperforming recruits by characterizing them as feminine or as homosexual. One scholar noted, "the linking of the military function with sexual identity, the exacerbation and promotion of violence and aggression, and the repeatedly hammered ideal of seeking dominance at all costs" served to create in the recruits "a well honed emotional edge" to allow them to "kill the gooks." As a result, the author argues, "accomplishment of mission, violence, and aggressiveness became equated with masculinity" and "masculinity was affirmed through completion of a military function."[35]

The drill instructors employed several tactics to instill the desired masculine traits, ones that many athletic coaches throughout the country employed, although probably not to the same degree. At the first level, DIs questioned whether the recruit was really a man. "Can't hack it, little girls?" and similar denigrating questions echoed out in many bases. On the first day, some Marine drill sergeants would yell out, "Awright ladies! . . . We're going to begin today by learning how to dress. These are trousers . . . Not pants! Pants are for little girls! Trousers are for marines!"[36] They enjoyed using terms such as "pussy" and "cunt" to describe someone who did not measure up to the masculine idea of aggressiveness.[37]

While the women's movement gained momentum during the 1960s, the overall attitude of most people remained mired in the conceptualization of the male as dominant and the woman as subordinate. The use of language reinforced existing societal norms, especially in working-class and lower middle-class homes. Drill instructors and others in the military employed gendered language to embarrass, humiliate, and feminize recruits who failed to conform to expectations. Most recruits never questioned the gendered terms and focused more on avoiding the actions that led to being feminized in a highly charged masculine environment.

Beyond stereotyping underperformers as feminine, drill instructors utilized the more insulting tactic of questioning of a recruit's sexual orientation to force compliance. Strong currents of 1960s America reinforced stereotypes of homosexuals as effeminate sissies with questionable loyalty to the United States.[38] As a result, drill instructors challenged the recruits' sexuality, understanding that many would desperately try to avoid such labels for fear of being marginalized within the unit. Characterizations such as "you dirty faggot" commonly spewed from the DI's mouth, assaulting the masculine self-image. Shaming the individual or group for having homosexual proclivities clearly pushed conforming to the perception of the masculine soldier and created a groupthink that often marginalized individuals who appeared in any way gay.

A Minnesota draftee, Tim O'Brien, provides a good example for the use of feminization and sexual orientation. One day, the sergeant caught him and a friend who shared his reservations about the war in back of the barracks shining his shoes. Already singled out for being "college boys," the DI verbally assaulted them. "Out behind them barracks hiding from everyone and making some love, huh?" he asked, adding, "You're a pussy, huh? You afraid to be in the war, a goddamn pussy, a goddamn lezzie?" He continued hurling insults, "You two college pussies out there hidin' and sneakin' a little pussy. Maybe I'll just stick you two pussies in the same bunk tonight, let you get plenty of pussy so tomorrow you can't piss." Instead, he punished them with guard duty and continued the harassment.[39]

Race in Training

In the effort to break down the recruit, minorities often faced additional challenges because of their skin color. Racism, both institutional and individual, existed within the military as many officers, instructors, and recruits carried long-standing racist proclivities. In training, minorities often found themselves having experiences similar to those on the outside, being singled out by DIs for negative attention and finding isolation in the process unless other minorities were in the group. While it often made a tough task even harder, most minorities were accustomed to racism and coped with the trials.

The dread of training started for some minorities even before they left home. Many feared heading to the South, where African Americans would encounter more segregated societies in South Carolina, Kentucky, Georgia, North Carolina, and Louisiana than at home. One African American from New York wrote in his diary that "most of the Negro fellows I've met worry most about being sent down South. I worry, too. I'd rather freeze the rest of the winter than do my basic in Dixie. . . . The farthest south I've been is Greenwich Village, and I'd like to keep it that way." He was happy when he ended up at Fort Leavenworth, Kansas.[40]

Race often played a significant role in the drill instructors' treatment of the recruits. As one Marine noted, he had a drill instructor who was a "Southerner from Arkansas that liked to call you chocolate bunny and Brillo head."[41] Another remembered, "I was next to this big Puerto Rican dude. Smokey catches the dude looking at him out the corner of his eye. He says, 'Are you eye-fucking me, boy?' . . . I hope you fuck up. I hate you Puerto Rican cocksuckers."[42]

Similarly, a Mexican American Marine remembered that the "DI's liked to zero in on Hispanics. They threw around a lot of racial slurs like 'wetback' or 'beaner.'" To him, they often meant it, especially the "redneck" DIs, but he also recognized that the DI's wanted to test how far they could push the Marine before he started fighting back. "I didn't let the racial slurs bother me very much. As I saw it, boot camp was a sort of game. I took it seriously, but I was not going to let the DIs conquer me, no matter how hard they hit me or what kind of names they called me."[43]

Not every DI regarded race as a distinguishing factor. One Marine remembered his instructor telling the recruits: "There are no niggers in this platoon, there are no spics, there are no wops, there are no kikes, there are no poor whites whatever. . . . You are all fucking maggots and maggots you will remain until you've earned the right to call yourself United States Marines."[44]

While DIs often employed racist language, typically they applied it uniformly across racial lines, which actually created some unity between different groups. The process also had other effects. In fact it eased the transition to racially stereotyping the enemy, even among minorities sensitive to the issue. This process built on long-standing hostilities in American society toward Asians that had been exacerbated by World War II and the Chinese Communist Revolution.[45] As Christian Appy observes, "If the drill instructors' use of racist language served to defuse internal hostilities among the trainees, it also served to legitimize racist stereotypes when projected onto external groups such as the Vietnamese. If racist language seemed to lose its venom when used to homogenize American soldiers, it preserved its poison when used to demonize a foreign enemy."[46] This trend would have significant consequences when some recruits became soldiers and headed to Vietnam.

College Boys in Training

Class could also play a role in how DIs responded to individual recruits and in their efforts to break them down. A veteran remembered, "The people in the Army were not intellectuals. Most of them were from working-class backgrounds. A lot of them were Southerners. . . . Certain economic groups like blue-collar kids and city kids adjusted very quickly to the Army." He added that "most of the middle-class kids like me didn't fit into what was going on. . . . We grew up in a secure environment where a lot of things were taken for granted."[47] The initial training quickly destroyed any vestiges of the comfort many of the young men had known as civilians.

The same recruit also emphasized that his vocabulary and accent ensured conflict with a guy from Georgia who went out of his way to pick fights. "This kid was quite a bit bigger than me, plus I had really lost my bearings and was sort of helpless. So there were fistfights which were quickly broken up—nothing much really happened. But the feeling of being an outsider was reinforced, because I had this antagonist all the time looking for an opportunity to get at me. I had to be on my toes. It was a whole new education."[48]

Another recalled that DIs often singled out those with a college education. Some delighted in asking, "Oh, little college boy, you think you're smarter than us?" Most DIs, coming from lower socioeconomic positions, enjoyed channeling their resentment against the more privileged recruits. They also looked at reservists, many of whom were from middle- or upper middle-class backgrounds, with disdain and asked, "What do you mean you don't want to go to Vietnam? That's where the Marines are; combat!"[49]

In addition, class affected how recruits integrated. One Massachusetts veteran from the middle-class suburbs of Boston noted that when he arrived at basic "most of the people were poorly educated. I was amazed at how stupid some people were." He found that when he got to Fort Polk, Louisiana, "it was about 50 percent black and the other 50 percent were poor whites." Most were from Tennessee and Texas and "I never had anything to do with people like them. Really poor people. You don't like to think that because, well, if I'm with all these guys that are just from the lower classes then how the fuck did I get here."[50]

Many of the young middle and upper middle class swept into the military during the conflict faced difficult challenges from the DIs and isolation from the majority of recruits whose backgrounds were significantly different. Things improved some over time as more college educated kids found themselves snared by the draft, but class antagonisms never fully abated and if anything sometimes carried over onto the battlefields in Vietnam.

Singling People Out

Minorities and college boys faced special challenges, but most completed training and moved on. That was not the case for everyone arriving. Recruits failed for a variety of reasons, including injuries, many times an aggravation of old ones from accidents or athletics. The vast majority, especially the draftees, finished as the instructors learned how much pressure to exert without causing the recruit to snap. Uncle Sam needed troops during wartime and by 1966 the process of weeding them out assumed a greater urgency than normal. Still, peer pressure and extraordinary duties ensured conformity and cooperation, except among the most difficult recruits, although sometimes only after significant hardships.

Certainly, some recruits had a harder time making the adjustment. The timing was important. One recruit remembered that on arriving in March 1968 several people in his basic training platoon had bad attitudes. These were people who "had the feeling that they didn't care what anybody told them. I think they'd just as soon be thrown into the stockade. They figured, 'Well, what the hell can you do with me? I'm going to Vietnam anyway.'"[51]

To try to maintain discipline, drill instructors often singled out the people who did not perform their duties up to expectations. In one case, a DI inspected the recruits to make sure that they had shaved properly. When he discovered that one had not, he called him in front of the platoon and ordered him to dry shave (no shaving cream). The young man who had a bad case of acne did as instructed and according to one of the onlooker, "it just tore his face up." As he observed, "I thought it was pretty nasty of them, but . . . that was one of the ways they kind of show everybody, to pick on one guy and make an example of him, keep us all in line."[52]

Sometimes the DIs relied on other recruits to discipline their counterparts. One Marine recalled that he had risen to lead a group of seventy-five recruits. Each day, the DIs would call him to their hooch and work him over with the instruction, "You make sure that everything goes well today. . . . Anything that goes wrong we are taking care of right now, so when it does go wrong it is your job to straighten it out." He told the four squad leaders beneath him that if any problems arose with a recruit, "you correct him. And if you can't handle it, I'll correct him." That meant the use of whatever means necessary to ensure compliance, as he wanted no part of having to answer to the DIs.[53]

The efforts to ensure conformity could often change people. One person observed that "a perfectly regular guy could come into the Army, and before he knew it, he was doing things he'd never done before. Making fun of some poor fat guy after the sergeants kicked him around. Talking about what it would be like to get a gang together and take the café waitress out in the alley."[54]

The Marines developed particularly strident measures to deal with under-performing or recalcitrant recruits. These included the use of "motivational" platoons. According to Marine Colonel William C. Joslyn, there were two types. The "incentive" was "for the mama's boy, the cry-baby who's never been in a fight" while the "achievement" was "for the hard-nosed kid, the rebel who doesn't want to be a member of the team."[55]

In both cases, the recruit endured additional physical training and abuse. The days started with ten-mile forced marches followed by viewing films such as President Johnson awarding a Medal of Honor to a fallen Marine. Then, runs over the 225-yard infiltration course soaked a recruit in sweat and mud to yells of "If you don't make it this time, we'll just stay here until you do." Other duties included filling buckets of sand and trekking across the base to deposit them or digging ditches and then filling them back up again. This continued until the recalcitrant recruit learned his lesson, or he snapped and ended up in the harsher Correctional Custody with more serious offenders who experienced even tougher duties and harsher living conditions. As one Marine noted, once finished, "guys either come out with laryngitis because they're completely hoarse from screaming all the time, or they come out like vegetables—completely passive from being buffeted back and forth, ready to take orders from anyone."[56]

Religious and racial differences could intensify how officers and DIs singled out a person. A Black Muslim lamented that his time at Fort Jackson, South Carolina, included intense harassment. When he arrived, the officers stood him in front of the company and stated, "This guy is a Muslim. He cannot be trusted. If you are in training with him, watch your back." "I feared for my life out on the rifle range," as his sergeants would tell him that "guys like you should be dead." He encountered other challenges. Knowing that Muslims should not eat or touch pork, officers assigned him to KP duty cleaning the grease traps. Fortunately for him, a chaplain intervened and removed him from the duty. Other actions included being consistently grilled by Army intelligence and doctors who questioned his loyalty and asked if he was a Communist and trying to turn other GIs against the United States.[57]

The persecution created a virulently antiwar activist. He began carrying around a book by Marx and "after duty hours I would preach Marxism and

Islam" to interested recruits. He admitted, "If I had to pick up a gun, let me pick it up and turn it on the system, not somebody in Vietnam who I know nothing about." The system responded by ordering his deployment to Vietnam as a two-star general told him, "Well, you're going to die all right. But to hell with this fighting and dying in the streets. You're going to die in Vietnam." An assistant chimed in, "Since you love the Vietnamese people and the Communist way so much, you going to go out there and be with them. Boy, we going to make sure you die in Vietnam."[58]

DIs also liked singling out those who they believed were homosexuals. One veteran remembered being at Fort Lewis, Washington, where others accused one recruit of being gay. "So consequently he was followed around by a sergeant and called faggot and queer. . . . And he was kicked, and made to crawl on his hands and knees and police cigarette butts. And he was made to keep his eyes averted downward to the ground and ridiculed in front of everyone." The humiliation took its toll. The veteran recalled, "I saw that kid sitting in his bunk one afternoon and he was just rocking back and forth, banging his head against his pillow."[59]

The marginalization of individual recruits had consequences. The most obvious was a recruit going AWOL (Absent Without Leave) or UA (Unauthorized Absence) in the Marine Corps or deserting. Going AWOL was not uncommon in the history of the U.S. military and typically happened for short periods, with many of the people ultimately returning and facing a wide variety of punishments for the offense but remaining in their units. These could include soldiers leaving for R&R and returning late after having too good a time. Others involved thoughts of deserting, but returning after thinking it over.

Desertion, a much more serious offense, involved absences beyond thirty days and with a demonstrated intent to leave permanently. High rates had occurred even during World War II when in 1944 there were 63 desertions per 1,000 active duty personnel, a number not matched in Vietnam until 1971, when they rose to 73 per 1,000. In fact, the numbers through 1968 were much lower than World War II, being only 21 per 1,000 that year.[60] In raw terms, the numbers rose in the Army from 27,000 in 1967 to 39,234 in 1968 and peaked at 65,643 in 1970.[61]

Only a fairly small percentage of the desertions occurred during training, but if the recruits became "runners," the Army branded them as criminals. With the assistance of law enforcement agencies, including the Federal Bureau of Investigation (FBI), the military began a manhunt. Deserters constantly lived a life of watching over their shoulder. The threat of being returned to the service was great enough, but often more serious punishments awaited them, with hard time in a military prison being the most feared. Some fled to Canada or elsewhere, but officials often caught and punished those who remained stateside.

Among the thousands of examples of desertion and punishment, Jim Allgood's experience offers particular insights. At first, he refused to report to Fort Ord, but ultimately did. When a chaplain refused to refer him to a psychiatrist to help with a discharge, he bolted and fled to his home. After a month, he turned himself in and while awaiting trial for charges of being AWOL, a psychiatrist recommended a discharge, noting the "subject is basically unsuitable for military service." As he waited, he struck a corporal during an altercation. The officer in charge ordered him to start basic so he ran away. For two and half years, he eluded capture while working in the San Joaquin Valley. Ultimately, FBI agents caught him at a gas station in Santa Cruz in October 1968. They handcuffed him, threw him in their car, and took him to the Fort Ord stockade to await trial.[62]

The process of deciding his fate continued for several years. Another psychiatrist found that he was an unsatisfactory candidate for the military and an officer assigned to be the Article 32 investigator (the equivalent of the grand jury) recommended his discharge and the dropping of charges. When the commanding officer of the post recommended trial, Allgood retained a civilian attorney who went to a U.S. District Court, which ruled against the Army and issued a writ ending the military's custody over him. Immediately, the military appealed the decision in a higher court while Allgood returned to his wife and job.[63] The case ultimately was settled in Allgood's favor, but only after a significant amount of wrangling and a stain on his record.

In extreme cases, the stress of training led to attempted suicide. In 1968, at Fort Dix, New Jersey, more than 200 recruits attempted suicide and six succeeded. In 1969, David Swanson of New Britain, Connecticut, became another such casualty. He had arrived on August 4 and reported to sickbay with chest pains the following day, but doctors ordered that he return to his platoon. Four days later, he slashed his left wrist. After receiving medical care and having a short consultation with two Army psychiatrists, he went back to duty. On August 29, he tried killing himself again. This time, the psychiatrist characterized him as an "immature and dependent personality," but certified that he had no signs of mental illness, so he marched back to his platoon.

His worried parents contacted their congressman, whose office tried warning Army officials about the seriousness of the situation. While some steps were taken to address the problem, by September 20 he went AWOL and returned home. There, he took an overdose that killed him, leading an angry Congressman Thomas Meskill (R-CT) to charge the Army with being "grossly negligent and responsible for the man's death." The Army instead blamed the problem on the young man's "long-standing personality problem" and claimed that with "time and leadership" he would have been able to "adjust to military life and perform satisfactorily."[64]

While some people snapped under the strain, the vast majority of recruits simply endured, and in some cases enjoyed the challenges of training. The Army and the Marines, especially as the war intensified, needed the soldiers to fill slots created by deaths and completed tours. Training was psychologically and physically demanding, but those with some background in sports and those from families with strong disciplinarian parents found the process challenging, but not overwhelming. The majority finished and moved onto Advanced Infantry Training or other specialized training courses.

Dangers of Training

Training held potential dangers beyond the self-inflicted ones, although they intensified in advanced training when soldiers began handling more sophisticated weapons. Because many of the recruits lacked experience with weapons and there was the ever-present danger of malfunction, accidents happened. Injuries typically ranged from minor to more serious ones, but the possibility of death permeated camp life. The military worked hard to prevent problems, but some occurred.

Sometimes, the stress of training combined with access to weapons created a volatile situation. One Army veteran recalled being at the rifle range one day and returning from the armory with a functioning rifle to find his unit in disarray. One of the recruits who "was getting picked on really bad" had shot an instructor. The ultimate fate of the instructor remained a mystery, but the MPs hauled off the perpetrator to await an unknown fate.[65]

In another case, an instructor showed the recruits how to use a white phosphorous grenade. To the horror of the onlookers, "the thing exploded right in his hand and he just disintegrated. He virtually disappeared before our eyes. We had to go around and search for body parts and the only thing we found was the palm of one hand . . . and a couple other fragments of body. White phosphorous just ate the guy right up."[66]

While chances for mishaps in basic training existed, perhaps the greatest danger that weighed on the recruits was the continuing specter of Vietnam. One Army recruit at Fort Riley, Kansas, remembered that one week saw three funerals for KIAs (killed in action) in Vietnam who had trained at the base. "It's depressing to hear the gun salute and the last bugle call for them. You can't help thinking they might be sounding taps for you someday." As time passed, though, he observed that the thought "begins to disappear after awhile."[67] Ultimately, however, they played taps for him in 1967.

Daily reminders of the fighting in Vietnam confronted the recruits in training. A Marine described an NCO (non-commissioned officer) who "had almost no face. His face and head had been burned and scarred beyond recognition. His ears were just stubs and his mouth and nose were more or less gone. . . . We were in awe of guys who had come back from Vietnam, but seeing him jarred us."[68] Such visuals reminded the trainees of how close they had moved toward possible combat and combined with everyday dangers to force recruits to recognize that they were not at home any longer.

What Kept the Recruit Going

Even in the face of danger and the constant degradation and fatigue associated with training, many forces drove the recruits to succeed. The most obvious one, especially for draftees, was the threat of punishment and continued time in basic if they failed. If they tried to go AWOL, they faced time in military jail, a significant threat given the reputation of the military penal system. But there was another: the sense that failure was not an option. As one observer noted, "The structural mechanism for insuring . . . success was basically the same as that used in primitive rituals: forbidden to quit, he was forced to persevere. He had no choice but to conform."[69]

Fear of failure proved another strong incentive. Philip Caputo, after entering the Marines and starting The Basic School (TBS) for potential officers summed up well the feeling of being classified as an "unsat." "I endured these tortures because I was driven by an overwhelming desire to succeed, no matter what. That awful word—unsat—haunted me. I was more afraid of it than I was Sergeant McClellan. Nothing he could do could be as bad as having to return home and admit to my family that I had failed." He added, "It was not their criticism I dreaded, but the emasculating affection and understanding they would be sure to show me. I could hear my mother saying, 'That's all right, son. You don't belong in the Marines but here with us.'" He went to great lengths to avoid being identified with the "marginals," whom he described as carrying "the virus of weakness."[70]

While fear of punishment and failure pushed many recruits forward, others remembered the Army adopting various methods to ensure completion. According to one veteran, to discourage desertion, DIs told the draftees that "only 17 percent of us were going to Vietnam. And of that small percentage, only 11 percent would actually be combat troops. That eased my mind a great deal. Hey there's still a chance that I won't have to go and get my guts blown out." However, a certain cynicism developed afterward as he lamented that "at the end of our training, with only three exceptions—one fool who had gone Airborne, one guy who kept fainting and another kid who had a perforated eardrum—every single one of us went to Vietnam—200 guys."[71]

Many others developed coping mechanisms to keep going, some related to trying to maintain elements of their individuality. In one case, a North Carolina trainee used his liberty to go to the nearby Augusta College and mingle with students, over time establishing friendships that allowed him to maintain touch with the world that he had left.[72] In another case, W.D. Ehrhart stressed that he and many other Marine recruits looked forward to Sunday. "Everybody always wanted to go to church because it was the only hour in a 168 hour week when you weren't doing push-ups or close order drill or bayonet training while livid DIs swarmed all over you like horseflies."[73]

Another part of the equation was that the military, especially the Army, wanted as many people to finish the process as possible to fill their manpower needs. One author noted that "one of the most striking achievements of the drill instructors is to create and maintain the illusion that basic training is an extraordinary challenge, one that will set those who graduate apart from others, when in fact almost everyone can succeed."[74]

The Turning Point

A significant part of survival of the initial training occurred in the fourth to fifth week when the training changed from breaking down the recruit into building a soldier. When recruits moved to weapons train-

Group photo of Marine Training Platoon 1055 in San Diego, California, September 1966. Many of the young men ended up in combat in Vietnam, including members of the Morenci Nine. *(Photo courtesy of the family of Clive Garcia Jr.)*

ing, giving them something to focus on that was new and constructive, attitudes changed. As one observer noted, "for the first time, the recruit feels that he is being given something useful to do, that he is acquiring a skill that is of some interest and value." He added that "he is tested on his proficiency with the rifle and he passes the test. Suddenly, he is no longer a worthless human being; he has a worthwhile skill for which he is rewarded by a lessening of harassment." When combined with the reduced physical and emotional stress and the process of being in better shape from running and physical activities that had developed in the first few weeks, the recruit began to believe that he would make it and be ready for the future challenges.[75]

Along with new training opportunities came changes in the DI's tactics. While there remained a tendency to marginalize "unsats," the goal of unit cohesiveness and teamwork, a building of espirit d'corps, became even more important. When a comrade faltered during long hikes or runs, a Marine remembered that "somebody would take his rifle, somebody would take his pack, and two other people would take his arms, and you always bring your fellow Marine along because we're a unit."[76]

The results could be very satisfying for many young men. An Iowa veteran remembered the pride associated with his platoon winning the award for best barracks. "When the lieutenant announced we had won the award it made all the sweating and slaving worth it." By the end of basic, he also wrote, "I am beginning to acquire a different attitude towards things. I don't give up on a difficult challenge."[77]

For the final few weeks of training, the drill instructors moved toward rebuilding the recruit in the image that the military sought, a well-conditioned, reflexive soldier who responded to orders and subordinated individual desires to the group. The verbal assaults often continued, although typically more restrained and often as positive reinforcement. At this point, the goal turned into building a man who thought he was the meanest, toughest soldier in the world, able to defeat any enemy.

Training Results

By the end of initial training, most young men looked back on the experience as one that had proven their manhood and fulfilled a rite of passage that many men like their fathers had completed while weaker members of their generation had failed or never tried. Questioning anything became anathema to the soldiers. Unit cohesion, discipline, and a willingness to work for the common good marked success. By the end, the drill instructors had instilled these values, although strong vestiges of American individualism remained in many recruits who subordinated them temporarily for the sake of survival.

The results were often clear. In one case, a Marine remembered his unit completing boot and walking back to their barracks in new uniforms when an instructor yelled, "Hit the dirt." Without thinking, they did and immediately began crawling along on the ground in their new uniforms. The instructor proudly exclaimed, "There, now you're Marines. You did what you're told, when you're told."[78]

Another Marine veteran who completed boot camp at Parris Island reported that at the end, "When I came out I was convinced that I could beat anybody in the world. I didn't have enough sense to be afraid of anything. I didn't question why or how to do something, I just did it."[79] In a different case, a veteran recalled, "Boot camp was a bitch, but you came out feeling good and looking good. We all knew that the DIs were brainwashing us, but we loved it. . . . You felt you could kick anybody's ass and that all the girls would just jump all over you."[80]

Despite the enthusiasm of some of the recruits, others questioned the entire process and called for reform. Toward the end of the war, Lieutenant Colonel William E. Datel and Lieutenant Colonel Llewellyn J. Letgers at Fort Ord instituted a merit-based system of rewards rather than punishments. Each new recruit received a punch card, which the drill instructor reviewed three times a day and gave punches for performance. In addition, once a week, there was an overall evaluation. Bonuses such as movies, two-day passes, and other things accumulated for the best recruits. This concept provided positive reinforcement and reduced the "stripping of self," thereby easing the transition from civilian to soldier. While recommended for overall adaptation, drill instructors and many training officers resisted and appeared unwilling to accept any drastic change.[81]

The initial training experience, no matter the techniques, when combined with future instruction, created a man who had survived and often excelled in a very demanding physical and psychological test of manliness. The recruit left with a new confidence and often viewed himself as separated from others in his generation who he believed could not handle the task he had just completed. In addition, as one observer noted, the recruits had reoriented "their thinking to identify with the group, many new soldiers insisted that they belonged to the best platoon of the best company of the best branch of the armed forces in the history of war."[82]

Advanced Training

Upon graduation from basic training or boot camp, the recruit received an assignment determined by a Pentagon computer, despite some recruiters promising different assignments. The most dreaded designation for many young men was the MOS 0311 for the Marines and 11 B for the Army, infantry. A certain gallows humor evolved relating to the designation of "11-Bravo" as they often referred to themselves as "11-Bulletstoppers" or "11-Bushes."[83]

Frustrations often arose with the Pentagon computer-generated assignments. One complained, "I don't quite know what to think of the good ol' USMC. They looked at my college calculus, chemistry, and physics and said I'd make a good infantryman."[84]

Once designated for the infantry, most Army recruits received a short leave and then reported for Advanced Infantry Training (AIT) while many of their colleagues with different MOS designations headed off to different sites for training in areas such as mechanics and communication. They traveled to various training sites across the country and often confronted signs such as the one at North Fort Polk, Louisiana, a place called "Tigerland," which read: "Training ground for the infantry soldier of Vietnam."[85] For many, this reinforced what many already feared was their ultimate fate.

AIT built on the process begun in basic training or boot camp. Recruits received more instruction in firing weapons, although many worked with the M-14 and did not fire the regulation M-16 until in Vietnam. Bayonet training and hand-to-hand training continued, with advanced techniques taught. Trainees still spent some time in the classroom learning basic warfare and tactics. The overall changes were noticeable to many as they realized that they were one step closer to combat to Vietnam.

A major transition into AIT was the advanced training in firing specialized weapons. Recruits received more instruction in weapons such as the 50-caliber machine gun and other automatic weapons, laying Claymore mines and other anti-personnel ordnance, and sometimes operating more advanced weapons. Increasingly, they began spending time in the field on maneuvers, and some trained at places like Camp Pendleton, where mock Vietnamese villages had been constructed. The troops performed attacks and operations on the sites, which were often populated by Asian American troops.

Some found advanced training easier than others. In one case, a Texan moved to Fort Huachuca, Arizona, after basic in Louisiana. A star tennis player in college, he was pulled aside by the base commander, who had him travel the country representing the base in tennis tournaments, although he took some time to work on Morse code as he prepared for a specialty in communications. At other times, Army brass flew in, and he and his doubles partner played with the generals and their staff. It was cushy duty, and in fact, the base commander worked up orders for him and his partner to transfer to West Point to serve on the athletic staff. However, a couple of weeks before this happened, the command changed and the new general cancelled the move. A few months later, he found himself in a forward firebase only a few miles from Cambodia. In his first night, he received guard duty with a machine gun. He spent the entire night trying to figure out how to load it, a job he should have learned in advanced training. Fortunately, he did not have to use it that night.[86]

Establishing the Purpose of the Job: Kill! Kill! Kill!

Advanced training built on the efforts of basic training and boot camp in creating men who responded to orders and further pushed the job of the soldier: to kill when ordered. This contradicted almost every impulse embedded by civilian society throughout most of their lives. Civil society considered killing wrong, a criminal offense. As a result, the military labored hard to reprogram the recruits, and it often took much time and effort to accomplish the goal.

This reprogramming required the dehumanization of the Viet Cong and North Vietnamese. Training officers employed a variety of tactics to achieve the objective. One included listening to the instructor order: "First two rows down!" They would drop and respond, "Kill, kill, kill the gooks!"[87] In another point, during bayonet drills one guy would scream "The spirit of the bayonet is" and then everyone would respond, "To kill." He followed with "I can't hear you," and the response grew louder, "To kill, to kill." Once worked into a frenzy, the instructor would order an about face and the group waiting to practice the drill would yell, "The United States effort in Vietnam is a peace keeping mission." [88] Such irony was not lost on many observers.

The training suffered from serious lapses. The military prepared recruits to enter into a combat zone with little to no training in dealing with civilian populations who looked like the enemy. Stories filtered back, through veterans and media portrayals, of how women and children often were Viet Cong who set booby traps or tried to kill Americans with grenades. Vietnam was not World War II, with clear front lines and a more easily identifiable enemy typically separated from the civilian population. It was a guerrilla war that on a daily basis brought U.S. soldiers into contact with an alien people among whom many Americans could not distinguish the enemy from the ally. The training made it much more difficult to deal with such a situation as all Vietnamese became "gooks," and by extension the enemy.

Some veterans, especially minorities already familiar with racial stereotyping in their own lives, recognized this problem. One African American veteran observed that after entering the Marines in 1963 he took guerrilla warfare training at Camp Pendleton. At that time, the Marines practiced as if the Cubans were the aggressors, which he noted was easy "because you had a lot of Mexicans" who served as Cubans. Over time, things changed as the Cuban targets on the firing range changed to "silhouettes" of Vietnamese and "getting people ready for the little gooks." Increasingly "any Hawaiians and Asian-American in the unit . . . played the roles of aggressors in the war games."[89]

Another African American recalled that during training "right away

they told us not to call them Vietnamese. Call everybody gooks, dinks."
By the time he received his orders for Vietnam, he was convinced that
the Vietnamese "were like animals, or something other than human. They
ain't got no regard for life. They'd blow up little babies just to kill one
GI. . . . They told us they're not to be treated with any type of mercy or
apprehension. That's what they engraved in you. That killer instinct. Just
go away and do destruction."[90]

Another explained how the dehumanization process worked. "We
didn't look on the Vietnamese as human beings. They were subhuman.
To kill them would be easy for you. If you continued with this process,
you could stack them up like cordwood and you didn't have any bad
feelings about it because they were a subhuman species." He added that
the use of terms like "gooks" and "zipperheads" became equated more
with insects and the instructors would say, "there's a gook, step on it and
squash it. . . . These were gooks and you had to kill them."[91]

The final result often led to sarcasm about the success of the military
in training their recruits to kill. One joked that he saw the preparation as a
lesson in "one thousand and one ways to easily kill your mother-in-law."[92]
Yet, in reality, the training also had turned young men into soldiers able
to kill to defend themselves and their colleagues. This was necessary for
those young soldiers thoroughly indoctrinated with civilian concepts that
condemned killing. Some harbored serious reservations about taking a
life, but most readied for the challenge of firing on the enemy, and like
many other generations of warriors, worried that they might not be up
to the task.

Views of the Instructors

Typically, the relationship between trainee and instructor changed significantly from basic to AIT. While verbal harassment continued, the severity
that had begun to ebb toward the end of basic continued diminishing as
instructors began focusing more on building individual abilities and confidence. Many of the recruits, especially those expecting that they were
bound for Vietnam, began concentrating even more on the task at hand
as they realized its potential importance to their survival. As a result, the
respect for the instructors and their knowledge intensified.

One veteran commented that after reaching AIT that "most of the
instructors were returnees from Vietnam and they were real knowledge-
able about what was going on. . . . They trained and taught us about a lot

of things that had been overlooked because it was such an unusual type of war, guerrilla war."[93] As the war dragged on, another noted that AIT instructors "were more intense . . . We had a lot of Vietnam Veterans that were training us in different phases, so we were really getting close to the war then as far as talking to these guys, they . . . no, they weren't really on our case, they were more into teaching us how to survive the jungle which was in front of us. . . . I learned a lot from these people."[94]

The instructors' efforts typically had a positive effect and by the end of advanced training, most recruits exhibited a new pride and understanding of themselves. One Marine commented that at training's end, "I had developed a hardness and a confidence of which I had not thought myself capable. . . . I found that I had actually come to enjoy the unsolvable problems and pitfalls placed before me, and if I could not master them, I at least developed a capacity to know what I was doing."[95] A paratrooper added, "I came home on leave and I swore to God there were no five men alive who could beat me up. They might win for a while, but eventually if I persevered I would overcome them because I was Airborne. Hell, I could do anything."[96]

The Evaluations of Training

The evaluation of the training and its preparation for the rigors of combat in Vietnam differed among the individuals and their experiences. The amount of time devoted to training also affected its effectiveness, as the number of hours decreased when the need for replacements increased significantly in 1967 and 1968. While no amount of instruction readied someone completely for the rigors of combat, the uneven training clearly affected the infantryman's chances of survival in Vietnam. While some praised the training, many considered the preparation inadequate for the fighting in Vietnam.

Whether the soldier trained as a replacement or within a unit structure that ultimately deployed to Vietnam affected perceptions as well as who provided the instruction. One grunt observed, "I didn't go over as a replacement," rather "I went with the unit." He added, "We had real good training. Real good training."[97] An officer candidate acknowledged that the overall training in OCS, especially that provided by captains and senior NCOs just back from Vietnam, was effective and gave him "skills that really paid off in Vietnam."[98]

Even those who praised elements of the training found significant challenges once they arrived in country. A West Point graduate, Lieutenant Bruce Heim, wrote: "There is nothing the Army or West Point has in its training program that will prepare you to see your first dead GI, your first wounded child, your first crying widow. Military Art and Tactics never told you of the butterflies and near nausea that are continually with you as bullets fly over your head."[99] A Marine echoed his feelings: "How do you prepare somebody for that type of carnage? You don't! . . . I learned way more my first two months in Vietnam about war than they could [ever] have taught me."[100]

Even specific programs designed to promote survival had limitations. A Marine who took advanced training that included attacking mock villages emphasized that such training "gave you a basic idea of the villages and stuff but of course they couldn't portray the . . . fear, they couldn't portray of course going into an actual village with people in it and having them stare at you and hate you and things of that nature." He added that it was the people missing that taught "you of that prickly feeling on the back of your neck of, 'is this little kid going to come up and give you candy or a hand grenade.'"[101]

Another common criticism was that "we weren't really ready for all the different booby traps that there were there. . . . We had booby trap training in the states . . . but they were kind of Mickey Mouse compared to what we really ran into because it was too dangerous—you can't make a trap that . . . simulates what's going to happen without really getting hurt. You have too many casualties to practice that, so that's something you get used to and you get that just by instinct."[102] Booby traps accounted for a significant number of casualties, but few changes occurred in training at home, although the Army and Marines developed some projects in country.

The most biting critiques of training sometimes came from military officers, both during and after the war. In his study *The Army and Vietnam*, Andrew Krepinevich focused on the mentality of the military during the Cold War and its preoccupation with waging conventional wars like World War I, World War II, and the Korean War. It was a "comfortable, familiar frame of reference in which to approach conflict," according to Krepinevich, but it failed to take into account the nature of the guerrilla war in Vietnam. Instead of preparing troops for counterinsurgency, which required more emphasis on long-range patrolling, night operations, and intelligence gathering, the Army primarily continued its exercises in large battalion-style operations. The result was a "misplacement of training emphasis" that made it "easy to understand how the Army entered the war so unprepared in 1965."[103]

Another damning indictment of the training originated with the controversial Colonel David H. Hackworth. A highly decorated Korean veteran, having enlisted in the military at fifteen, he experienced his first tour in Vietnam as battalion commander for the 101st Airborne from 1965 to 1966. He ultimately received other assignments, including a stint in the Pentagon, before becoming the training battalion commander at Fort Lewis.[104] At Fort Lewis, Hackworth infiltrated the training, pretending to be a private, a "Korean retread." He characterized the AIT as "criminal" and "virtually everything these trainees got was wrong in terms of applicability to the war in Vietnam." He found incomplete and incompetent instruction in the use of the M-60, the night vision gear, and particularly mines and booby traps. He complained bitterly that the Army provided only five hours of instruction in the nine-week course on the mines and booby traps and that no instruction film existed, expressing dissatisfaction to a general that "almost every U.S. full colonel in Vietnam has an air-conditioned trailer, but we don't have a training aid that could save legs and lives." Other problems included instructors who never taught recruits how to change an M-16 magazine while in prone position or deal with a jammed weapon, a common problem with the M-16. He considered the fact that "graduation" field-training exercise (FTX) was conducted in the winter snow, while most of the troops would have a short time between leaving AIT and being in the tropics of Vietnam the ultimate insult.[105]

Hackworth fought the system and it won. Minor changes were made after his stint at Fort Lewis, but he encountered an entrenched bureaucracy. He returned for another tour in Vietnam, where he continued to butt his head against the wall. Ultimately, his outspokenness cost him his career. In June 1971, he gave an interview for ABC's *Issues and Answers* in Saigon with correspondent Howard Tucker. In it he responded to the question, "Did poor training lead to higher casualties in Vietnam?" He answered: "I am convinced of it. I think that our casualties were at least . . . thirty percent higher because of troops that were not properly trained." Such problems resulted in losses in areas such as friendly fire incidents. He also criticized the leadership, including political leaders, for the problems. Recognizing the military's displeasure with his statements and the unlikely probability that he would become a general or take his next assignment at NATO, he decided to retire from the Army.[106]

The problem that Krepinevich, Hackworth, and others failed to fully acknowledge is that changes occurred in training as the military learned lessons as the war continued. Equally important, the U.S. military in the 1960s had to prepare for different types of conflict, not just the one in Vietnam. Garrison duties in Korea or Western Europe required troops prepared for conventional warfare. In other areas, the U.S. military needed to plan for police actions such as the one in the Dominican Republic in 1965. These competing demands created problems of emphasis in training and contributed to significant challenges for the officers implementing military policy in Vietnam with troops not particularly well trained for the conditions and tactics of the enemy. While some troops received more specialized training at bases in places such as Panama and once in country, these efforts often stretched resources. Similar problems plagued the U.S. military well into the twenty-first century, when it found itself embroiled in an urban guerrilla war in Iraq.

Next Stop Vietnam

By 1966, the general perception upon completion of AIT was that a soldier was bound for Vietnam. Manpower strengths had dramatically increased in the country and remained near 500,000 for the period from 1966 to 1970. However, with the military having several million men in uniform, this meant that many of the soldiers remained stateside or headed to other duties in bases in Germany, Korea, Japan, or Guam. A small number headed off for specialized training in organizations such as the Rangers and SEALS, but the vast majority waited for service on the front lines in a ground war in areas besides Vietnam.[107] No matter what the odds, the specter of Vietnam remained omnipresent for the infantrymen in the Army and Marines. It was an ominous one for most, although some wanted to get into the thick of battle. Whether excited or not, many headed toward combat in Vietnam, sometimes with only a short interval between training and fighting.

3

The First Wave

The American Infantryman in Vietnam, 1961–1968

Marine Philip Caputo waded ashore in South Vietnam in 1965 convinced that "like the French soldiers of the late eighteenth century, we [Americans] saw ourselves as the champions of 'a cause that was destined to triumph.' So, when we marched into the rice paddies on that damp March afternoon, we carried, along with our packs and rifles, the implicit convictions that the Viet Cong (VC) would be quickly beaten and that we were doing something altogether noble and good." Later, he observed, "We kept the packs and rifles; the convictions, we lost."[1]

Like Caputo, in the earliest stages of the conflict most American infantrymen expressed few doubts about their mission or America's eventual triumph over the Viet Cong guerrillas and their North Vietnamese Army (NVA) allies. Yet, most left for Vietnam with significant apprehensions about how they would react in battle and whether they would survive. Once in the country, they battled the enemy, the environment, and often the military bureaucracy. They would fight and 58,000 ultimately would die in Vietnam, thousands of miles away from their homes and families. Those who returned often experienced physical and psychological trauma; and by the end of the tour, many doubted both the mission and the effectiveness of U.S. efforts to build a stable nation-state in South Vietnam. For many, like Caputo, convictions wavered, but most GIs remained steadfast in their commitment to their comrades and their country.

Last Goodbyes

The difficulty of the goodbyes when the recruits left for boot camp paled in comparison to those shipping out for Vietnam. Apprehension, fear, and anxiety hung like a dark cloud over everyone. The fear of death was especially acute for the infantryman who, depending on the method of transportation, might be in heavy combat within a couple of days. Leaving proved hard for everyone, but it was much more severe for the many young men who often traveled individually, not as a group, to the jungles of Southeast Asia.

The departures were difficult for many parents watching their sons, and in some cases daughters, leave. Even the most battle-hardened veteran had a hard time. Lewis Puller Jr. remembered that as he left, his father "tried to tell me again and for the thousandth time the parable of the Spartan mother who, on sending her own son off to war, advised him to come back with his shield or on it, but he was unable to complete the quote." As he turned to walk to the car, he hugged his father and "finally and after what seemed an eternity, we broke our embrace, and my mother led him back into the house with tears streaming down both their cheeks." He observed, "It was the first time I had ever seen my father cry."[2]

In another case, a South Dakotan who had been a POW in a Japanese camp during World War II shocked his son at the steps of the plane in Pierre. All his life, the father had promoted a young man's duty to fight for his country, but that day he approached his son and said, "You know, Son, you can go to Canada; I wouldn't mind a bit." He then pointed to another plane and said that if he wanted to go there or to Canada that he should do it. While caught off guard by his father's statement, the young man stressed, "I was still proud that I was going, but when he said that, it floored me," and "it brought tears to my eyes."[3]

Leaving wives and children was even harder. The grunt already faced the uncertainty of a year living under the cloud of death, but also having a spouse and typically young children created even more strain. The stress placed on marriages, many of them new ones done under the pressure of soldiers leaving and wanting a short time together, was significant. The wives also faced uncertainties of a life alone or returning to their families for the duration, often saddled with children, including newborns. The dark cloud of a spouse's possible death just added to the worry and tension.

One West Point graduate, James McDonough, described leaving his wife and newborn son at National Airport in Washington, DC. He told her, "Don't worry, I'll make it back. The words sounded weak, but I wanted her to believe them. I wasn't sure I did." After a kiss, "I broke the contact, forced myself to turn and walk away. I could not bring myself to look back even once at my wife and child. The pain was too great; my guilt at leaving them was too deep."[4]

The family members left behind faced a great deal of uncertainty, especially the wives of those leaving, many of whom remained traditional housewives in 1960s America. One Marine wife, Kathryn Fanning, summed up the feeling of many: "I felt lost when Hugh told me he had orders to Vietnam. I couldn't bear the thought of his leaving. Who would make me exercise? Who would put the cap back onto the toothpaste? I tried to kid with him about how things would go to hell in a handbasket, but the truth was, I was terrified."[5]

The military made some efforts to support the families. In one case, the Army created the Schilling Manor at an old airbase in Salina, Kansas. Army wives and children stayed in government-provided housing for the duration of their husband's tours in Vietnam along with some wives of MIAs and POWs. The base became known as "The Home of the Waiting Wives of the United States Armed Forces." Originally, a small group of wives from Fort Riley whose husbands deployed began living on the base. What began as a small experiment grew to hundreds of families. The military provided not only housing, but also schools, playgrounds, activities, and social support services. The assistance helped, although the periodic appearance of those bearing the president's condolences had an impact. Still, the positives outweighed the negatives.[6] Nonetheless, the vast majority of American wives waiting at home lacked this network and most experienced severe dislocations due to the absence of their loved ones.

For both the soldier and his family, the departure often was very traumatic. Many had dealt with similar problems during preceding wars, but the fact that the soldier often deployed alone combined with the rapidity of the insertion into combat added tension. Regardless, millions turned their backs on their homes for one year and headed off to war, like so many of their parents. One certainty for most, when contrasted with their fathers who fought in World War II, was a limited number of days to endure, 365 days for the Army and thirteen months for the Marines. The countdown began almost immediately and each grunt knew his DEROS (Date Eligible for Return from Overseas). For many, it proved a very long year.

The Trip Over

Soldiers traveled by either ship or plane to Vietnam. In the early stages of the war, many went as units on troop ships, mostly from West Coast ports. Others, especially those going as replacements as the war continued, simply boarded a plane for the long trip from the West Coast to Vietnam, typically with stops in Hawaii, the Philippines, or Japan. In either case, for most soldiers, apprehensions heightened the closer they got to Vietnam until they landed on the beaches, docks, or at the airport.

Early on, many troops traveled by ship, often with the units with which they had trained. The ships lacked creature comforts, especially for the enlisted men, as one Army soldier, David Parks, found when he boarded the U.S.S. *Patch* on December 16, 1966. Packed like sardines, they had bunks four layers high and ten across with little air circulating, especially in the lower decks. Once at sea, he complained that most of the grunts had never been on the ocean before and that "we are practically swimming in vomit."[7]

With little to do, the young men had a lot of time to think. Parks talked about lying in his bunk and daydreaming of better times back home. "It gives you a creepy feeling, this looking back over your whole life. You're practically telling yourself that you won't make it back. I try and shake this feeling by imagining something good happening to me after next year, when I'll be out. It's a little game that's hard to keep up, because you know you're trying to fool yourself." He thought about death and lamented, "If death does come, I hope it won't play around polite like. I want it to be fast and clean. I don't want to know what happened."[8]

For more than two weeks, the troops remained on the *Patch* traveling through the seemingly endless Pacific, heading into intense heat and humidity, which made the trip even more uncomfortable. Christmas passed and New Year's followed with the crew noting it by the blowing of a whistle, a few people opening contraband bottles of alcohol, and a weak attempt to sing "Auld Lang Syne." Finally, on January 2, 1967, the ship anchored off the coast of Vietnam and the next day Parks and his comrades finally touched dry ground. They carried their M-16s with six clips and prepared to meet the enemy, some envisioning themselves hitting the beach like their heroes at Normandy or Iwo Jima. Instead, they disembarked in orderly fashion, boarded trucks, and traveled up Highway 15 to their base camp, Zulu. While the lack of action reduced apprehension and thoughts of glory, Parks and his fellow soldiers liked that they were on dry ground and the countdown had begun for their return home.[9]

Another common transport for troops heading to Vietnam was the airplane, a comparative first in the American experience in war, with the time significantly shortened between leaving the United States and arriving in a combat zone. Often within twenty-four hours, the young soldier left home and landed in a different time zone in an alien country on the other side of the world. There was no time to acclimate like those on the ships, who at least had been traveling through the tropics, and there was less time to reflect on the impending change to their life. Still, the eighteen to twenty-four–hour trip seemed like an eternity to some and created a surreal experience of one day being stateside and the next in war.

The perception of the flights depended on the experience. One stewardess noted how some of the young men were rowdy, something she learned to expect when you put more than 200 soldiers on a plane bound for Vietnam. Sometimes, they would ask for a pillow or blanket in the overhead storage and then run their hands up her leg. In another case, the airline stupidly put sanitary napkins in the bathrooms that caused someone to think it would be funny to smear some ketchup on it and leave it in the aisle. While many GIs often apologized for the behavior of their comrades, she noted, "Fortunately, I came out of it not hating them. I knew a lot of girls that ended up that way."[10]

Grunts also held many different perspectives on the trip. One veteran remembered traveling from Fort Dix to San Francisco and then boarding a commercial plane for the trip over. He found the presence of the stewardesses with all the extras as "kind of ridiculous going off" to war as they served drinks and dinner.[11] Another recalled that during the trip, "I kept thinking that soon an announcement would come over the speakers stating that this was just a test to see how I would respond to pressure. It still hadn't hit me that I was on my way to a war zone. I wasn't issued a weapon when I boarded the plane, so how could I be going to a place where I was expected to shoot people?"[12]

No matter how the soldier arrived in Vietnam, it was a severe shock to the system. Many had never left their homes before joining the military and most could not have located Vietnam on the map before their induction. But, suddenly they were in an exotic and alien country, thousands of miles

A young Marine waits on the beach during a landing at Da Nang, August 1965. *(National Archives)*

from home. Many headed right to the front lines as replacements with little time to adjust to the new surroundings. The immediate immersion left many disoriented and desperately searching for some semblance of normal life. Living in a combat zone often made that nearly impossible.

First Impressions

Most veterans, whether front-line troops or rear echelon, shared first impressions of the heat, humidity, and rancid smells of South Vietnam. Most had never seen the Third World and its poverty and filth. In addition, most were truly unfamiliar with any Asian culture beyond occasional visits to a Chinese restaurant in the States. The shock of the weather and cultural change made many long for home even more. One grunt who received an assignment in the Central Highlands emphasized that "if I'd been on the coast I might have tried to swim east 'til I drowned." [13] Nonetheless, most accepted the challenge and began counting the days until they returned to the "world."

One veteran, Robert Peterson, summed up the feeling of many when he said that as he left the plane, "I felt like Alice stepping through the looking glass." The intense heat and humidity enveloped the soldier as soon as he departed the plane, making it especially hard on those who had just left winter in the United States. Peterson described the air as that of a "very smelly sauna" punctuated by the heavy smell of jet fuel that caused him to stop and take a deep breath. As he looked back at a stewardess who mouthed, "Good luck," he "turned back to the task at hand. I knew my life would never be the same from this moment on. This was the initiation into my Rites of Passage." [14]

The foul smells of rotting garbage and decaying plant life combined with the incessant sweating only compounded the agony that most of the soldiers were on their own. Early on in the conflict, troops often arrived as units with familiar faces. However, many of the grunts traveled as individuals. One draftee expressed his frustrations that "even though in a crowd of several individuals who felt exactly the same way, each man was on his own. Each man was an island. Each man had to face the future using his own inner strengths and dealing with his own inner weaknesses. I owned plenty of both." [15]

Once on the ground and processed, the soldiers not receiving rear-echelon jobs began filtering out to the units. "One of the things I remember was it [the bus] had all of these screens and things over the windows like we were prisoners. I thought, 'well that's stupid. I'm not going to try to escape.' I found out later that it was to keep them from throwing stuff at you!" [16] Others observed the olive drab buses had heavy armor over the wheels and strategic parts of the bus including the engine and the gas tanks, leading one to think to himself: "Wait a minute, now, let's see if I've got it straight. We're here to help defend the South Vietnamese against the Communist invaders, right? Why do we need protection from the people we're protecting?"[17]

Ironies often added to confusion. A veteran remembered arriving later in the war at Long Binh and "on the bus from the airport to this camp, the first thing I saw was some Vietnamese guy peeing on the side of the road. And I thought, 'Oh, geez, this is a backward country.' And the next thing I saw was Coca-Cola signs. I thought, 'this is very strange. This is a very unusual mixture.'"[18] Another wrote his parents that "this country is so beautiful, when the sun is shining on the mountains, farmers in their rice paddies, with their water buffalo, palms trees, monkeys, birds and even the strange insects. For a fleeting moment I wasn't in a war zone at all, just on vacation."[19]

For most, any illusion of being on vacation ended quickly. Many leapt immediately into the fray. While some received advanced training in booby traps and jungle warfare at special bases, the vast majority of grunts went right into front-line units to replace the killed, wounded, or those who had finished their tour. Most began counting down the days to the end, many battling apprehensions that they would not return home alive. While some thought about a chance for glory, most focused on survival.

The FNGs

When they arrived at their new bases and duties, the soldiers often experienced heightened feelings of isolation and disorientation. Once in camp, veterans labeled them the "fucking new guys" (FNGs) unless they had the good fortune to arrive with their own units. Like most organizations, there was an initiation ritual as the FNGs had to earn the respect of their peers. It was often a very perilous time as green soldiers found out that their training had fewer applications than promised. They learned on the job, all the while enduring the worst assignments.

Often, as part of the hazing, the new guys received the most dreaded duty of "burning of the shit." It was a disgusting, albeit necessary task to prevent disease. Because of the absence of widespread plumbing and sanitary conditions, enlisted men received the job of moving the cut-off fifty-five gallon oil drums from the bottom of the wooden outhouses into an area where they poured gasoline and crude oil onto the waste. Once they began burning it, they stirred it until it was gone. One GI remembered that "when lighted, the concoction produced a pungent odor and thick, dark smoke" that drifted upward into the often stale Vietnamese air.[20]

While the hazing was often disgusting, integrating into the unit was the more important task for the grunt. One Marine wrote that when he arrived "the old-timers who had been in Vietnam for a year wouldn't have anything to do with me." They made him earn their respect, as one corporal warned him that "you mess up and you're on your own. Mess up twice and I'll kill you." He admitted that he stayed at the back of the line during patrols. "I figured the best way not to screw up was to stay in the back and watch everybody else. New guys in the back of a line couldn't trip bouncing betties or step on mines. But if a new guy took the point, people started getting very nervous."[21]

For many others the shock of what they would be doing for the next year often was overwhelming. A future Medal of Honor recipient, Franklin Miller, admitted that when he arrived at his base camp at An Khe in March 1966 he enjoyed taking an M-16 without signing for it and all the ammunition and grenades that he wanted. However, as he prepared to board the helicopter to head to a recon unit, the door gunner asked, "Are you the replacement for those guys that got greased last night?" He remembered that the statement made "my skin crawl" and that the flight to the forward camp "seemed like the longest I'd experienced in any military aircraft."[22]

Like many others, Miller suffered a significant shock when he arrived. The first few weeks were very dangerous and many died learning on the job, including 997 who perished the first day.[23] Ultimately, most learned the ropes and integrated into the units, making sure to inflict on the other newcomers the same hazing that they experienced, sometimes more, sometimes less, depending on the person. The reality of most units after 1966 was the constant cycling of troops as some died, other suffered wounds, and some finished their tours. The overall unit cohesiveness that characterized World War II and to some degree Korea was lost. While all struggles had FNGs, the Vietnam War made it more common because of the rotation system.[24]

Why They Fought

Once in country, the reasons that the young men fought, often heroically, differed among individuals. In the early stages of the war, the majority were volunteers, committed to the mission. In fact, 20 percent of the soldiers who had comfortable duty in Europe requested a transfer to Vietnam during the period 1966–67. They actively submitted requests, Form 1049s, and in many cases the military granted them.[25] Whatever the reason for their choices, many grunts continued to write home about their commitment to defeating the Communists, while others stressed the common thread of soldiers throughout the ages, that of fighting to protect one's comrades and to survive.

Especially in the early stages of the war, idealism played a more significant role for some grunts. One Marine wrote in his last will and testament in December 1965: "I am fighting an inevitable enemy that must be fought—now or later. I am fighting to protect and maintain what I believe and what I want to live in—a democratic society. If I am killed while carrying out this mission, I want no one to cry or mourn for me. I want people to hold their heads high and be proud of me for the job I did." He died a couple of months later on Valentine's Day 1966 at the age of nineteen.[26]

Another raised this theme when he wrote what he called his last letter: "Believe me, I didn't want to die, but I know it was part of the job. I want my country to live for billions and billions of years to come. I want it to stand as a light to all people oppressed and guide them to the same freedom we know. . . . I can hold my head high because I fought, whether it be in heaven or hell. Besides, the saying goes, 'One more GI from Vietnam, St. Peter; I've served my time in hell.'" He died on February 1, 1966, while on patrol, at the age of twenty-one.[27]

More commonly, the average grunt fought primarily for survival and that of his buddies. One commander wrote years later about the grunts with whom he fought that "they were tough, dirty, and often profane but loveable characters who fought more for each other than for the cause in Vietnam." He added, "Ideology is not tangible when people start shooting and you depend on those to either side of you to help defend you. You do not create a personal relationship with the Constitution, Declaration of Independence, democracy, or capitalism. That only occurs with other fighting men in the heat of battle."[28]

In another case, during especially ferocious fighting, a sergeant in the 1st Cavalry wrote: "I was so surprised last night to see that the men here were willing to risk their own lives to save a buddy's. It really makes you have faith in people again."[29] Another veteran who arrived in 1969 echoed those feelings and noted that the arguments for fighting for democracy for the South Vietnamese rang hollow as "the waters had been too politically muddied by then. And I'm not sure that in most wars by the time a man gets to the front lines that kind of appeal works. He'll die for the man on his left and his right, maybe for his platoon leader or company commander. What drives him on day to day, moment to moment, is the strength of personal bonds within the unit itself."[30]

Whether fighting for ideology or comrades, or a blending of the two, the American soldier in Vietnam went into the field against a tenacious enemy. While the commitment to the stated goals of extending democracy wavered as the war continued and the grunt constantly complained about the conditions, for many, the experience was the seminal event of their lives. They created long-term friendships with men with whom they shared their memories and suffering through the daily struggle to stay alive. This intense bonding affected people in many different ways.

Dealing With Fear

Besides the constant companion of boredom, fear marched along with soldiers in Vietnam as it had with every other soldier in the history of man. Many soldiers went into battle as a test of their manliness. Those raised on literature such as Stephen Crane's novel *The Red Badge of Courage* asked themselves how they would deal with the fear.[31] Would they stand tall in the face of danger, or cower and run as Henry Fleming originally did? The ever-present nature of combat in Vietnam with the snipers and booby traps, the elusive enemy that chose their time and place of contact, and other dangers of disease and pestilence exacerbated the fear.

There were always exceptions as an arrogance of power sometimes dominated the grunts' attitude, especially in the early stages of the war. One veteran wrote: "We were young men in search of our destiny, our kismet; filled with the piss and vinegar of our years. . . . We were ready to be tested, if the test wasn't too severe." He added, "I wondered—how tough could it be? This was just a little pissant country that nobody could find on their map. This wasn't a real war—this was just Vietnam."[32]

Despite such arrogance, most young men fought back the fear. A young volunteer from upstate New York wrote: "I was nineteen when I arrived in The Nam, and scared to death. Six feet and a hundred and twenty-five pounds of skin and bones, glasses, silver fillings in my teeth. Scared to death; never a hero." For him, the thought of returning home "was so far away, so far beyond the imagination. You knew The World existed, but deep inside you knew it was spinning without you, and damned few people even noticed you weren't there."[33]

Others talked candidly about the fear. One grunt emphasized that over time the "worst thing is the fear that grabs you. A horrible fear that won't let you sleep . . . and since you can't sleep, you don't do anything but think." He talked about thinking a lot of home, the friends and family remembered there and "that you cry at night when you're on guard and nobody can see you. You cry for the suffering, the pain, and for the fear that invades you because you don't know when you're going to die . . . the terror goes with you all the time."[34]

While there were exceptions, most entered the war zone afraid on many levels: dreading death or maiming, letting his comrades down, or being labeled a coward. Sometimes the fear became too great for some men to function, but the vast majority dealt with it, partly as a result of training and largely due to a survival instinct. Most American soldiers performed capably under the stress of combat, but the fear factor rarely went too far away. When it did, people became scared of that person and avoided the burnt-out comrades who endangered the unit.

Getting Down to Business

While U.S. politicians proclaimed South Vietnamese liberty the primary goal of American policy, Vietnam veterans recognized their principal duty was to kill the enemy. Some soldiers, with little supervision and very dependent on role models and group mentalities, became cold-blooded killers, while others fought for survival and continued questioning the basic assumptions of the killing. No matter which, the survival instinct proved very strong for almost all except the completely burned-out or depressed.

A major function of the training had been the dehumanization of the enemy, reducing them to non-human status to ease the transition toward killing. Modern technology, especially artillery and aircraft, had made the killing cleaner and more disengaged, easing the psychological damage done to the soldier. Yet, in Vietnam there were different standards as the enemy was more elusive and less likely to directly confront Americans. The proximity of civilians and limited rules of engagement in many areas created additional frustrations; as one Texan exclaimed, "The trouble is, no one sees the Vietnamese as people. They're not people. Therefore, it doesn't matter what you do to them."[35]

Race often played a role, one thoroughly indoctrinated by society and military training. One Marine remembered that "the only thing they told us about the Viet Cong was they were gooks. They were to be killed. Nobody sits around and gives you their historical and cultural background. They're the enemy. Kill, kill, kill. That's what we got in practice. Kill, kill, kill. . . . I felt that if people were killing Americans, we should fight them." The grunt acknowledged that "As a black person, there wasn't no problem fightin' the enemy. I knew Americans were prejudiced, were racist and all that, but, basically, I believed in America 'cause I was an American."[36]

Whether race was a factor or not, for some killing proved easier than they thought. A platoon leader remarked, "You'd be surprised how similar killing is to hunting. I know I'm after souls, but I get all excited when I see a VC, just like when I see a deer. I go ape firing at him. It isn't that I'm so crazy. I think a man who freezes killing a man would freeze killing a deer. I'm not perverted, crazy, or anything else. . . . He runs, you fire. You hunt so I think you'd feel the same way. It isn't all that horrifying."[37]

Another infantryman observed that "the frightening thing about it all is that it is so very easy to kill in war. There's no remorse, no theatrical 'washing of the hands' to get rid of the nonexistent blood, not even any regrets." During combat, "you're scared, really scared, and there's no thinking about it. You kill because that little SOB is doing his best to kill you and you desperately want to live, to go home, to get drunk or walk down the street on a date again." Such sentiments were prompted by the suddenness of most fighting, where the firing stopped and "it's all over and you're alive because someone else is either dead or so anxious to stay alive that he's run away and you are the victor—if there is such a thing in war."[38]

The duty to kill could waver, largely according to a person's own background, sense of situational ethics, and sensitivity to others. A veteran remembered that "one day during a fire fight, for the first time in my life, I heard the cries of the Vietnamese wounded, and I understood them. When somebody gets wounded, they call out for their mothers, their wives, their girlfriends. There I was listening to the VC cry for the same things. That's when the futility of the war dawned on me."[39] A Native American veteran recalled the first enemy that he saw dead and how it affected him. "I had to think about it because he looked like me, you know—dark eyes and black hair. This shook me up."[40]

For others specific events caused a reevaluation, especially when the "fog of war" created casualties among civilians who found themselves in the cross fire between Americans and the enemy. In one particular incident, U.S. soldiers of the Tiger Force entered an area where a man emerged from a small thatched hut with an AK-47. Without hesitating, the group fired on him, riddling the flimsy structure with M-16 bullets. The leader, Lieutenant Donald Wood, entered the hooch to find the dead man lying beside a woman and a baby who had been ripped apart in the intense barrage. Visibly upset, his colleagues tried comforting him, telling him that these things happened. Inconsolable, the lieutenant retreated into silence, unable to forget the dead child and asking how he would ever be able to talk about it. While others moved on to read their mail and put the day behind them, he could not escape the scene. For some like Wood such images haunted them for most of their lives.[41]

Few veterans admitted to enjoying killing and most counted down the days until their tour ended. One wrote in 1967: "I can't wait until this bloody mess is over. Time can't go fast enough. Every day you go out looking for someone to kill. And you're disappointed if you don't find a victim. Death as I have seen it here so far is awful. I hope the memory of it won't stay with me."[42] Another complained bitterly, "I never had the opportunity to directly save lives. My responsibility was to kill and in the process of killing to be so good at it that I indirectly saved my men's lives. And there's nothing, nothing, that's very satisfying about that. You come with a high body count, high kill ratios. What a fucking way to live your life."[43]

For many, the painful memories of killing haunted them long afterward. Others compartmentalized the event and pushed it deep into the darker recesses of their minds. All depended on the intensity and frequency of the killing, combined with the depth of existing moral and cultural standards. Other factors included whether the soldier identified the enemy as a soldier or a civilian and the context of the encounter. Many killed for survival, which allowed for justifiable rationalizations of the use of violent force. In the end, they recognized it as part of the job and moved on, happy in the realization that they had lived.[44]

Booby Traps and Snipers

The killing process and the chances of death and dismemberment often differed in guerrilla wars, even those that combined elements of conventional war, especially in the setting of a jungle where the element of surprise formed a fundamental component of the fighting. In Vietnam, most contact with the enemy on a daily basis came from booby traps and snipers. Months sometime passed without a major contact, but each day soldiers on patrol dealt with the frustrations of an often-unseen enemy whose booby traps or long distant shots could take your life as easily as someone with a bayonet charging into your front lines. With these constant specters of death, one soldier noted, Charlie is "a twenty-four-hour-a-day problem."[45]

In the guerrilla war, snipers can play a significant role. The VC and NVA snipers had many advantages. The knowledge of the area and often the cooperation of the civilians cemented optimal conditions for the snipers, some of whom were women. A common NVA tactic was to fire on the lead element of the American patrol, hoping to slow its advance and draw it toward the fire where additional NVA snipers would be on the flanks. Officers, the radio operators, and heavy weapons personnel were prime targets. The enemy also repeatedly slipped up behind a patrol and picked off the rear elements and then disappeared to cause "slow attrition and eroding morale."[46]

Some Americans noted the effectiveness of the enemy. One veteran Marine sniper emphasized that "for the record, the Viet Cong and NVA fielded some of the finest sniper teams in history. When it came to field craft, silent movement, camouflage, noise discipline, and tactics, the Communist snipers were superior to anyone on the battlefield." He added that "the Marines combated the VC and NVA jungle skills with accurate and deadly marksmanship, courage, better weaponry, and the quick ability to learn how to play the game."[47]

In another case, a patrol from the 25th Infantry Division ran into some expert snipers. Corporal Gary Heeter only had three days left on his tour and acknowledged that "there were the best snipers I'd seen as long as I'd been over there." Within a short time, the group "lost eight men in one platoon, shot between the eyes." Their captain had left the area, so the group just hugged the ground until he returned. Finally, he ordered them to get behind the VC and kill them. Unfortunately, along the way, they had to cross a minefield where Heeter stepped on a "bouncing Betty" mine that blew off his leg. While he survived the sniper, the other enemy weapon of choice ended his time in Vietnam and ensured two years of hospitals in the United States recovering from the wounds.[48]

While snipers inflicted damage, equally wearing on the psyche of the grunt were the booby traps. They differed in degree of complexity and sophistication, with some designed to maim as much as kill. The enemy understood that it cost more to deal with a wounded soldier, both in time and money. The costs started with the evacuation of the wounded and escalated with medical treatment and the impact on civilian morale when a soldier missing a limb or in a wheelchair returned stateside.

The NVA and VC employed a variety of booby traps. They included the simple punji sticks, sharpened bamboo buried a few feet in the ground where U.S. troops would step on them, impaling the victim. Often, the VC put human or animal feces on them to ensure an infection. In other cases, the enemy strung a wire across a path, hooked to a grenade in a can (sometimes from American C-rations) that when tripped, pulled the pin and exploded the ordnance. Other times, the enemy rigged captured or black market U.S. Claymore mines and detonated them as Americans walked into an area. The enemy also buried Chinese and Russian mines capable of crippling a large vehicle.

Veterans remembered the effectiveness of booby traps. One grunt stressed that of the mines "the Bouncing Betty is feared most.... It leaps out of its nest in the earth, and when it hits its apex, it explodes" usually about waist level, which terrified men fearful of losing their manhood. "Step on them, and the unlucky soldier will hear a muffled explosion; that's the initial charge sending the mine on its one-yard leap into the sky. The fellow takes another step and begins the next and his backside is bleeding and he's dead. We call it 'ol step and a half.'"[49] Another veteran remembered, "I earned the Purple Heart, not as a result of a wound received in the heat of battle but rather from clumsily stumbling over and impaling my leg on a shit-smeared punji stake."[50]

The result was, as one Marine emphasized, a pressure "maintained by an unseen enemy that would try to pick us off one or two men at a time with booby traps, snipers.... Both approaches were equally lethal, but the frustration . . . would be greater because of the near impossibility of retaliation."[51] Most Americans understood their advantages if only the enemy engaged directly, but its failure to do so created anger and aggravation. For long periods, the soldier went without seeing the enemy, all the while sustaining the constant psychological pressures of the enemy lurking at a distance waiting to shoot him or just walking along and being blown to bits. This difficult environment where one could not see the enemy or retaliate had negative consequences, especially when Americans interacted with South Vietnamese civilians, who seemed to always avoid the traps.

Hot Zones

When there was significant enemy contact, the experience was intense and left an indelible mark. Most enemy contacts in Vietnam consisted of short firefights with sudden bloody exchanges that ended quickly, often with the enemy withdrawing before the Americans could call in heavy artillery or air cover. The fighting could be brutal and often bore more of a resemblance to the jungle fighting of World War II in the South Pacific than traditional conventional fighting that had characterized World War I and World War II. When large, sustained full-scale combat with substantial NVA or VC forces occurred, such as during the Tet Offensive, the Americans typically held the field with overwhelming firepower from artillery, helicopter gun-ships, and fixed winged aircraft like the massive B-52s that rained down destruction on the enemy. In either case, the havoc wreaked on both sides was often horrific and created a lasting impression.

In one case of close combat, an experienced Special Forces soldier, Tom Roubideaux, was out on patrol with Vietnamese airborne when his unit came under attack. Suddenly, a young NVA regular jumped up with a bayonet and attacked him, striking him on the first pass, driving the bayonet into his arm. He pushed him aside and removed it. Enraged, he began beating the NVA to death with the blunt end, with ultimately his radioman and another adviser pulling him off, telling him "that's enough, that's enough." Finally, he stopped and later examined the NVA's gun and found three rounds in his rifle, meaning he would certainly have been killed if the NVA had responded properly and shot him. He noted that it was "probably the first American he tried to kill and it was the last."[52]

In another case, a Marine, Walter Sudol, arrived in Vietnam and immediately went to a front-line unit. He remembered celebrating his twentieth birthday in the A Shau Valley as his detachment headed toward a reported enemy arms cache around Hill 1044. The area looked like the moon, with bomb craters everywhere from the massive air strikes by B-52 planes that left no foliage, only fallen trees. As his squad rounded a bend in the road, a huge explosion lifted him in the air and pounded him to the ground on his back. As he desperately tried to catch his breath, his commander, Lieutenant James Simms, ordered his unit to advance on a series of bunkers.[53]

A furious fight ensued with enemy machine gun fire killing the point man. As Sudol and a Navy medic made their way forward, Sudol remembered that "the machine gun rounds and AK-47 rounds were going past my head so close that I could hear the snap of the rounds as they barely missed me." He looked up long enough to see his lieutenant killed by an AK-50 machine gun round and the medic's right ankle shot away. As Sudol ran to him, the enemy finished him with a burst of machine gun fire to the head and chest, leading to blood and body parts being sprayed on the young soldier. Traumatized, he "tried to dig a hole into the ground with my hands, trying to get away from the intenseness of the death around me." Fortunately for him, a M79 round blew off the head of the NVA. "All the time, I could not get the thought out of my mind that I was going to die on my twentieth birthday and of the pain my parents would have to go through." He survived and his unit marched up the hill, but after losing five KIA and a number wounded.[54]

One of the most challenging duties in Vietnam involved going underground to search out the enemy who had established hundreds of miles of interconnecting tunnels during the war, especially in the Iron Triangle area northwest of Saigon. There, specially selected American soldiers, usually because of their diminutive size, endured the dangerous duties of searching for the enemy and his supplies in the maze of tunnels. Nicknamed "tunnel rats," some volunteered for the extra pay and adrenaline rush of combing the tunnels that often were only large enough for the small Vietnamese to transverse while commanders ordered others to participate. They encountered tunnels full of booby traps, snakes, and Vietnamese guerrillas who guarded the area. Armed often only with a revolver and K-Bar knife with ropes often attached to their ankles or necks so that they could be pulled out, they waged battle in areas where no one could see or hear them.[55]

A tunnel rat, Art Tejeda, remembered one of his most harrowing experiences in the tunnels as he helped break in a new rat named John Riley. One day, they began investigating a tunnel. Forty feet in, they uncovered a huge quantity of RPG-2s (rocket-propelled grenades), complete with night scopes. Further in, they found new AK-47s, never fired, with huge quantities of munitions, and finally through a trap door, additional weapons that could have outfitted more than 500 fighters. An excited Riley kept bragging loudly, "I told you; I told you," to which the veteran Tejeda kept responding, "be quiet," knowing that the voices echoed through the tunnel.[56]

They crawled on, coming to another trap door Tejeda had seen before during an earlier trip in the tunnels with a canteen and pistol belt not far from it. They decided to change places as Tejeda had been following Riley. As they did, their flashlights illuminated three Viet Cong immediately in front of them. They fired, "and the next thing I saw was this green, yellow, and red-colored flash and a loud bang," Tejeda recalled. The blast flipped him on his back and he took out his .45 and emptied the clip toward the VC. He decided it was time to pull out and reached for Riley. He put his hand to his chest, which was not pounding or pumping so he knew he was dead. "Get out; it's time to get out," he kept telling himself as he began backtracking.[57]

Wounded, he crawled for what he recalled felt like an eternity. He remembered seeing his mother's face, then the face of his fiancée, who kept telling him, "Art, you're hurt. Get out of the tunnel." When, he responded, "No, I'm tired," she cursed him, "Damn you, Art, get up and see the sun for one last time." Finally, he saw a light and scrambled out to find himself soaked in blood as a bullet had passed through his comrade and hit him in the jaw and thigh. Walking around, he demanded, "Give me a gun! Dig him out! Dig him out!" referring to Riley. After he punched out one medic, a captain tried to calm him down, but finally the blood loss caused him to black out and allow treatment. When he awoke at a medical station, he had a strong sense of loss, but he knew that in uncovering the weapons they could not "be used against us anyway because we had uncovered them." He had done "something good."[58]

No matter what type of service, the combat soldier faced significant dangers. As one writer emphasized, "In a typical twelve-month tour, an infantry soldier stood a 3 percent chance of dying, a 10 percent chance of being seriously wounded, and a 25 percent chance of earning a Purple Heart."[59] While the odds favored the grunt, the constant specter of death that hung over him frayed the nerves and provided lasting images of combat and especially death and destruction in the modern age of war. Few ever forgot the sights, smells, fear, and experiences of combat.

Losing a Friend

The loss of the friend delineated the true loss of innocence and often ignited cynicism toward the war or rage and a desire for revenge. For most people, watching anyone die was very traumatic, but watching a close friend die, often ripped apart by a modern weapon, was especially difficult. The intense bonds established by those in combat made the loss even worse for the soldier already enduring a very traumatic event.

While many developed coping mechanisms to continue to function after the loss of a close friend, it was difficult and for many the deaths severely shook them and created a memory not easily forgotten.

Memories of grunts losing a friend and its impact fill Vietnam-era letters and journals. One Marine wrote his parents about the death of his best friend, a husband and father with only sixty-seven days left to serve in Vietnam, who succumbed after a 60mm mortar exploded next to him. "I carried him over to the aid station where he died. I cried my eyes out. I have seen death before but nothing as close as this." A few days later, four others died when a rocket hit their bunker. "I think with all the death and destruction I have seen in the past week I have aged greatly," he wrote to his parents; "I feel like an old man now. . . . Payback for my buddies is not the uppermost thought in my mind. My biggest goal is to return to you."[60]

Another veteran, a member of the 101st Airborne, wrote his pen pal in Tucson that his friend named Foreman, who had forty-two days left in country and who "kept me going when I said I'd quit, died today in this damn country." "With 42 days left for each of us, we lost a real friend that seems to make this war worthless. The odd thing, I feel no hate or revenge. You might say a feeling of complete disgust or agony at the thought, 'But why him?'" He added, "I feel like I did when my father died. NOTHING! Nobody was around then it seemed either, but everyone was." He expressed his feeling that "I'm lonely and everybody is around and cares. I believe I'm a bit crazy. Tonight I'm full of love and one of my best and reliable friends is waiting to go home because of what seems to be the unnecessary."[61]

For most, the key was to mourn and then move on or risk losing themselves. One veteran spoke of always knowing that death hovered near and "you don't know whose turn it is." Yet, there were "times when you lose the fear because something happens, like they kill a friend of yours. For five or six days it goes away because you're so shook up from losing your friend that life means nothing to you. Then it passes, and you started to be interested in life again." The week in between could be characterized by taking chances and not being careful, but eventually the will to survive returned fully.[62]

The loss of a friend compounded the feelings of frustration, anger, and depression. Most learned to bury the memory deep to prevent it from interfering with their own ability to endure, although none ever completely erased the loss. They often stopped associating with the FNGs

Marines walk along a rice paddy dike in search of Viet Cong,
December 1965. *(National Archives)*

and kept more to themselves. Regret and depression typically arose when
they had time to think, which occurred a lot for many of the grunts in
Vietnam as the war was one with a significant burst of energy followed
by long, arduous tasks of humping through the terrain in search of the
enemy. During those treks, the grunt had time for reflection on friends,
family, home, and the losses.

The Boredom of War

Death remained a constant companion, but boredom characterized the
majority of the experience in war for most grunts. While preparation for
combat such as cleaning weapons and walking about in search of the

enemy occupied most days, much time was left to think and reflect and find ways to pass the time, whether through card games, reading and writing letters, or becoming numb from drinking and sometimes harder drugs when in base camp. Like most soldiers before them, the grunt in Vietnam battled boredom in a variety of ways.

One Army paratrooper summed up the feeling of many grunts. He had excitedly accepted his assignment to Vietnam in 1967, hoping to realize his life-long dream of winning glory like his heroes in books and movies. Yet, as he endured his service, he noted: "My romantic notions of war began to dull as the exhausting, frustrating months passed with nothing but a few snipers' bullets and the shells of mortarmen to break the tedium." He lamented further, "In many ways the despair which often overcame me on lonely, eventless nights of staring into the jungle gloom from the parapet of a sandbag bunker was even greater than the oppression of the garrison. So close to battle but yet still so distant. I had crossed 6,000 miles of ocean to seek my destiny but had only deepened my sense of loss."[63]

A Marine stressed that the "war was mostly a matter of enduring weeks of expectant waiting and, at random intervals, of conducting vicious manhunts through jungles and swamps where snipers harassed us constantly and booby traps cut us down one by one." He added that "the tedium was occasionally relieved by a large-scale search-and-destroy operation, but the exhilaration of riding the lead helicopter into a landing zone was usually followed by more of the same hot walking, with the mud sucking our boots and the sun thudding against our helmets while an invisible enemy shot at us from distant tree lines."[64]

With down time, the soldiers had occasion to reflect and homesickness invariably set in for many of them. One veteran of World War II and Korea wrote his family that "some nights (and days) a guy just gets homesick—even an old solider like me—and tonight is one of those times. If I close my eyes, I can just hear all the 'sounds of home,' kitchen, TV, kids fights between Carol and Jaime, etc. Sure would give the world to be there."[65] A second lieutenant wrote his wife in Indiana: "I can picture your face in front of me, and our home and our children. Oh! How much the things we take for granted can mean so much. The smell of cut grass, the wind blowing over the lake and making the trees and grass sway. The smell of autumn, the bareness of the world during winter. All of this means so much, and how little it is appreciated."[66]

Boredom has been a constant feature of war as the enemy often chooses the time and place of contact, especially in a guerrilla war. The same was true in Vietnam as soldiers fought boredom like the mosquitoes and other pests. As in other conflicts, they challenged boredom by writing letters, partying with friends with large quantities of alcohol provided by their government, played games, and found other diversions. Often, the boredom was most omnipresent when they were in base camp, surrounded by large numbers of the support staff, which left time for idle hands to often find trouble, whether they went looking for it or it found them. The result was that like other wars, there were minutes, sometimes hours of terror, followed by many more hours of sitting and waiting.

REMFs

When bored, the grunts had time to think about many things, including the unevenness of their sacrifice compared to the large group of support troops, numbering higher in Vietnam than other wars as the conflict became more mechanized and bureaucratic. There were the often self-described Rear Echelon Mother Fuckers (REMFs) in Vietnam, but their service typically differed dramatically from that of the infantryman. While much more at risk than previous rear echelon troops because of the constant potential of attacks at any place in the country as evidenced by the Tet Offensive and the terrorist attacks on areas where GIs congregated, many enjoyed the privileges of air conditioning, hot meals, and luxurious accommodations that were denied the grunts.

A photo interpreter for the Air Force highlighted the differences between those in the front lines and those in the rear. He noted that he would travel with friends from the Tan Son Nhut airbase just outside of Saigon to the city. "We would sit on the 6th floor of the Ritz Hotel eating steaks and drinking cocktails and watch the tracers coming out of the helicopters as they strafed the banks of the Saigon River 3 or 4 miles away."[67] Another REMF lamented, "We're just 'paper soldiers,' that is, the people doing administration, although somebody has got to do it. The 'roughness' we endure is only the water rationing, being hot, and the somewhat dreary atmosphere of it all."[68]

Those on the front line often established a distance from the REMFs and created a pecking order in terms of the commitment and value of the soldiers. One Marine noted that while there was rivalry with the Army, "we were proud that we were in the bush." In Vietnam, he observed,

A Viet Cong soldier armed with an SKS rifle crouches in a bunker. *(National Archives)*

"it wasn't so much being a Marine as it was being a grunt, being in the infantry" that instilled pride. "In fact, we had more respect for an Army infantryman than we did for a Marine Corps person in the rear." He acknowledged that "there were lots of guys in the rear who did some dangerous things, but you couldn't have told us that at the time."[69] Another soldier after R&R was not so kind, writing about the troops stationed in Saigon that "the guys stationed there really have the life. No wonder the war is lasting so long. The officers and noncoms don't want to give up the kind of living they have up here."[70]

In another case, an officer emphasized that on visits from the bush to base camps "the field soldiers got a snapshot view of the base camp lifestyle the support troops led, and they despised them for it." He noted that the REMFs had "warm showers, freshly laundered and pressed uniforms every day, mess hall meals three times a day, and access to PX [post exchange] items such as stereo equipment, hard liquor, and cigarettes. . . . When the men were off duty they had access to live entertainment and liquor at the air-conditioned clubs. . . . The grunts weren't impressed that the support troops put in long days repairing trucks, typing up paperwork, building barracks, and performing an endless number of other tasks." The result was often that "it didn't take more than a couple of beers and an off-hand remark to start a brawl."[71]

Conflict between the grunts and REMFs permeated the war. Only a relatively small group actually fought on the front lines, as there were plenty of clerks, technicians, and others such as mechanics required to maintain the fighting force. Many of those not in the infantry in heavy combat areas, including engineers, helicopter and aircraft pilots, and truck drivers, endured tremendous dangers, but there was a clear distinction between the REMFs and grunts that even carried over into postwar debates about the sacrifices of the soldier in Vietnam.

The Enemy

Other debates about the soldier in Vietnam arose, many related to American allies and enemies. As the war heated up and larger numbers of NVA moved southward, the battles reinforced American views of the stubbornness and hardiness of the enemy. While sometimes having less admiration for the Viet Cong, the American ground soldier genuinely respected the enemy, one they saw as more and more determined to endure great hardships in the face of the more heavily armed and technologically superior Americans. The question often turned to the perception that these men and women had more dedication to a cause than the ARVN, which over time created cynicism and ambivalence about the mission.

From the outset, Americans typically respected the enemy, especially the NVA. A veteran of the 1st Cavalry, Dennis Deal, admitted that after Ranger and airborne school "I thought I was a really bad ass, and what five-foot, one-hundred pound little Asian punk was gonna hurt me? I soon found out." After brutal fighting in the Ia Drang Valley in 1965, he remembered surveying the battlefield and finding a NVA who "had his buttocks shot off and his insides were leaking out a large hole. . . . But what this guy did is an amazing story of human endurance. As he was lying there . . . he had taken a hand grenade, armed it, and wrapped it around the upper hand guard of his rifle stock. He had booby-trapped himself. I thought, 'Man, if we're up against this, it's going to be a long-ass year.'"[72]

Another veteran stressed that he viewed the enemy as "some of the hardest fighters in the world. I respect them to the utmost. . . . I don't believe in their concept, I don't believe in communism" but when "another soldier that plays that strong and fights that hard you've got to respect him."[73] Another veteran echoed a similar feeling. "I just kept getting a higher and higher degree of respect for who we were fighting—the North Vietnamese were good—and they at least knew what their purpose was, and we didn't." [74] Another added after the war about the NVA: "I could sit and drink a can of Diet Coke with one of those guys and not feel any animosity. And I really think they could probably sit down and do the same with me. I think they would really respect us, and I had tremendous respect for them."[75]

While the NVA often provoked positive comments from many American veterans, the same was not always true for the Viet Cong. This resulted often from a sense of frustration of fighting an elusive enemy. "I had no idea that the enemy was every man, woman, and child," one grunt emphasized. "I thought perhaps the enemy might be in civilian clothes, and armed, but at least I'd be able to identify him. Didn't work out that way. I barely ever saw a live enemy soldier in combat. I always saw women and children and little tiny babies, and after firefights I would see dead enemy soldiers, but to see them face to face was a rare occasion."[76]

Nevertheless, most Americans viewed the Viet Cong as tenacious and pesky, although lacking the formal training and firepower of the NVA. A particular incident stood out for one veteran. One day, a VC mortar team lobbed several rounds into his compound, which meant that "two Viet Cong, each maybe five feet two in height, 110 pounds, between sixteen and eighty years of age" with a "rusty piece of metal" caused the Americans to launch helicopter gunships which plowed the area with machine guns and then a jet dropped napalm and finally some large 105 mm and 175 mm cannon pounded the area. "Then everything dies down. And you hear pop-pop-pop—they fire three more rounds at us. At that point I knew there was no way we could win that fucking war. . . . To stay there, take it, and then shoot back! Forget it. They got more than we've got."[77]

In another case, a veteran of the 25th Infantry Division commented that the VC "there were not as well trained as the NVA, but they were trained well enough." He talked about how they could organize, put together an ambush, fight, and then melt back into their villages and return to live as a farmer. "But they were still damned good fighters. I had a lot of respect for them. They kicked our butts a couple of times. If it wasn't for artillery and air strikes, we'd have just never got out of there."[78]

However, other times, the NVA and VC provoked disgust for their tactics. One Marine remembered finding the remnants of a farmer who had been chained to a stake in the ground and ordered to discharge a command-detonated mine when U.S. troops entered an area, killing the farmer and the Americans.[79] The NVA also inflicted many atrocities during the war, which provoked revulsion, especially when directed toward Americans. The number of POWs remained small as neither side typically gave or expected quarter.

In one case, an Army officer stressed that most of his officers "have a grudging admiration for the courage and steadfastness of the North Vietnamese, but only active dislike for the Viet Cong, who seem to specialize in acts of terror against the defenseless." He wrote how "just two days ago they tortured a 17-year-old girl who was to marry a government soldier. They smashed her face with rifle butts and tore off part of her scalp, then left her dying in the road. Needless to say, not much mercy is left in anyone's heart after an atrocity like that."[80]

Despite the negative views of the NVA and VC, the tenacity of the enemy often led American soldiers to question their commitment to the South Vietnamese, both the troops of the Army of the Republic of Vietnam (ARVN) and the civilians. Throughout the war, many Americans asked why the North Vietnamese and the Viet Cong endured the hardships and battering inflicted on them by the technologically superior American forces. In some cases, the NVA and VC began to achieve a near mythical position, partly in an effort to explain why the people of a Third World nation could ultimately emerge victorious in their efforts to expel the western powers, first the French and then the Americans. The same was rarely true for the Vietnamese allies.

The Vietnamese Allies

The United States desperately tried to create a viable fighting force in the form of the ARVN. Despite propaganda highlighting the ARVN's hard work and commitment to defeating the Communists, the majority of grunts, as well as those in command, typically held their South Vietnamese allies in contempt, arguing that with few exceptions, they avoided fighting and let the Americans bear the burden. Many also viewed them as riddled with the Viet Cong who secretly aided the enemy. These factors translated into an ambivalent relationship at best, a dysfunctional one at the worst.

From the earliest stages of the major fighting, negative perceptions persisted of the ARVN. Lieutenant Colonel John Paul Vann provides a good example. A top adviser to the Seventh ARVN Division, Vann had told a *New York Times* reporter in the early 1960s that the South Vietnamese "may be the world's greatest lovers, but they're not the world's greatest fighters. But they're good people, and they can win a war if someone shows them how." On the flip side, he added that the VC could be defeated "if they would only stand and fight."[81]

Despite Vann's initial optimism, he grew disenchanted after the Battle of Ap Bac in January 1963. A force of more than 1,200 ARVN troops, supported by heavy artillery, helicopters, and bombers, moved against 400 VC whose heaviest weapon was a mortar. Led by a political appointee, the ARVN troops advanced cautiously, despite the constant urging of Vann and other American advisers who wanted more aggressiveness. A poorly performed air assault further exacerbated problems. By dusk, the VC melted into the night after inflicting significant casualties, leading Vann to quip that it was "a miserable fucking performance, just like it always is."[82] In contrast, he told reporters that the VC "were brave men. They gave a good account of themselves today."[83]

When Vann's superiors exaggerated the ARVN's successes at Ap Bac, he and several colleagues wrote a scathing indictment of the ARVN. Working internally within the military while creating alliances with journalists such as David Halberstam, Vann called for better preparation of the ARVN and new leadership, hoping to prevent the escalation of the presence of American troops, which he argued would create a bloody battlefield with the peasants caught in between and "we'd end up shooting at everything—men, women, kids, and the buffalos." His calls went unheeded, and he ultimately resigned in disgust over the incident and other complaints.[84]

For the most part, negative perceptions of the ARVN remained throughout the conflict despite efforts by American propagandists to portray them in a positive light. Challenges developed, many rooted in

American racism and elitism. As one Marine observed, "the problem was that we were always better. All of the American forces were always better; so you can understand how that makes a person feel. If you're always better and probably, you always tell them you're better, then you get a tremendous complex and the typical military just doesn't handle . . . personalities very well. So we kind of just came in and took over and ran over them and while we were doing it, told them how bad they were. So, they just kind of wanted us to go away."[85]

The most common perception was that the ARVN were unwilling to fight. One Marine summed up the feeling of many in that the "enemy was a tough, hard, dedicated fucking guy and the ARVN didn't want to hear about fighting."[86] A Marine officer, Bernard Trainor, who advised a secret CIA program to launch attacks on northern targets by former North Vietnamese Catholics, talked about why the program failed. He observed: "Our guys wanted to draw their rice and pay but were not overly interested in getting shot at."[87] Another complained that while preparing for an operation in fall 1968 "as was often the case with the South Vietnamese units, the ARVNs never showed up, and late in the afternoon the word came down from battalion that their sweep had been scratched. There was a good deal of grumbling up and down the line about wasted effort and unreliable allies when the word was passed, but no one was disappointed at having avoided another enemy confrontation."[88] Such experiences led one veteran to emphasize, "I started hating ARVNs because they were so unreliable and a couple of times in ambushes the ARVNs disappeared."[89]

Such negative attitudes affected American interactions with the ARVN. In one case, ARVN soldiers stopped a Marine truck and requested evacuation of a wounded comrade missing a leg. At first, one Marine replied, "Fuck him. Let him hop." When they finally relented, the truck commander complained that the "fucking little slope grabbed my leg" and that he been around enough of them "to know that most of them are queer. They hold hands and stuff." Then another Marine kicked the man out of the truck with the admonishment, "Fuck you, you slope. Out you go."[90]

In another case, a U.S. military doctor stressed that "the ARVN troops had the lowest priority for treatment on the list of all the casualties you could get. The highest was any U.S. person. The second highest was a U.S. dog from the canine corps. The third was NVA. The fourth was VC. And the fifth was ARVN, because they had no particular value." He observed that only the Vietnamese civilian ranked lower than ARVN and that they prioritized the NVA and VC because they could provide information. The fact that the American dog ranked higher perplexed him, but he noted that the dog represented about $10,000 worth of training.[91]

While the majority viewed the ARVN negatively, there were some exceptions, usually among those who trained specialized ARVN units or tribal groups such as the Montagnards or worked closely with them as advisers, such as members of the Green Berets. In one case, a U.S. rifleman gained a great deal of respect after spending a lot of time with some ARVN Rangers and airborne units. One in particular impressed him, a North Vietnamese named Nu who had joined the NVA but changed sides after witnessing Viet Cong atrocities. "And the South Vietnamese put all the guys like him into the Rangers and gave them the worst combat duty," he observed, adding, "they were tough, tough guys. I loved them. Spirit—they'd fight to the end. They had the same kind of esprit de corps that we had, they really believed."[92]

Overall, despite a few positive exceptions, the Americans viewed the ARVN soldier with contempt. The Americans walked into the relationship with a belief in their cultural, thereby, military superiority. Racial sentiments influenced the perceptions, but not without limits, as Americans respected the enemy's fighting prowess. While a few Americans acknowledged the combat ability of some ARVN, particularly those who were well equipped, trained, and led, the vast majority viewed the ARVN as a handicap. This created significant animosity, as the American grunt believed that the ARVN wanted him to do the work that they should have been doing for their own country. While clearly ignoring the structural difficulties of building an effective fighting force in an artificially created country where generals often earned their positions by political patronage and the central government dispersed the ARVN in irrational directions because of the fear of coups, the Americans viewed the limitations as a cultural deficiency of the southerners and responded with disdain and sometime brutality toward their allies.[93]

America's Other Allies

While the grunts often viewed their ARVN allies contemptuously, the same was not true of the other allies who sent troops to Vietnam under President Johnson's "many flags" campaigns. Soldiers from several nations, including Australia, New Zealand, and South Korea, made significant contributions to the war effort. In return, Washington rewarded the sacrifices handsomely with military and economic assistance. U.S. leaders would have preferred an even more international force like the one in Korea; nonetheless, American soldiers generally developed very favorable views of the allied soldiers.

The most important contingent that assisted the United States in Vietnam was from South Korea, whose government provided more than 300,000 troops, a number peaking at more than 50,000 in country in 1968. Ultimately the Republic of Korea (ROK) had more than 4,400 KIA and many more wounded. In return, the South Korean government of President Chung Hee Park received significant concessions from the Johnson administration, including modernization of the ROK equipment and private contracts for Korean companies, helping to create a powerful economy.[94]

The ROK troops developed a reputation for brutality and savagery, both toward their own troops and the enemy. In one case, a Marine observed that the "ROK discipline was unbelievable." He watched as a sergeant ordered a subordinate to get the American a chair. When the Marine refused because he had been sitting for hours, the ROK sergeant thought it was because there was dirt in the chair and proceeded to grab his countryman by the collar and to slap him. "It was overpowering, it was not necessary but that's how disciplined these guys were," the American commented.[95]

The discipline paid significant dividends for unit responsiveness, however. A Mexican American veteran remembered being on patrol one day with the ROK when a sniper fired on them. "One Korean soldier blew a whistle and they went straight into the jungle. The VC were scared of them because the Koreans didn't give a shit. You shoot at them and they went right after you, and they didn't take prisoners either."[96]

The brutality of the ROK toward the VC and NVA was legendary. One Asian American veteran noted, the "ROKs used to chop a lot of heads. . . . Those were tough guys. They were the most inhuman motherfuckers I ever saw in my life. Their methods of interrogation—I once saw one of them kicking somebody's head. He kicked it until the head exploded like a watermelon. So he kept kicking it until it was just goop. It was unreal. . . . It was almost like a Fellini movie."[97] In another case, a Marine remembered capturing an NVA lieutenant and turning him over to the ROK for interrogation. They promptly "took him up in a chopper, and after they got the information, they threw him out anyway."[98]

Americans sometimes used the brutality of the ROK to their own advantage. In an operation against a hamlet know as Viem Dong, a Marine captain decided to settle a score with the village for assisting the enemy. According to one of his lieutenants, the captain "knew that our South Korean allies were free to operate without the political constraints that figured so heavily in all our planning." The Americans surrounded the village while the South Koreans swept through and flushed out the enemy. "Whatever else the Koreans did in the village was their own business, but with their reputation for brutality, we all knew that the village would be loath to support the Vietcong so openly in the future." The final operation ensured that "if we got our kills, we could take full credit, and if the ROKs became overzealous, we could plead our lack of control over our allies."[99]

The Australians also committed significant numbers of troops, peaking at more than 7,600 in 1969, losing more than 400 KIA and 2,300 wounded. Concerned about Communist expansion in Southeast Asia, the Australian government at first proved an especially strong ally.[100] In the summer of 1965, the first Australian forces arrived in Bien Hoa and commanders attached them to the U.S. 173rd Airborne Brigade. Immediately, tensions arose as the Australians disliked American tactics. The Australians, trained extensively in jungle fighting and veterans of the Malaya campaign, preferred smaller scale actions designed to limit their casualties and those of noncombatants. The well-trained Aussies also liked to brag that "one Australian is worth ten Yanks." Ultimately, the Aussies received permission to control Phuoc Tuy Province, forty miles east of Saigon, and the important port of Vung Tau. For the duration of the war, they operated along with a small contingent of New Zealanders from a base camp at Nui Dat with their own air and naval cover, achieving significant successes without the massive casualties experienced by American forces.[101]

Despite limited contact with the Australians when contrasted with the ROK soldiers, Americans viewed them very positively. One American commander talked about how the "Aussies used squads to make a contact, and brought in reinforcing elements to do the killing; they planned in the belief that a platoon on the battlefield could do anything, 'including get out.'" American leaders, he added, resisted the idea of breaking down their units "into such seemingly devourable chunks," but "in any event, I still maintained the Australians understood the war better than our guys ever would."[102]

Another American who served as an artillery forward fire observer for the Aussies and New Zealanders emphasized his positive experience. He wrote his parents that "as a whole so far, the Aussies and New Zealand officers seem much better than ours. They're all so darn professional. They really impress me." He praised the equipment that the Aussies had adopted for jungle warfare and noted "that given the opportunity, the 'digger' (Australian soldier) was a tremendous fighter."[103]

Other forces, including Thais, also fought alongside the Americans in Vietnam. In the end, however, the Americans and ARVN fought and died most, although Koreans made a substantial commitment. The American soldiers developed positive images of their allies, especially the Koreans and Aussies, although suspicions remained on all sides and the size and scope of the cooperation never matched that of World War II or Korea. Still, when juxtaposed against perceptions of the ARVN, the Allied forces fared much better, which further underscores the severe strain between Americans and the ARVN.

The Vietnamese People

Because the Vietnam War remained primarily a guerrilla conflict between 1965 and 1968, the Vietnamese people often found themselves trapped between the Americans and the enemy. Over time, the South Vietnamese people evoked hostility as well as much sympathy from the American soldier. Many watched as Vietnamese peasants easily circumvented minefields and booby traps that killed their comrades. The ability of the enemy to blend into the villages exacerbated animosities and sometimes led to atrocities. On the other hand, the American GI often demonstrated sensitivity toward the Vietnamese, especially the children. Some GIs often spent their off-duty time helping the Vietnamese. The ambivalence of the experience and collateral damage affected almost all of the GIs involved and added layers of complexity to their relationship to the war.

The abject poverty often shocked the Americans and further strengthened feelings of superiority, but also evoked sympathy. One American wrote: "The people live like pigs. They don't know how to use soap. When they have to go to the bathroom, they go wherever they're standing, they don't care who is looking. . . . The houses they live in are like rundown shacks. . . . We are more than millionaires to these people—they have nothing. I can't see how people can live like this."[104] Another noted that he had to guard a trash dump. The civilians always wanted in to scrounge and one day, he decided to let in two older women. "We expected they would sift through the stuff and take a couple of loads out." Instead, they ran in and dove into garbage cans and began fighting each other for the garbage. "That just blew me away to see that, fifty-year-old women rolling and fighting each other in the garbage. That was just not a dignified way to live."[105]

As a result, the Vietnamese evoked great feelings of sympathy from many good-hearted GIs who spent their extra time helping out, especially with orphanages and other relief activities. One GI lamented, "The soul of this nation lies in its youth. The elders, the parents, are tired. They've lived with war, and the hardships involved, for too long. They no longer believe another kind of life is possible. The children do, though. They want to learn. They want to do things the way we do, have things like we have. They have hope for their future." He asked his mother to send school supplies, toothpaste, and notebooks for the school at the Vinh-Son Orphanage. "These children . . . are the victims not of their generation, but of yours and mine. Many of their parents have been killed . . . by terrorism while defending their homes, their country, their freedom . . . You and I must do something for these children."[106]

In another case, a Marine wrote his grandmother: "We have been doing a lot of work in the villages lately, of the community-development type, so it looks as though I will never get away from my Peace Corps days." He worried however that "we must be really messing up these people's minds. By day we treat their ills and fix up their children and deliver their babies; and by night, if we receive fire from the general direction of their hamlet, fire generally will reach them, albeit not intentionally." He believed that "they must be really going around in circles. But I guess that just points up the strangeness of this war. We have two hands, both of which know what the other is doing but does the opposite anyway."[107]

While there were acts of kindness, overall, ambivalence characterized most Americans views of the South Vietnamese. One Marine lieutenant lamented that for his first two months, he had been in an area where there were only hard core NVA, which removed the "ambiguity" of the situation, no "good guy, bad guy" issues. Then, he transferred to a coastal area around Cam Lo. "The Vietnamese did not like us and I remember I was shocked. I still naively thought of myself as a hero, as a liberator. And to see the Vietnamese look upon us with fear or hatred visible in their eyes was a shock." He talked about how "the people that I thought would regard us as heroes were the very people that we were fighting, and all of the sudden my black-and-white image of the world became real gray and confused."[108]

In another case, a veteran remembered capturing a suspected VC. During the interrogation, he kneed him in the chest, provoking the Vietnamese man to grab his leg. He began punching him, but he would not let go. "Soon as I stopped punching him, he let go of my leg and looked up at me with this wide grin on his face. He didn't crack his lips at all, but looked up with this blank expression—it was all for me to read." Afterward, he recalled, "I started seeing that look everywhere I went."[109]

Overall, many Americans remained suspicious of the Vietnamese, building on the initial shock of taking buses with chicken wire over the windows on their first day in country. One Native American veteran expressed the frustrations of many grunts as he talked about how there were three enemies, the Viet Cong, the NVA, and "the third type of enemy, at more times more deadly than the other two, . . . the South Vietnamese people themselves." He added that "when among them, you had no way of knowing whether they were the enemy or not. The enemy could be a cleaning lady, a barber, a laundress, or even an innocent-looking child." He knew that they performed duties such as laying booby traps, marking American base camps, and intelligence. Therefore, he noted, "The enemy was all around you. The only territory you held was where you stood."[110] Other Americans began to ask questions about the South Vietnamese and whether they were worth fighting and dying for in the first place.

This ambivalence toward the South Vietnamese had significant effects. It often blended with anger about how ungrateful they were to the Americans saving them from the Communists. The significant acts of kindness and efforts at community development lost effectiveness in the face of the rage that sometimes provoked individual and corporate acts of inhumanity, from killing livestock to destroying homes or creating "free fire" zones that uprooted people from their ancestral homes. The resulting confusion over the mission led many Americans over time to adopt negative views that ultimately led to atrocities.

The Other Enemies: Disease, Climate, and the Local Non-Human Inhabitants

The enemy and the people were not the only challenges that the grunts faced in Vietnam, as U.S. leaders could not have chosen a much more inhospitable environment in which to fight. U.S. forces encountered many non-human threats that could easily kill or emasculate even the hardiest soul. As in many guerrilla wars that the United States had waged in the

Third World (the Philippines, Nicaragua, Haiti, Dominican Republic), the setting had difficult terrain, primarily jungles, mountains, and rice paddies where the climate and local pestilence exacted a heavy toll, both physically and mentally. It made the fighting even more difficult for the young men in South Vietnam.

An Army sergeant summed up the feelings of many when he wrote: "This is hell. Besides killing and maybe being killed there are many other things that make life almost unbearable. Leeches that suck our blood, insects of all kinds, snakes, spiders. . . . The heat, the rain and mud. The long marches with heavy pack, going two or three weeks without a bath, wearing the same clothes for weeks at a time, not having a place to sit down or even lie down except in six inches of mud."[111] The surroundings and method of fighting just exacerbated typical feelings among grunts relating to combat.

Outside of the mud, the grunts talked most about the mosquito as the source of the greatest afflictions. One Army officer wrote his wife: "Your particular enemies, the mosquitoes, are not to be seen or heard. We do sleep under nets which are fully effective if tucked in carefully. However, the hum of 20 to 30 hungry lady mosquitoes is a rather unsatisfactory lullaby, net or no."[112] Another veteran emphasized, "At night mosquitoes plague me while I'm lying on the ground with my poncho wrapped around me."[113] Nets and repellents sometimes worked, but the aggressive mosquitoes often found their way through even the most elaborate defenses.

The mosquitoes were a particularly difficult enemy because they spread malaria. While the soldiers adopted preventative measures, the disease still struck. One veteran who contracted malaria stressed, "We were supposed to get a white pill every day and a bigger pill on Sundays. Well, we were lucky if we got one on Sunday. We didn't get one every day." He complained that the military "have such high standards and yet they don't follow through on their part of the standard."[114]

Malaria also could kill as easily as a bullet. In one case, a nurse wrote home to her parents about how a soldier suffering from malaria had spent the day running to the latrine to vomit. He woke up and ran toward it in the middle of the night and slipped and fell, cracking his head on the hard floor. "The nurse who was on duty said you could hear his skull fracture." He went into cardiac arrest and later died of severe brain damage, largely as a result of a mosquito bite.[115]

In some cases, the GIs stopped taking their malaria prevention medicines, hoping to catch it to escape duty. A doctor remembered that despite threats of a court-martial for failing to ingest the pills some soldiers thought, "Forget it, we're gonna get killed anyway. That's no threat. Put us in the brig? Terrific, we love it." As a result, he traveled around to educate troops that malaria besides possibly damaging the liver could also induce "cerebral malaria—being delirious and losing part of your brain is something that scares the piss out of people." His goal was to say, "Look, you should know if you do this, there could be consequences."[116]

Besides mosquitoes, other abundant forms of blood-suckers, including flies that ate at rotting flesh and sores, populated the jungle.[117] However, one of the most common and dreaded was leeches. As GIs waded the streams, rivers, and rice paddies, the leeches attached themselves. Removing them was a challenge: many grunts used burning cigarettes, while others employed lit matches, and others just pulled them off, although that left the head and the possibility of blood poisoning. One Mexican American developed a novel approach. One day, in desperation, he decided to put some tabasco sauce on the leeches. "Those little bastards just wiggled their little heads out and started coming off . . . they were falling off like flies." Everyone around started asking to use the sauce. The soldier concluded, "That's about the only experience in Vietnam that I could think of humorously, but it was so funny watching those little buggers fall off."[118]

While mosquitoes and leeches aggravated the GI, the most feared non-human inhabitants were the snakes. Of the 140 different snake species in the country, 30, including the king cobras, Malayan pit vipers, and Malayan Kraits, are poisonous. One veteran remembered being warned that "in Vietnam you'll find that there are 1,001 different species of snakes, 1,000 of them are poisonous, and the other one'll eat you whole."[119] Another related hearing many stories about the mythical twenty-two-step snake: when it bit you, the average person died after taking twenty-two more steps.[120]

The snakes were a constant source of tension. One person noted, "Even a boring task in a combat zone can rapidly become exciting, and often in completely unexpected ways" when dealing with snakes.[121] There were many encounters, most not ending in death but clearly frightening. In one case, a medic trekking through the jungle remembered sitting down and feeling something crawling on his leg. He did not really pay attention, believing it was a lizard at first but when he turned around to look, he saw a Malayan Viper staring at him, less than six inches away from his face as its tongue went in and out of its mouth. He simply pushed the snake away into the bamboo, but remained extremely agitated. His commander tried to quiet him, but he responded, "I would rather be in ten firefights than to have a snake crawl up my leg."[122]

In response, many Americans took extra precautions. In one case, a GI decided to take some logs from a local family's fire and place them in an open field. He stacked them in a pile, placed his poncho on top, and laid across it. When a colleague protested that a VC sniper would nail him, he responded: "I'd rather be shot than bitten by a snake. I figure the VC will think I'm dinky-dau (crazy) and won't waste a bullet on me."[123]

Besides the creatures, the heat and humidity added to the discomfort, although cooler climates and seasons prevailed in parts of South Vietnam. A South Dakotan Marine remembered being up on the Demilitarized Zone (DMZ) and in the mountains where troops required a constant supply of water and food by helicopter. "We never had enough water. We had to ration it and God, it was hot. We'd be so thirsty and we'd sit there with canteen in hand. You'd open up the canteen and take a sip, close the canteen, put it down and sit there and think about how thirsty you still are." It would get so bad that in the early mornings, Marines would lick the dew off leaves to satisfy their thirst.[124]

American soldiers, especially those from colder climates, struggled with the heat and relentlessly beating sun. One Army veteran remembered that "it seemed like someone on every mission, would fall out due to heat exhaustion or they would pass out and we had to get them dusted off and usually by the time they got back to Chu Lai with higher altitude and the cooler air, they were okay."[125]

The jungle also extracted a significant toll in terms of constant pain, often from jungle sores and rot. "Slight cuts and insect bites refused to heal as sweat and dirt turned broken skin into vicious festering red welts that would not scab over," one lieutenant wrote. The lack of clean water with which to wash and the constant sweating made it impossible for wounds to heal, especially blisters from humping through rice paddies, wading rivers and streams, and climbing hills. Whenever possible, the lieutenant ordered his soldiers to "take your boots off, change your socks, air out your feet." Despite such precautions, the pain never stopped for many.[126]

For many the jungle rot became a constant source of irritation. In one

In September 1965, soldiers took time out for a surfing contest sponsored by the United Service Organizations. *(National Archives)*

case, an African American veteran complained, "I had jungle rot. I was all fucked up. My feet would turn white from the water, and that water was nasty." After days in the jungle or rice paddies, "the only thing you could do was air 'em out. Don't wear any shoes for days, 'til they're completely dried out. It itches, man. When you take a shower you start scratching—scratch, scratch, scratch, scratch."[127]

The jungle rot, diseases, and pestilence made Vietnam a living hell for many young GIs. There were just over 10,000 non–combat-related deaths in Vietnam, with some caused by the environment. The constant threat of malaria, typhoid, dysentery, and other diseases when combined with the threat of snakes, the vermin, and heat exhaustion added to the psychological toll endured by the American soldier.[128] Most moved on, with a great deal of griping and searching for relief, and by the end of the tour, few wanted to return.

Rest and Relaxation

Because of the severe strain of fighting in Vietnam, a prosperous industry developed during the war to service GIs on short or extended breaks
from the bush. A liberal leave policy provided time away from the fighting, mostly in the cities that developed around American bases and the
larger towns that already had thriving industries catering to tourists and
businessmen. During the second half of most tours, the GI received a
brief reprieve. Most had opportunities to travel to Thailand, Australia, the
Philippines, Japan, or Hawaii for rest and relaxation. The breaks often
created very vivid memories of time in the foreign locales, as well as
the surreal quality of being in combat, going on vacation, and returning
to the fighting.

The most common form of R&R for the front-line troops occurred
when they returned to base camps. While only allowed a short time
to resupply, soldiers could take advantage of the local luxuries, which
included showers, beds, and clubs stocked with cold beer and food. In
one case, an officer remembered during one stand down that he arrived
at the field grade mess where white linen tablecloths covered the table
along with china and flatware. A variety of main courses graced the menu,
including his choices, steak and lobster, along with a nice selection of
wines. He admitted that "rank has its privileges, but this was carrying
it a bit too far."[129]

The South Vietnamese in these areas learned quickly how to live off
the Americans. Bustling Vietnamese businesses sprang up overnight as
the Vietnamese provided everything from a haircut and shaves to laundry
service, as well as the small bars and brothels that prospered, especially
around the major bases such as the Dogpatch near Danang. Prostitution
flourished, as it had in every conflict in the history of man. Many young
women found employment, sometimes pimped by their family members.
In one case, an engineering battalion even outfitted a mobile van with
several prostitutes to accompany them when they went outside the camps
to more isolated areas to construct a bridge or road.[130] In another case,
a veteran recalled that near his base camp, the "Vietnamese built these
little bars out of cardboard and tin cans. Most of the time we didn't even
have to go to town to party because they were right there. They'd sell you
anything. . . . They built little whorehouses real quick."[131]

The military tried to regulate many of the businesses, especially prostitution to prevent the spread of venereal disease. One veteran remembered

that two things kept him from partaking in the world's oldest profession. One was the large number of Amerasian children that he saw in an orphanage not far from his base. The other was a "rumor going around about the Pacific Island—there was supposed to be some really virulent strain of VD going around and there was nothing they could do about it. Antibiotics didn't even dent it. If you caught it, they just took you to this island and you'd spend the rest of your life there. I didn't really believe it, but I didn't have any desire to participate."[132] Nonetheless, many grunts took advantage of the services provided.

Many also traveled to various other places in South Vietnam, with Saigon, the capital, being one of the most popular for short leaves. It was also often a source of hard-to-obtain items. As veteran recalled, if grunts really needed something, they traversed the streets of Saigon to deal on the black market. On one occasion, he found four 81 mm mortars for sale, as well as jeeps and drugs. "Socks were something we could never get hold of. I bought military socks in the damn black market down there in Saigon. You weren't supposed to buy that stuff, but you needed it. All kinds of medical supplies. I couldn't believe it."[133]

While Saigon was a popular destination, others went to places such as China Beach or Vung Tau for several days to recuperate. Nice facilities including clubs, rest centers, and beaches awaited the soldier. One soldier wrote: "The greatest pleasure of the three days in Vung Tau was my big double bed in the villa. There I slept late on clean white sheets in a room with electric lights, a bath, windows, and a clean tile floor." He added: "I could just lie there and stare up at the ceiling without having to peer through mosquito netting. Nor, when I finally got around to getting dressed, did I have to first empty my boots and check for crawling wildlife."[134]

Besides the in-country leaves, during the middle of a tour grunts received a short reprieve to travel to Japan, Australia, the Philippines, Thailand, or Hawaii. They returned to soft beds, hot showers, and good food as vast service industries such as restaurants, hotels, and brothels catered to the American GI and provided him with a brief respite from the boredom and strain of combat duty.

The experience often took on a surreal nature. One GI described his time in Japan as "I got off the bus here tonight, looked at that full moon, and said, 'What a night for an ambush.' Mentally I'm still in Vietnam. I can give you a pretty good idea of Vietnam by telling you my first impressions of Tokyo." There were other things that stood out as "I noticed no barbed wire, which is everywhere in Vietnam. I also noticed that car windows weren't shot up, and no curfew. Weird. Also they don't carry weapons here."[135]

Another GI, who took his R&R in Australia, observed that the time away from Vietnam gave him too much time to think. Afterward, he stressed that "it was weird. Getting back to a completely English-looking and -speaking country made me feel kind of ashamed of the way I've thought and acted over here. I realize that I've actually enjoyed some of the things I've done which would be repulsive to a healthy mind. This place does make you sick in the head. When one starts to enjoy the sickness of war, he is sick."[136]

Young, single men, many with money piled up from their time in the bush, often chose Thailand as their destination. The close proximity meant less travel time, something important to those measuring their R&R in days, not weeks. Much cheaper than stateside, and with less regulation of sex and booze, Thailand was exotic, unlike any place most GIs had visited and reminded them of the movies they had seen before going to Vietnam about the Orient. Early on, stories trickled back to other GIs, and Bangkok in particular became the popular choice to blow off steam and escape the trials of combat in Vietnam.

Many of the grunts remembered vividly their short time in Thailand. A lieutenant from Danville, California, wrote to his brother about his week in Bangkok where it cost $30 for a room for the week, $30 for a chauffeur who was on call twenty four hours a day, and $3 for a sumptuous meal. "The sights are fantastic: 'Bridge on the River Kwai,' Ramakien murals, temples, markets," but he complained about the prices back home, noting that a night on the town in San Francisco cost $200 while it was only $10 in Thailand. He added that he had met a Thai girl "who looked like Nancy Sinatra" who "had three roommates, and they thought I was Number 1." Clearly, he enjoyed his time in Thailand immensely.[137]

While the single men often flocked to Thailand, for many married couples Hawaii was the most popular destination. Direct flights from the mainland allowed wives to make plans in advance, and the increase in air travel made it an ever more popular destination. Despite the positives, strains always existed. For the soldier just out of the bush, any place with clean sheets, showers, and room service was a shock to the system. The tropical paradise further created a surreal experience. A realization dawned on many grunts in Hawaii that life outside of Vietnam for most people proceeded as normal, with few thoughts of the fighting in Southeast Asia.

Equally important, for many being with their wives added to the dislocation. Outside of career soldiers who were familiar with long absences from family, most of the young men had only recently been married before shipping out. Suddenly, they found themselves thrust together with someone they loved, but realized that they had changed because of their combat experience. In some ways, they felt alienated and distant from their spouse.

On the other side, a wife might find herself dealing with someone she barely knew for only a few days before he left for Vietnam. One wife from Tennessee, Seawillow Chamber, had been married only few weeks when her husband shipped out for Vietnam, so they arranged a rendezvous in Hawaii in March 1968. She had never flown before, and the trip itself was a shock. After arriving, she waited as soldiers disembarked buses. "I'd see one after another, and I never could see him. Then finally . . . this strange person came over and grabbed me. . . . It was Ron." She remembered, "I had the strangest feeling. I thought, 'Here, I'm going to a hotel room with a man I barely know.' . . . Everything was so strange. My mind was just so messed up because I'd had so many shocks to my system. . . . He was so unfamiliar, and everything around me was unfamiliar." It took a day, but they reconnected and for three days they enjoyed the islands, but before they knew it, he was on a plane back to Vietnam to complete the last four months of his tour.[138]

R&R could have drawbacks. The psychological edge that many had held in the bush dissipated quickly. Equally important, the grunt faced a return to the dangerous duty after having had some time in a safe place and being reminded that there was a world outside Vietnam. One expressed that fears engulfed him as he returned from R&R, ones exacerbated by the fact that he had only thirty days left on his tour. "I had lost the hardness necessary to say, 'Hey, I may not survive, but so what? If I lose my leg, I'll still keep going. If I'm dead, who's going to care?'" For him, this self-described delusion kept him going. Yet, upon his return "it took about two weeks to get that back."[139]

Short Timers

Most Vietnam veterans knew exactly the number of days left on a tour, which became even more important as they neared the end. Many talked about watching jealously the "freedom birds," planes leaving for the states flying overhead with soldiers who had completed their tour. Yet, often as their date neared, apprehensions and excitement heightened. Fear gripped some, while others tried to put it out of their minds, always a difficult task. In some cases, a grunt escaped early due to a bureaucratic snafu or luck of the draw, while others decided to extend their tours by months and sometimes years. For many, becoming a short timer put the reality of returning home in more focus and when the day arrived, mixed emotions surfaced, although for most elation trumped all other emotions.

Jokes circulated around Vietnam about the short timers. "He's so short he needs a ladder to get into his tent" went one, while another emphasized, "He's so short he can walk under the yellow line in the road."[140] One medic remarked that they would give some of the guys "a short-timer's stick. That was a stick about a foot and a half long that he could cut notches in, one for every day left in-country." He also remembered that "if a 707 happened to fly over, everybody would just go wild. That was the freedom bird to home."[141]

Having the end in sight created problems. One Army psychiatrist wrote about the "short-time syndrome" where GIs became even more tense in the latter stages and "a large number of persons become psychotic at this time, and [some] soldiers do something wrong and get thrown in jail." On another level, the psychiatrist found that the "short-time syndrome" actually led to soldiers extending their tours. In particular, he found some of the soldiers reluctant "to face relationships and responsibilities back home." "Promises made prior to departure in the anxiety of going to war must be kept, and the person no longer has an excuse why he hasn't done this or that to further himself."[142]

While there were exceptions, the majority of grunts could not wait to board the freedom bird. The short timers often became more cautious, and sympathetic commanders often tried to ease the transition by rotating men into safer duties farther away from the combat zones as the departure time neared. However, 1,448 soldiers died on their last day of service in Vietnam.[143] Most, nevertheless, finished the tour and headed home, elated but apprehensive that they would find things had changed, both in themselves and in the world.

Leaving Vietnam

The last views of Vietnam evoked different responses. For most, it was a sense of elation at having survived the year and being on the way back home to normalcy with family and friends. For others there was an ambivalence of leaving behind colleagues and returning to a strange, alien world that they had left seemingly an eternity ago. In either case, they remembered the trip in vivid detail as it signified a break with everything that had been central to their lives for at least a year.

Most veterans left by air for the trip home. When asked about flying out of Vietnam, one veteran remarked: "The joy. Boy everybody stood up and cheered when the pilot announced we were crossing into the United States. You didn't really think, you know you asked about physical and mental stress, I don't think we really realized that until right when we crossed into the United States and we knew."[144] In another case, a soldier remembered, "I expected everyone to have a big yell and a holler, a hoot and a holler that we're leaving on our Freedom Bird." Yet, "I know it was only in my mind, but I thought I heard this scream and a yell and a cry of everybody who got killed and wounded in Vietnam—Vietnamese, Americans, all at one time. I bet it lasted for twenty or thirty seconds. Just a roar that builds, and it was men, women, Americans, GI's. . . . I'd call it a holy experience." It stopped and he "realized that I heard it and no one else did."[145]

Flight attendants who transported troops in and out had special insights. One flight attendant remembered waiting at Bien Hoa to take a group of GIs back to the States. One named Andy stood out as he made a spectacle of himself, jumping up and down and holding out his process papers while waiting to board the plane, all the while dressed in camouflage and heavy boots. He had "the biggest smile on any face in all of Asia." When he boarded he took a seat, and she admitted being drawn to him despite the fact that he reeked of the smell of the jungle. His first words were "I'm goin' home." The young man from a small town in Alabama told her during the trip about the 250 people in his hometown, all of whom wrote to him during his tour, encouraging him not to be a hero and come home safely. As the plane touched down at Travis Air Force Base, everyone cheered, but not him. "I looked toward his seat and he had his big face pressed against the window as far as he could press it without breaking through. Tears were streaming down his face and he wasn't trying to cover them up. He was saying in that still soft voice, 'I'm home, I'm home.'"[146]

Most anxiously awaited their return home and gladly jumped at the opportunity to board the plane and head stateside. Yet, there were always apprehensions. Stories of the antiwar activists spitting on soldiers funneled back to Vietnam as the war escalated and passions intensified. A significant number also returned home with wounds, both physical and psychological, that would require time and assistance to overcome. Some worried about readjusting from combat into society, while others regretted the loss of camaraderie. Whether apprehensive, sad, or elated, the grunts experienced the full gamut of emotions. Still, when they stepped off the plane in America, most greeted the cooler air, beds, and hot meals, and absence of the specter of death with relief. They had survived their rite of passage.

Conclusion

Those returning home often found a different country than they had left. Many, especially those who had entered combat for the first time, found themselves changed men. The intensity of the experience and the relationships they formed affected their view of the world. Teenagers returned home aged far beyond their years. In addition, as the war escalated, many encountered an ungrateful country that ignored their sacrifices, something that worsened as the war turned into a quagmire by 1968 when the Tet Offensive shocked and disillusioned many in the American public. The experience was a powerful one and left a lasting impression on all that served, but especially the grunt who endured the most difficult conditions, both physically and psychologically. No one left Vietnam unscathed, but the grunt especially came home a different man.

4

The Winter of
Their Discontent

After Tet Until the Withdrawal and
Fall of Saigon, 1968–1975

As the war intensified and subsequently became more controversial by early 1968, a South Dakotan noted that he had two weeks leave before shipping out to Vietnam. Then, he went AWOL an additional fifteen days to determine whether he could really kill someone. He played a pacifist message in his head, but ultimately the question boiled down to whether he worried more about shooting someone else or being shot himself. "Between not knowing that and not wanting to look over my shoulder the rest of my life I decided to go."[1] Others held a different view. A Tennessean, firmly imbued with a sense of duty, remembered that as he trained in 1968, "In fact, I had some anxiety over the possibility that my training was going too slow, . . . they could straighten it up at any time, and I might miss the action."[2]

These two extremes highlight the varying attitudes of American soldiers, the former becoming more prevalent as the fighting escalated and U.S. casualties grew significantly after the Tet Offensive in January 1968. Draftees on the front lines increased after Tet, and they ever more encountered a muddled mission where neither politicians nor most

During the heavy fighting of the Tet Offensive, in early February 1968, some U.S. soldiers rest along a wall in Hue City. *(National Archives)*

military leaders articulated concrete objectives. With dwindling support at home, the grunt often encountered a more difficult position than those who had arrived before 1968. Most continued fighting bravely and some remained firmly committed to defeating the Communists, but many increasingly focused on their own survival and that of their comrades as the United States began withdrawing and turning over fighting to the South Vietnamese.

The Year of Living Dangerously

The most intense fighting of the war for the Americans unfolded in 1968. In living rooms across the country, Americans watched on television as U.S. troops fought off assaults on Khe Sanh and then Saigon and Hue during the Tet Offensive. The brutal aftermath of often house-to-house fighting raised U.S. casualties significantly and undermined predictions of an American victory. In 1968, more Americans died than in any other year, and the decision by President Johnson to withdraw from the presidential race after his near defeat in the New Hampshire primary by antiwar activist Eugene McCarthy further shook the nation's confidence. In response, Republican presidential nominee Richard Nixon promised to extricate the United States from Vietnam through a secret plan that allowed peace with honor. Nonetheless, many Americans and Vietnamese died during the lengthy withdrawal that culminated in 1973.[3]

As January 1968 opened, the most severe fighting centered on Khe Sanh, a Marine base on a plateau surrounded by commanding hills near the demilitarized zone (DMZ). Four Marine and one ARVN Ranger battalions, totaling nearly 6,000 men, faced two divisions of between 30,000 and 40,000 NVA. American leaders feared the North Vietnamese wanted to replicate the French defeat at Dien Bien Phu, so they concentrated on defending this crucial base. However, while U.S. commanders focused on Khe Sanh, the enemy planned a coordinated strike throughout South Vietnam during the Tet holiday.[4]

At Khe Sanh, brutal fighting occurred. In one case, a young lieutenant led his platoon outside the wire with orders to assess the area but not advance more than 400 meters. Inexperienced, he ordered his troops to chase several snipers, who led his men into an ambush. A Marine remembered, "We just watched our guys get chewed up right in front of us." When the other Marines asked permission to aid the survivors and retrieve the dead, commanders denied it, fearing more casualties. "We just watched every one of those guys get zapped," one Marine lamented, adding that "I can tell you it's a fact that we had 27 men lying dead out there for over a month. And we weren't allowed to go pick up the bodies. I'll tell you, morale was really rotten, really bad."[5]

When the Marines ultimately tried to recover the bodies, all hell broke loose. As the Americans took casualties, one of the Marines, Ken Korkow, began jumping out and retrieving the wounded, risking his life in the constant enemy barrage. At one point, he left his rifle and only took a K-Bar knife. As he passed a major in a trench, the officer ordered him to get his rifle. Korkow responded that he could get "whatevered," thinking "what was he going to do to me, court-martial me out there? My attitude toward him was, 'Sucker, if you're a man get out here and fight the war. Get out of the trenches, . . . get up and be a Marine'." Finally, he suffered wounds to his hand and leg but told medics to work on the more seriously injured. For his heroism, he received the Navy Cross.[6]

With the country transfixed on Khe Sanh, the enemy launched a major nationwide offensive in late January. The attacks surprised most Americans as well as the ARVN, which had many of its troops on leave to celebrate the Vietnamese New Year. As the NVA and VC began their assault, one helicopter pilot remembered being at Can Tho where "they breached the perimeter, and they were coming in. We had cooks and typists and whoever could carry a gun out there." A pea-soup fog kept the helicopters on the ground, so pilots jumped in their new Cobra gun ships and began flying just a foot off the ground. "Using their many guns, rocket launchers and grenade launchers, cruising along in the grass," the garrison "managed to blow Charlie right back out of the perimeter but not before he blew up just about every helicopter on the flight line."[7]

The most vicious fighting occurred in the old royal capital of Hue. Early on, the VC overran the town and brutally murdered thousands of people. For more than a month, they held the central area of the Citadel. One Marine rifleman remembered the house-to-house, room-to-room fighting, as he and his fellow Marines fought up Le Loi Street near the Perfume River. In one case, he saw a doctor merely cut off the skin holding a man's foot with a pair of scissors. In another area, he watched as a fellow Marine lay on the ground as VC snipers waited for others to rescue him. VC snipers hit one wounded man seventy-four times before his comrades retrieved him. In the meantime, the VC shot four others. "I saw guys beg somebody to come out and get them and then I saw guys say, 'I'm all right, don't do it.'" He speculated some feared for their comrades, while others worried about being shot again if someone tried to help them.[8]

The Americans and ARVN fought back bravely and decisively defeated the VC and NVA. The planned general uprising never materialized. Many NVA and VC units retreated into their sanctuaries in Laos and Cambodia where they licked their wounds, often for more than a year. The enemy found itself momentarily on the defensive and morale at a low point.[9] Nonetheless, they recognized that the Americans had decided to start withdrawing and turning over their responsibilities to the ARVN. Enemy strategists understood the need to rebuild and wait until the Americans withdrew before beginning any additional major operations. Without American support for their opponents, they believed in their ultimate victory.[10]

Despite being a tactical victory, the battles of the Tet Offensive ended in a strategic defeat for the United States. American leaders had created unrealistic expectations beforehand that casual and concerned observers began questioning. General Westmoreland had told reporters in late November 1967, at the National Press Club: "We have reached an important point where the end begins to come into view. . . . Whereas in 1965 the enemy was winning, today he is certainly losing."[11] Soon after, President

Johnson made a surprise trip to Vietnam in December 1967. At that time, he underscored American victories on the battlefields and "in the cities and the villages all over Asia."[12]

Tet undermined Johnson and his advisers' optimistic reports about victory being around the corner. Americans watched VC sappers penetrate the perimeter of the most fortified position in South Vietnam, the U.S. embassy in Saigon. Television brought them the images of the bloody battle of Hue, where it took months to expel the enemy, and they witnessed the summary execution of a suspected VC by the Saigon police chief. In response, distinguished newscaster Walter Cronkite quipped: "What the hell is going on? I thought we were winning the war." After he made a short trip to Vietnam he told his viewers that it appeared "more certain than ever that the bloody experience of Vietnam is to end in a stalemate."[13] A crisis in confidence spread across the country, and among many U.S. soldiers, at the same time that more Americans began dying in South Vietnam.

The Dreaded Visit

During the entire conflict, more than 58,000 Americans died from combat and accidents, including more than 37,000 after January 1, 1968, as ferocious fighting followed the Tet Offensive. The appearance of an Army or Marine official to report the death of a son (and in a few cases, a daughter) in Vietnam constituted the worst nightmare of a grunt's spouse or parent. A terribly traumatic event, few people forgot when and where they received the news. For many, it took years to come to grips with the loss of the loved one, and some never did fully.

The whole process, for example in the Marines, began with a call from the casualty section at Marine headquarters, often to recruiting depots near the hometown of the person killed-in-action (KIA). In one case in late spring 1967, a Vietnam veteran-turned-recruiter in southeastern Missouri, Harry Spiller, received a call reporting the combat death of nineteen-year-old John W. Williams from the small town of Chaffee. Spiller gathered himself and jumped in his car for the twenty-mile drive from his station in Cape Girardeau. Once there, he searched for a church, hoping to find a pastor to accompany him. Ultimately, he found a Catholic priest who provided directions to the house, although he hesitated to accompany Spiller since the family belonged to a Protestant church.[14]

As Spiller pulled up to the home and exited his car, he heard someone cry out, "Johnny! Johnny! You're home." When he turned, an older woman with silver streaks in her hair faced him. Soon, her expression changed from excitement to sadness, "You're not John," and she began crying, "Oh, my God! What's wrong?" Snapping to attention, Spiller began: "Mrs. Williams, as a representative of the commandant of the Marine Corps, it is my duty to inform you that your son, John Williams, was killed in action on April 27, 1967, in the Republic of South Vietnam in the defense of the United States of America." She fell into his arms, stammering amid the crying, "I thought you were my son. He was due home any time." Spiller continued into the home where he instructed the grieving mother on the procedures for the return of the body and burial.[15]

The absence of Mr. Williams forced Spiller to continue his trek through Chaffee. Finally, he arrived at a field where he emerged in his dress blue uniform and trudged through mud toward an older man working on a tractor, grease all the way to his elbows. Looking up, the man queried, "My son's dead, isn't he?" As the man's eyes filled with tears and his arms dropped hard down to his side, Spiller repeated his report. When finished, the Marine observed, "Mr. Williams sat back and hung his head as if all life had been drained from his body."[16]

A distraught Spiller returned to the recruiting station in Cape Girardeau, feeling "like I've ruined their lives." A colleague comforted him, "You can't feel that way, Spiller. You were just delivering the message." Yet, the ordeal continued, as a few weeks later he and several other Marines returned to Chaffee. In dress uniforms, they entered the Jackson Funeral home, filing to the front as a soft rendition of "Amazing Grace" played. They sat in the front row and listened to the short service, Spiller's first funeral since his father's death many years before. The sermon included an often-repeated recitation during wartime of John 15:13: "No greater love than the man who lays down his life for a friend."[17]

As the service ended, the formally dressed Marines took their positions on each side of the casket and escorted it to a waiting hearse. At the cemetery, they quickly exited, grabbed rifles, and marched 200 feet away from the grieving family and friends gathered around the casket hovering over a deep hole. On command, they fired a salute as a local band member played taps. Then, two Marines folded the flag on top of the casket and one took it to Mrs. Williams and recited: "We present this flag to you in recognition of your son who gave his life in the defense of the United States of America." Then, he placed it on her lap, saluted, and walked away. For Spiller, this only started the process of "plant one, enlist one."[18]

Being a self-described "death angel" represented an extremely difficult duty, but those receiving the news, sometimes young wives with little children, endured the worst experience. In one case, the wife of a draftee, Pauline Querry, remembered being under a big sycamore tree in her family's back yard in Illinois on May 12, 1968 (Mother's Day). As she read the paper, a story about her husband's unit's (the 3rd Battalion, 39th Regiment, 9th Infantry Division) recent battle caught her eye. Suddenly, she began crying and trembling, thinking, "Howard is dead. I know it. I don't know how I know. I just know." When her alarmed mother came out, Pauline whispered, "Howard is dead."[19]

Three days later, a green sedan with the letters "U.S. Army" painted on it, pulled up outside her parents' home. Slowly, two men exited and entered the house. The officers looked anxiously at Pauline, obviously several months pregnant. "We regret to inform you that your husband, Sergeant Howard E. Querry, was fatally wounded on the afternoon of May 10 by a penetrating missile wound to his right shoulder." She thought to herself: "I must be alone to sort this out. Leave me alone," but she continued to listen as they outlined the details of the funeral. She ran to her room and threw herself on her bed, leaving behind her hysterical weeping parents. As she gasped for air, "my unborn baby starts kicking and squirming . . . and I sob. I'm shattered, blown to pieces. It can't be true. No medics come, no helicopters fly me away to an emergency room. I struggle to save myself but I cannot. I die." Then a half hour later, "a ghost of my former self gets up off the bed and begins planning Howard's funeral."[20]

As she waited for her husband's body, Pauline kept hearing people tell her to be strong for her baby. "I went through the motions of living, but every morning when the sun came up and the realization of his death would hit me, I'd sink into despair again." Finally, the body arrived. Anxiously, she drove to the funeral home, hoping to see her husband's body lying neatly in Army uniform in the coffin. She met his escort, formally dressed with white gloves, but did not speak "as I blamed him for Howard's death. He was part of the institution that killed Howard— The United States Army." Then, she suffered a shock when the funeral director described his body as "non-viewable," having been divided and individually wrapped in three pieces with a strong stench that caused him to close the casket immediately. Her brother, a former Marine, offered to view the remains, but Pauline declined.[21]

Soon after, they held the funeral complete with a 21-gun salute and taps followed by an officer handing her a folded flag. She recalled that she "pressed it to my heart, bowed my head and didn't shed a tear." All she wanted was to "go to my room and be alone for the rest of my life. I just wanted to be alone. I didn't want to be seen in public. I felt enormous shame that such a terrible thing had happened to me and my husband." Struggling daily to deal with the loss, she stressed, "The only thing that kept me going during that time was the life I had growing inside me. I couldn't give up." The kicking of her baby gave a "very good reason to live . . . and sometimes I pretend he's coming back." This ensured her "love affair with denial continued for many years. But pretending didn't make . . . grief go away—it just buried it deeper and deeper."[22]

For widows like Querry as well as parents and siblings, the pain remained a constant companion. While many moved on, often remarrying and starting new lives, the memories remained, images of the young men forever frozen in time. For a small number, the pain continued longer because of the uncertainty of their husband or family member being listed as missing in action (MIA). Helicopter pilots and their crews or Air Force, Marine, or Navy aviators shot down comprised the majority of MIAs. The tendency of neither side to take prisoners limited the number of infantrymen captured. Nonetheless, there were some, and the grief of not knowing affected the families of servicemen terribly, as one mother of an MIA lamented: "You can't kill your own son in your mind. I can never stop thinking, 'My God, if he's alive, what must he be going through?' If he was dead maybe I could accept it. But you never know."[23]

Heartbreaking examples included Humberto Rosario, a U.S. Army machine gunner from New York City who remained MIA for more than a decade. In August 1968 while engaged in a firefight, the enemy overran his position. A subsequent sweep of the area uncovered his weapons and uniform, but no body. The Army duly reported to the family "it is the belief by this command that Cpl. Rosario was captured by enemy forces. Efforts will continue to obtain additional information."[24] During the interim, the Army listed Humberto as MIA. The family received periodic reports about the progress to find him. His brother, Alberto, who joined the Army at about the same time, held his breath in 1973 with the release of the POWs following the Paris Peace Accords. Hoping for some sight of his brother, his heart skipped a beat when he heard the name Rosario announced by a TV broadcaster, but "this man stepped off the plane. I saw him and then I heard his full name. It was not Humberto— his was a Mexican name." Finally, in 1978, Alberto received a call from his father reporting that he had cancer and could no longer work to support the family in Puerto Rico. "Alberto, I must ask the Army to declare Humberto dead. We need to collect his insurance and back pay." The Army granted the request and declared Humberto officially dead in 1978, although his name remains absent from the Vietnam Memorial in Washington, DC.[25]

No matter whether people held out hope for an MIA or experienced an immediate loss, the wives, children, and parents of the fallen serviceperson endured a gut-wrenching trauma. For some, it took years to heal and move on with their lives. For others, full recovery never came. The deaths, whether from enemy bullets, friendly fire, disease, or an accident, left a void in the lives of many Americans. The loss of more than 58,000 Americans directly affected family members and friends, literally millions of Americans who lost loved ones in Vietnam.

Heroes

Many heroes fought in Vietnam, some recognized for their valor, others not; some who died, others who returned home. During the war, 244 Americans received their country's highest honor, the Medal of Honor, with 153 dying during their act of courage. The numbers compared favorably with other conflicts including World War I (124), World War II (464), and Korea (131). Many others received the Distinguished Service Cross, Silver Star, Bronze Star, and Purple Heart. While they never received the recognition afforded heroes such as Audie Murphy, whose face graced *Life* magazine, many Vietnam veterans distinguished themselves with similar gallantry, even as the war wound down.[26]

Many heroes arose throughout the conflict, and not everyone fit the stereotype of the American hero. One included Private Lewis Albanese, the son of Italian immigrants who moved to Seattle after World War II. A draftee, Albanese admitted to hating the Army and actively seeking to avoid difficult physical duty. One sergeant even characterized him as a "goof-off." He entered the Army in October 1965 and deployed to Vietnam with his battalion in August 1966.

Once in Vietnam, Albanese's unit fought throughout the dangerous Binh Dinh Province where the 18th NVA and 2nd VC regiments operated. On December 1, 1966, his platoon went on an operation to relieve fellow Americans pinned down by enemy fire near the hamlet of Phu Muu. As they crossed through a graveyard, the enemy sprang an ambush, utilizing a long ditch with bunkers and firing positions to chew up the Americans. As his colleagues tried to retreat, Albanese provided covering fire. Then, he fixed his bayonet and jumped into the trench.[27]

While there were no American eyewitnesses, commanders pieced together Albanese's exploits over the next fifteen minutes. Using his rifle and grenades, he moved down the ditch, killing at least six Viet Cong and disrupting others firing on his comrades. At the same time, another unit launched an attack on the main line of the VC resistance, killing more than sixty and taking several prisoners. The lieutenant and sergeant in charge returned and found Albanese dead at the end of the ditch with two VC right in front of him, his bayonet red with their blood. He had run out of ammunition and grenades and fought to the end. On February 16, 1968, his parents received his Medal of Honor with the citation stressing his heroism as "a tribute to himself, his unit, and the U.S. Army."[28]

Even as the United States began its withdrawal from Vietnam after 1968 and the war increasingly became unpopular, many soldiers continued to demonstrate extreme heroism. One example occurred in February 1969 when a group of Navy SEALS led by Lieutenant Bob Kerrey attacked an enemy sapper base on Nha Trang Island. Taken by Swift boats near the landing zone, Kerrey's party went ashore in two rubber boats. Once there, in the dead of night, they scaled a sheer thirty-five–foot cliff. Then, a VC defector led the small band to find the enemy.[29]

During the hunt, a firefight erupted as Kerrey dropped into a hurdler's position with his right leg extended. Suddenly, an explosion lifted him into the air, separating him from his weapon. When he regained his senses, he could smell burning flesh and felt a terrible pain in his right leg. Reaching down, Kerrey found his foot partially detached from his calf. While severely wounded, he continued fighting for an hour as he tied a tourniquet around his thigh, injected himself with morphine, and directed his troops. Ultimately, a helicopter crew lifted him out via a sling and injected him with more morphine. When he finally landed back at base, he thought to himself, "my war was over."[30]

Kerrey correctly appraised his situation. He went from Cam Ranh Bay to Japan and finally to a naval hospital in Philadelphia. After gangrene set in, the doctor's removed much of his right leg below his knee. He endured months of pain and agony in the healing process and then began the difficult task of rehabilitation, which included learning to walk with a prosthesis. He also battled the nightmares of a mission a week before being wounded in the hamlet of Thanh Phong, where many civilians died in a cross-fire. During his rehab, he found out his comrades had put him in for a Silver Star but his commanders had upgraded it to the Medal of Honor. "The news stunned and embarrassed me. I did not believe the action deserved the highest honor," he emphasized.[31]

Besides not believing that he earned the medal, a fact only changed by a friend who argued it reflected the heroism of the entire team, Kerrey had soured on the war. He remembered the turning point clearly, a televised speech by President Richard Nixon. One particular line infuriated him when the president said: "I've seen the ugly face of war. I know what you are going through."[32]

Nevertheless, he traveled to the White House with his family and on May 14, 1970, received his Medal of Honor in a ceremony with several other soldiers and their families. While disgusted with Nixon for invading Cambodia and the killings at Kent State, Kerrey maintained the dignity of the ceremony out of respect for his comrades. He walked away and became quite an example of determination and fortitude by developing into a successful businessman, then governor of Nebraska, and later U.S. Senator, all the while finding time to date a movie star and run a marathon.[33]

In another example of extreme heroism, on January 5, 1970, Franklin Miller and his small team of Americans and Montagards landed secretly in Laos aboard Hueys with Cobra gunships, searching for an enemy base. They had a soft landing with no enemy contact for more than three hours as they traversed the countryside. Suddenly, a massive explosion erupted and one of the Montagnards stumbled back toward Miller, his lower jaw gone. Enemy troops opened up while Miller, and the one remaining unit member not wounded, furiously fired back. Soon, Miller moved his men to a better position, pulling and dragging the severely wounded.

Ultimately, the enemy regrouped and spotted the blood trail. As they moved in, Miller found himself in deep trouble after he killed a point man. "Since I was the lone target they concentrated their fire on me. They threw rounds at me the likes of which I'd never experienced before." As he fired, he used a CS gas grenade to shield his withdrawal. Retrieving his colleagues, Miller dispersed another attack with grenades and automatic fire, although not before the enemy claimed the squad's other remaining healthy soldier.[34]

Miller hid his colleagues and moved forward toward a bomb crater that an overhead observer had spotted as a possible point to extricate the group. As he returned, "suddenly I was on the ground. Something was wrong. I wasn't moving—or even standing, for that matter. I was on my side, in tall grass." Soon, he vomited blood and found a hole in his chest. He stuffed his field dressing into it, and felt around his back to where the round had exited as "I felt bone fragments and flesh projecting from the wound." Closing the wound with a piece of his poncho, he sat there.[35]

As he recovered his senses, several enemy soldiers approached him. He fired on them, lifted himself up, and then stumbled back toward his wounded comrades, crawling the last sixty yards. Severely wounded, nonetheless he managed to drag everyone back to the extraction point. Soon, a sizeable enemy force attacked the crater where only three men could fire their weapons. A firefight ensued, one heightened by the sudden appearance of a Huey with guns blazing, hovering only a short distance above the crater. It took numerous hits before retreating, but it bought the small band time to regroup before another enemy assault.[36]

After the Huey disappeared, Miller left the crater and succeeded momentarily in breaking up another attack. Then, the enemy launched another furious assault on the crater, wounding Miller once again. Down to his last clips of ammo with night approaching, he went to the radio and began singing the Beatle's "Help." As he prepared to die, suddenly some Montagnards appeared with an American lieutenant, jumping in and yelling, "Motherfucker, this looks like Custer's Last Stand."[37]

Ultimately, the rescue unit drove back the enemy far enough to construct a safe landing zone. Eventually, the helicopters took the group back to base, where the wounded including Miller waited for evacuation to Pleiku. Although he had the shoulder and arm wounds, he remained in the best shape, so he thought at least "now I could get a little rest."[38]

Miller recovered from his wounds in Japan and his immediate superiors originally put him in for the Distinguished Service Cross, but commanders ordered an upgrade to a Medal of Honor. As he convalesced, he kept requesting a return to service in Vietnam, which he ultimately arranged with a clerk who pulled some strings. Within a short time, he arrived back at the base working with his old unit. Soon, he received a brief respite to travel to Washington to receive his Medal of Honor. He enjoyed the first-class travel and attention during five days in the capital in June 1971. At the ceremony on the fifteenth, only one other man stood with him among the seven honorees, the others awarded posthumously. He received his medal with a "rush of joy and sorrow intermixed." Afterward, President Nixon asked him if he needed anything. Miller replied that he wanted to return to his unit, to which the president gave General Westmoreland a nod. The Army granted his request.[39]

Miller returned to Vietnam. Although he had not changed, everyone treated him differently. Commanders started shielding him from action, fearful of having to explain how a Medal of Honor recipient died on their watch. Instead, he received more desk jobs, which caused him to chafe. Also, the American role had diminished, causing him to lament, "My world was coming to an end, and I was frightened at the prospect of life after the war."

Fate intervened when a commander ordered him to undergo a physical. He ended up in the psychiatric ward after some people reported seeing him saluting telephone poles. A few days later, he found himself at Fort Bragg undergoing tests, furious at the betrayal. Later, a doctor told him that officers often employed the practice to pull Special Forces soldiers from the field. Angry, he continued his service, noting how worthless he felt until he realized that he could help the next generation prepare for future wars. Ultimately, he retired from the Army in 1992 as a command sergeant major having received a Medal of Honor, a Silver Star, two Bronze Stars, the Air Medal, and six Purple Hearts.[40]

Throughout the conflict in Vietnam, many Americans such as Albanese, Kerrey, and Miller distinguished themselves, whether officially recognized or not. They came from different backgrounds, but possessed a commitment to their survival and that of their comrades and often the mission, although that priority diminished as American commitment to South Vietnam waned after 1968. Even as the war wound down for Americans and the morale of the military reached its nadir, young men continued to distinguish themselves. Still, they faced significant challenges on many fronts, often more than their comrades who arrived before the Tet Offensive.

A Racial Divide Widens

While there were many heroes in Vietnam, structural problems plagued the American military, especially after 1968 as popular support for the war declined precipitously. Many social problems continued, including racial animosities. For the first time, completely integrated units existed during the entire war and racial tensions persisted, especially as the military threw together people from different cultures and environments during a time of heightened racial conflict at home. As race riots increased in the United States after 1965, more challenges developed for the military. While combat typically cemented comradeship, divisions continued to survive throughout the war, which affected U.S. military operations in Vietnam.

African Americans constituted the largest minority group among soldiers in Vietnam, especially in combat zones. During the early stages of the war, African Americans volunteered in large numbers, many in the more dangerous duties such as Airborne, where soldiers received additional pay. At the onset, the African American community generally supported the war, partly out of loyalty to President Johnson, who had pushed through the most significant civil rights legislation in modern American history. However, as the war escalated, African Americans, led by Rev. Martin Luther King Jr. increasingly denounced it.[41]

Part of reason was that African Americans bore a disproportionate amount of the sacrifice in the first half of the war. Elevated African American casualties, higher than their proportion in American society, existed early on. The death rates of African Americans in 1966 stood at nearly 21 percent, high when compared to their 12 percent share of the population. This led to a concerted effort by the military to reduce African American deaths, which leveled off by the end of the war to 13.1 percent.[42] Such rates led one African American Marine in 1968 to complain bitterly while serving in Dong Ha that blacks constituted 60 percent of the fatalities. "I think we're being killed off. I think we're being used."[43]

Racism defined many relationships. One African American observed, "There were very definitely some racial problems. There were guys who really did hate the other race. Some brothers just didn't want to be around white guys. And in war zones people's anger gets magnified."[44] One white Army captain remembered being at Fort Knox in 1968. "I thought the wheels were falling off the country. I was concerned. Many of the soldiers that we got were draftees and we got them from Detroit, being close by. I don't know but it seemed to me that the racial relationships in Detroit must be the worst of any place in the country. We had Black kids come down there who had never been around White people to any degree before. They were suspicious. They were somewhat hostile."[45]

Despite the divisions, in combat, people generally worked well together no matter the race. One veteran noted, "Out in the field blacks and whites got along a whole lot better than in the unit that was way back." He added that the danger and shared burdens ensured that "people would go out and risk their lives for each other. . . . Like one for all; no racial distinctions. And that was one of the good things that came out of the experience, you know—that it can work."[46] Another African American veteran from Rhode Island who served as a medic emphasized: "Combat was horrible, but there was a beautiful side as well—the brotherhood between black soldiers and white soldiers and Hispanics and Native Americans. When we were in combat all that mattered was trying to survive together. I never imagined I could be so close to men. I can honestly say I felt closer to some of the people I served with in combat—of all races—than my own family."[47]

That same veteran also observed a significant problem with the unit cohesiveness once the grunts returned to base camps. "Unfortunately, it is very hard to get a handle on to that communion off the battlefield." He added, "It's like what you experience during blizzards or floods when people come out and work together digging out or filling sandbags. But when it's over they retreat back to their burbs or inner cities or barrios."[48]

A lack of understanding of different cultures, combined with pervasive racism, heightened problems, especially in the rear areas. One African American talked about how other African Americans increasingly greeted each other with the black power salute of a raised clinched fist. At other times, they gave each other the "dap," an elaborate handshake, or tapped each other on the forehead as a signal for giving knowledge. Such actions he believed caused some whites to feel "intimidated and I'm sure some got frustrated standing in chow lines behind a group of soul brothers who were giving up the dap and bullshitting and causing delays." He characterized it as their secret society "that could provoke anger."[49]

On the other side, whites, many raised in racist and segregated enclaves, provoked hostility with overt actions such as flying the Confederate battle flag and using racist slurs. While the Army and Marines tried reducing tensions by limiting the display of such cultural symbols, problems continued as all depended on the officers' enforcement of the edicts. Many clashes in the rear areas and base camps turned into race riots, often provoked by whites. In one case, after an assassin killed Martin Luther King Jr. in 1968, whites at Cam Ranh Bay put on white sheets like Klan members and marched around the base to celebrate King's death.[50]

In addition to black/white issues, divisions often developed within the African American community, especially as more radicalism entered the civil rights movement in the late 1960s. "Even though I felt a powerful communion with my African American brothers, I had grown

up in an integrated society and my best friends were Italian and Irish so
when the lines were drawn, I could sort of see both sides," one veteran
lamented. Other African Americans would question him "you mean
there are black people in Rhode Island?" so he would "fire back, 'Hey
man, I'm as militant as you are.'" He remembered "feeling jammed up
in the middle."[51]

Another African American echoed the problem of divisions within
the African American community. He talked about confronting another
black who told him "if you wasn't an NCO I would kick your ass." The
young man accused the NCO of being an Uncle Tom because he social-
ized with whites and insisted that people get their hair cut at a time that
Afros had become popular. "It was a personal thing—I wasn't black
enough for him, and he was too black for me."[52]

Racial problems also existed for many Latinos, although often not to
the same degree as for African Americans. The country, outside of the
Southwest, typically focused on race relations through the prism of black/
white interactions. Furthermore, Latinos had served in military units
with whites during most American conflicts. Latinos also often blended
with other groups such as Italians in terms of skin color and culture.
Finally, the Latino movement in the United States lacked the visibility
and sometimes the radicalism that existed in the African American community during the late 1960s.[53] Nonetheless, Latino soldiers shared some
problems with African Americans, including often facing discrimination
from whites at all levels who held various negative stereotypes that shaped
minorities' service.

A Mexican American veteran echoed the feelings of many African
Americans when he stressed that "out in the bush I've never felt such
affinity and togetherness with men of other cultures and races as I did
in Vietnam. But as soon as we got back to rear areas everything changed
again." "The blacks and some whites used to call us 'chingos,' I guess
because Mexicans use that word a lot. *No me chingo* means 'don't fuck
with me.' I used to say '*chingo* your mama,' and that used to piss them
off. We call the whites *gabachos* and *bolillos*—little white rolls. We
called the blacks names too, like *mayates*—which are June bugs—and
chanates—black crows," he remembered.[54]

Discrimination always existed, especially because of language differences and negative stereotyping. A Puerto Rican remembered being
wounded and while recuperating at the hospital he took a book with each
state represented where patients could write something and then pass it on

to the next one. When he opened it to the pages for Puerto Rico, someone had written: "You fucking spics, why don't you write in English that we can understand." Admitting to being shocked and angry, he wrote back: "If I'm good enough to fight and die for this country, I'm good enough to write or speak in any way I please."[55]

Problems developed for Latinos, partly due to racism but also from cultural standards. A desire to prove one's manhood led many Latinos to assume dangerous duties in the front lines. One Latino veteran observed that "the Raza" wanted to prove themselves. "You have pride in what you do and don't back down, the machismo. I think there was a propensity for Chicanos and Latinos to walk point or carry the M-60 machine gun and the radio as well sometimes."[56]

The machismo contributed to higher casualties among Latinos, which led to some disillusionment among the group with the war and how the leaders conducted it. One Mexican American veteran complained bitterly that after doing some research on his home when he returned he uncovered that Chicanos constituted 50 percent of the casualties from his rural California community.[57]

Like Latinos, Native Americans also faced significant obstacles in Vietnam. One Seneca veteran recalled, "When I got to the bush, my platoon sergeant tells me and the guys I came in with that we were surrounded. He said: 'The gooks are all out there and we're here. This is Fort Apache, boys, and out there is Indian country.' Can you fuckin' believe that? To me? I should have shot him right then and there. Made me wonder who the real enemy was."[58]

Other stereotypes abounded, often with tragic results. One veteran remembered that a "mystique" revolved around being Native American. He remembered one time being point on a recon patrol and a buddy tapping him on the shoulder and whispering, "Tommy, you're leaving tracks." When he asked "What?" the other man replied: "Well, Indians don't make tracks." In another case, a sergeant asked, "How old are those tracks?" He thought, "I didn't know how old those tracks were. You know, it could have been five minutes, or it could have been twenty years."[59]

Such stereotypes had a negative effect. Another Native American veteran observed that a number of Indians died "because they think all Indians are supposed to be good point men." He underscored that many Native Americans lived in cities, "but because of the heritage and because of what's expected of them and because of . . . pride or false pride or whatever, they never told anybody they were city folk."

As a result "a lot of Indians got killed just because they'd keep putting them on point."[60]

Army policies sometimes contributed to racial divisions, especially for Asian Americans. Because of problems of POWs' suffering brainwashing and then making anti-American statements during the Korean War, some soldiers endured POW training in Hawaii. "They had these guards," one veteran remembered, "a lot of them Hawaiian or Oriental who were obviously U.S. soldiers but of Asian descent, wearing Chinese padded uniforms and stuff like that." The anger created by the drills already played upon existing racial stereotypes and long-standing animosities.

Many Asian Americans recall the particular challenges they faced. One veteran remembered, "When I got there (Vietnam) my guys were talking about gooks, and zipperheads, and slants." He added, "I said to myself, 'Damn, I'm a gook, I'm a zipperhead, I'm a slant.' But it didn't take too long before my mentality became just like them. I should have known better, yet within a relatively short time we were all thinking alike."[61]

Another Asian American veteran experienced similar situations. On patrol in 1970, his unit received some green recruits. "They were all shiny and bright, and eager enough to be obnoxious," he remembered. During a patrol, the unit stopped to rest. As they sat, one of the new guys loudly proclaimed, "You know, I really want to kill me one of those slant-eyed bastards." The Asian American simply smiled and chuckled, acknowledging that he gave the guy an "oopsie." The veteran noted, "He was just a stupid kid who bought into the dehumanizing of the enemy. It was Army training. We were just killing gooks, it wasn't like they were real people." He concluded, however, that "but then and there, I wondered if I was fighting on the wrong side of this war."[62]

In some cases, being Asian American affected combat status, sometimes ensuring very difficult duties. One Asian American recalled being put in a special unit called a Peregrine Group with other Asian Americans who received special training in intelligence, hand-to-hand combat, and language training, including French and some Vietnamese. "The theory was that being Asians or half-Asians, we would look like the Viet Cong, live like the Viet Cong, and think like the Viet Cong. If you think like them, you can beat them at their own game." He observed, however, "but that was a big mistake. How can you take somebody out of Chinatown in Seattle and expect him to beat the Viet Cong when he doesn't even speak the language?"[63]

Asian Americans faced major challenges, much as they had in Korea. The racist stereotypes created barriers for many of them. The Army even played up many as in the filming of the *Green Berets* starring John Wayne; a Hawaiian Army major, William K.S. Olds, played the villainous NVA general.[64] Overall, the Asian American grunts faced serious obstacles in Vietnam. Racially, they bore more resemblance to the enemy, and culturally, most Americans continued to hold animosities dating back to the nineteenth century and exacerbated by World War II and then the fall of China to the Communists. Serving in Vietnam, as in Korea, proved very difficult for Asian Americans.

Throughout the Vietnam War, but especially in the late 1960s, the military faced considerable problems maintaining unit cohesiveness. The racial problems exploding at home undercut efforts to sustain an effective fighting force. While soldiers fought together well in the front lines, largely due to the survival instinct, once soldiers returned to base camps, the racial divisions resurfaced, causing many problems. When combined with other difficulties developing from the transference of domestic problems, the military by 1968 encountered many challenges in trying to fight an increasingly unpopular war.

Destroying the Military From Within: The Issue of Drugs

In addition to the racial problems transferred from home that heightened as the war continued, some recruits brought the drug culture from the States that became increasingly visible during the late 1960s. While always present in U.S. society, the drug culture that emphasized marijuana, heroin, and cocaine became more prevalent during the 1960s. War always brought about attempts to handle the rigors of combat and boredom of service. Drugs, primarily alcohol, had been the choice for most American soldiers, although cigarettes became more commonplace during World War I and World War II. Yet, in Vietnam, the problem intensified as the war bogged down and people tried to cope with their role in the conflict. Ultimately, drugs and alcohol had a corrosive effect on unit discipline and cohesiveness, although typically away from the front lines.

Alcohol remained the most abused drug in Vietnam and had significant effects on many veterans during and after the conflict. While the Army and Marines often limited the amount of alcohol for front-line soldiers, it was readily available in many base camps and through illicit sources.

"Juicers" often got drunk, just like they had with friends back home. Partly to forget, partly to loosen up, alcohol continued as the drug of choice of most young Americans. The abundance of alcohol, often hot beer, never surfaced as much of a concern to the military, although many young men developed severe drinking problems that later transferred back home with sometimes tragic results.

More soldiers increasingly used mind-numbing drugs including marijuana and heroin during the Vietnam War, especially in the second half of the conflict. Many soldiers abused the easily available drugs, especially marijuana, although many tried harder ones such as cocaine, LSD, and heroin. Many had tried them in the States before arriving, especially marijuana.[65] Some estimated that 28 percent of the military used hard drugs such as heroin and cocaine while in the service, creating more than 500,000 addicts, including many REMFs and those not stationed in Vietnam; others disputed such high numbers and exact percentages remain a mystery because a lot of GIs refused to answer questions truthfully about their drug habits.[66]

In most cases, few took drugs in combat zones, despite the availability as taxi drivers and street vendors in Saigon sold prepackaged marijuana cigarettes for less than a $1 per pack and a potent vial of heroin (with a street value in the United States of $200) sold for $2.[67] One Marine noted that "you didn't have time for drugs for the simple fact that if you were on drugs you couldn't make your mind work right in the jungle. . . . If they were on drugs they could get everyone killed." [68] In the jungle, some GIs relied on methametaphines, sometimes provided by medics, to stay awake and alert, but the majority avoided anything that dampened alertness and threatened their survival and that of their comrades, who punished anyone caught with drugs.

However, the same Marine observed, in the "rear there were drugs flying all over the place. Guys would go off someplace and do drugs. People were just giving it away."[69] A medic who served in 1970–71 commented, "There were drugs in Vietnam. When I was there you could see the vials lying on the floor. Maybe you walked in twelve feet, you'd see one or two vials just sitting there of white powder. . . . You'd see the guys smoking all the time."[70] A Marine on his second tour of duty in 1969 noted that things had changed since his first tour. "Now there was a drug problem that I hadn't seen before. Marijuana grew in every creek bed in Vietnam. Grunts were getting stoned on it, on hash and other drugs—you name it, and you could buy it. . . . I made up my mind not

During an operation, a medic searches the sky for a medivac helicopter to evacuate his wounded comrade. *(National Archives)*

to trust the men screwed up on drugs. I would do my duty, but I intended to come out alive."[71]

Sometimes problems developed as division arose between various groups. Both "juicers" and "stoners" clashed on the inherent dangers of using drugs in base camps or elsewhere. As one veteran noted, "Differences usually arose when the stoners, including myself, disagreed with the drinkers over whether at certain bases it was too dangerous at night to be stoned while on watch. However, the stoners I associated with could care less if the drinkers got so drunk they passed out, probably because the drinkers usually covered each other, as we stoners did."[72]

Alcohol, marijuana, heroin, cocaine, LSD, and others clearly affected the morale of the grunts. As the war dragged on, the use of drugs increased, although it typically was relegated to base camps and rear echelon areas. Nonetheless, it undermined discipline and contributed to divisions of the troops between juicers and stoners, exacerbating existing tensions, including racial ones. Other issues arose surrounding drug use and punishment such as fraggings of officers who tried enforcing restrictions. Clearly another domestic problem transferred from home, and as public support waned, some troops turned to drugs to try to help ease the strain of being in Vietnam.

Growing Frustrations

The racial and drug problems merely reflected the breakdown of discipline and cohesiveness of the military as the United States reduced its commitment to South Vietnam after 1968. As more deaths occurred and support for the war eroded in the United States, more soldiers (now more draftees) began to question the war and its goals. With the announcement of "Vietnamization" by President Nixon in 1969 in which he promised troop reductions and more focus on having the South Vietnamese fight the war, more soldiers became increasingly disenchanted and the survival instinct dominated more than the idealism and optimism that had existed earlier. Many soldiers increasingly denounced the politicians and their leaders, ensuring more of a search and evade policy as no one wanted to die for the unpopular conflict. As troop withdrawals accelerated after 1970, the military often struggled to sustain a quality fighting force.

Throughout the war, but more so after 1968, grunts expressed their frustration with political leaders. An Alabama Marine summed up the feelings of many when he declared that "one of the basic problems is that Johnson is trying to fight this war the way he fights his domestic war—he chooses an almost unattainable goal with a scope so large it is virtually undefinable, and he attacks this goal with poorly allocated funds, minimum manpower, limited time, and few new ideas." He continued by stressing that the enormity of the mission "can only be realized when you firmly establish in your own mind that Johnson is trying to take 5,000 villages living on a rice economy with a 2,000-year-old Asian tradition of chieftain rule warped by 100 years of ugly colonialism and build a nation with an industrial base and democratic tradition in the midst of a 20-year-old war."[73]

Such frustrations left many GIs bitter, and they vented their anger at the politicians in different ways. After a firefight, an Oklahoman veteran remembered seeing the body bags holding his colleagues and reported "something in me snapped. This was a turning point in my life, the way I view life." That day, he wrote a letter to his congressman, Page Belcher, and complained, "We, the Americans, were doing all the work and suffering all the losses." He queried Belcher: "Had he ever seen a friend lay in a body bag treated like so much trash?" The response only frustrated him more as Belcher sent "a form letter of his family's military service. I don't think I have the mastery of the English language to express my disgust at his response."[74]

The limits on how to conduct the war and the political micromanaging angered many grunts, especially those wanting to pursue the enemy into their sanctuaries in Cambodia and Laos. As an example, during one firefight with the VC near a French rubber plantation, an officer requested artillery support. A fire direction officer refused, noting that standing orders prevented damaging the rubber trees in the area owned by the French company Michelin. Livid, the officer screamed into the radio: "Send me the fucking bill for the trees! Fuck Michelin, and fuck the French!"[75]

Beyond the politicians, grunts vented their frustrations with their military leaders. As in all wars, the grunts expressed dissatisfaction with officers whom they often saw as enjoying better conditions and treating the GIs as expendable pieces on a chessboard. If anything, in Vietnam the animosities intensified as the war continued. By the late 1960s, some American infantrymen began writing on their helmets the letters UUUU. It meant "the unwilling, led by the unqualified, doing the unnecessary for the ungrateful."[76]

Many, including members of the officer corps, acknowledged the problems of leadership in Vietnam. One Army colonel wrote: "Some of the younger officers are very fine, but a few seem to avoid much real action by a display of fancy footwork. I intend seeing that all are tested before this is over, as there are too many prima donnas around who are more concerned with making general than killing the VC."[77] One observer noted that during his time in Vietnam "the only thing the officers wanted to do was get their six months in command and then split back to the States and be promoted and go on to bigger and better things. It doesn't take long for the average guy out in the field to say, 'Fuck it!'"[78]

A study commissioned by Westmoreland and conducted by the commandant of the Army War College, Major General G.S. Eckhard, in the late 1960s concluded that the typical commander in Vietnam was "an ambitious, transitory commander—marginally skilled in the complexities of his duties—engulfed in producing statistical results, fearful of personal failure, too busy to talk with or listen to his subordinates, and determined to submit acceptably optimistic reports which reflect faultless completion of a variety of tasks at the expense of the sweat and frustration of his subordinates."[79]

The rotation system, when combined with deaths and wounds that decimated units, created great instability. One infantryman complained that "toward the end of my tour, when I started knowing what I was doing in the jungle and started knowing what to do under fire, it was just about time to go home." He queried, "If that happened to me—if I was just getting good in the jungle and really knew what to do and I was going home—what good is it." He added that a newcomer replaced him and "by the time he gets good at it he's going to be replaced by a guy who is green. It's no wonder we never got a foothold in the place."[80]

Others, including commanders, denounced the system. An officer volunteered to return to his unit, but observed "to my dismay I was told that though I was rated as a highly successful company commander and had more combat experience than any officer in the battalion, they had many new captains." His superiors told him that these captains needed company command experience. Disenchanted, the officer stressed, "This war is not worth dying for if our attitude is locked into the career advancement approach. If that is the underlying ethic, then after two years of fighting this war, I am not going to waste my life."[81]

The frustrations mounted and by the start of the Vietnamization program, some of the leaders and their grunts had adopted different attitudes on the mission. A Marine commander, Bernard Trainor, commented that on his second tour "I wanted to do my job professionally with a minimum of casualties." He had listened when the commander of the 5th Marines, Clark Judge, told him, "You know, we're not out here fighting a war, we're out here campaigning." He understood Judge believed that their experience paralleled that of the British in the nineteenth-century as they fought along the Indian frontiers: "They were just trying to manage the unwinnable. In a sense, we were only biding time until we were pulled out of Vietnam."[82]

Another grunt entered the war more gung ho in 1970, but grew disenchanted with the ARVN and the South Vietnamese people as well as "our fearless leaders [who] wouldn't lead us." He recounted how a colonel landed one day and walked around examining the bodies "and as soon as he heard a shot he got back on his helicopter." Originally, the grunt walked point, but one day "I decided I wasn't gonna walk point anymore. I'll just walk in the middle and try to keep alive. At that point we practiced search-and-avoid. They'd tell us the enemy was coming from one direction and we'd say, 'Roger that' and go in the other direction."[83]

One platoon leader in Vietnam in 1968–69 emphasized that "we did our duty, but we generally were not very gung-ho. We did what we were told to do in a very conservative manner. That's why the artillery was called in on that sniper: we'd spend ten thousand dollars on artillery rounds before we'd take a chance on losing somebody, and I'll never apologize for that. Maybe that wasn't a very bravado way of doing it, but we did begin to think we were in a kind of holding action. There was very little of the charge-a-hill-at-any-cost mentality." Nonetheless, he concluded, "I believe that under different conditions these guys would have been as dedicated and motivated as any this country has ever sent to war."[84]

While frustrations among grunts arose in every war, the young men fighting in Vietnam, especially after the Tet Offensive, experienced more than their fair share. Fighting an elusive enemy with an often-perceived unreliable ally, under commanders facing pressures to provide body counts, and dealing with a high turnover rate, the grunts' attitude changed over time in concert with the officers in the field leading them. While some remained gung-ho, by 1969 and the onset of Vietnamization, their disillusionment with the politicians and their leaders accentuated the priority of survival and seeking to avoid dying for a perceived lost cause. While many continued to die and most fought bravely, disenchantment led the later grunts to approach the fighting differently than their 1965 counterparts.

Fraggings: Myths and Realities

The frustrations with the leadership sometimes translated into deadly actions. Throughout U.S. history, American enlisted men have often expressed contempt for their officers and bucked the chain of command, which sometimes led to violence. However, in Vietnam, by the end of the conflict, fraggings, an effort to kill an NCO or officer, usually by tossing a grenade into a hooch or tent, had increased. The Defense Department reported 788 fraggings from 1969 to 1972, while the Marines investigated more than twenty fraggings in an eight-month period in 1969. Others estimate that more than 1,000 officers and non-commissioned officers may have been killed at the hands of their own men.[85]

The incidents typically occurred in rear areas or base camps and resulted from disciplinary action often related to drug enforcement or racial conflict. Other actions, especially shootings, may have occurred in the front-line areas against cowardly or incompetent officers, but those incidents typically went unreported. Nonetheless, the numbers increased as the United States began withdrawing and the commitment to the mission wavered.

In one case, a white medic from Mississippi named Walter Ashford had trouble with some African Americans in his unit. According to another medic in the unit, "they were always finding some excuse to stay in the rear and trying to get some medical reason." Ashford typically responded by sending them back to the field, which made him very unpopular as "they thought he was quite prejudiced." One night as several medics slept in their tents, someone threw two grenades into it. The explosives did not kill anyone but wounded three as "the whole top of the bunk was just shredded . . . hundreds of holes through everything."[86]

In another case, an African American, Woody Wanamaker, from the tough streets of Jersey City, developed a strong relationship with a white, Al, from a small town in Vermont during a tour in 1968. People called them "Salt and Pepper" and they became inseparable as they typically avoided the other NCOs. One night, after a room-to-room search for drugs that ultimately discovered some marijuana, Woody and Al heard several soldiers making threats, "We're gonna get you motherfuckers."[87] The next evening, August 21, 1968, the two sat in their hooch talking about family. "And I heard the spoon pop from a grenade," Wanamaker remembered. It landed on the bed where Al lay. With little time, Al just doubled over it to save his friend. "He wasn't actually blown to bits, but there wasn't too much left of a human being." Wanamaker took some shrapnel and headed to the infirmary, angry and frustrated, as "I didn't know who it was."[88]

Wanamaker faced the unenviable task of accompanying the body home. The Army reported that Al died from enemy fire; a story Wanamaker reinforced by saying it was a mortar round. However, Al's wife remained skeptical. Wanamaker underscored the difficulty of lying and the frustration that he "couldn't explain to his son, age three, 'your father wasn't killed in combat. Your father got killed by another American over stupidity.'"[89]

He recalled that the grief "hurt me. It did a lasting thing on me. It destroyed me." He returned to Vietnam, where he became "very hard and callous." Regarding enlisted men, he felt "you did this to me. You took my buddy's life. You motherfuckers are gonna pay. It wasn't directed at one person, it was directed at everybody. I hated without malice." During his third tour, he went on a self-described witch-hunt, searching for the criminals. He received an assignment in a battalion where one of the suspects operated, but the soldier transferred out before Wanamaker's arrival. He ultimately gave up, but not before he had started drinking heavily to deal with the pain. Ultimately, he told Al's wife the truth after receiving therapy for his self-destructive behavior.[90]

The term "fragging" became well known during the Vietnam War and remained part of popular consciousness in films and literature on the conflict after 1973. While the exact number of fraggings and other forms of fratricide remains unknown, a lasting impression of the act and the war lived into the postwar period. The vast majority of troops never participated in the act, but unfortunately many veterans became associated with it and many other negative images from the conflict. The term permanently entered the American lexicon, and the Vietnam veteran became tainted as no previous group had been.

The War Protestor

The pressures and frustrations for the grunt in Vietnam heightened as the war stalemated and popular protests against the conflict intensified. Protestors became a major source of irritation. Longhaired college students and hippies confronting veterans returning home constituted the common perception of the war protestor, although the movement had a wide variety of participants ranging from U.S. senators to ministers from mainline Protestant denominations. Nonetheless, part of the disintegration of the gung ho spirit of many U.S. troops related in part to the decline in domestic support. By 1967 and 1968, major war protests had intensified and more troops saw them unfold. Increasingly, many questioned why fight a war for an ungrateful public.

From the start, many grunts viewed the protestors as undermining the mission, an attitude that continued throughout the conflict. One Marine noted that before he left for the Corps, "I didn't tolerate protest. I knew where I was going, so why listen to something that was simply going to make it harder for me to do what I knew I had to do? As far as I was concerned whether the war was right or wrong didn't matter. What mattered was that we had decided we were going to fight and once you made that decision to commit the troops, okay, we've got an obligation to do what's got to be done."[91] One Tennessee veteran emphasized, "These draft-dodgers, Jane Fonda, line 'em up against the wall. I'd gladly oblige 'em. I had a lot better people than they are die over there, and I ain't forgot them. Way I feel, they're just walking on their graves, what they done."[92]

Some grunts proved more understanding, but nonetheless were often upset by the acts of the protestors. A Marine complained, "I recognize the right of those to protest the war and the situation, but it makes me mad as hell that they protested me and my buddies."[93] Another agreed with the right to protest, but emphasized, "The only thing I disapprove of is when they raise and carry a Viet Cong flag. Something should be done about those few. But, even if a girl was lowering the U.S. flag and raising a VC flag, that would still be no reason for a group of men to attack her with sticks."[94]

Some went even further in acknowledging the right to protest and some actively supported the movement. A Marine observed, "I had some good friends from high school who were against the war, and I knew they weren't cowards. I knew they were good people. . . . I still believed at this time that the war was right, but I wasn't really bothered by the protests because I knew kind of where they were coming from, I guess."[95] Another GI wrote his brother, a Catholic priest: "If you do not get to go to that big peace demonstration [on] October 15th I hope you do protest against war or sing for peace—I would. I just can't believe half of the shit I've seen over here so far."[96]

The antiwar movement provoked strong emotions among most grunts, although no consensus existed. Tensions increased as the frequency and volatility of the protests intensified after 1968, peaking in 1970 with the killings of protestors at Kent State and Jackson State following the invasion of Cambodia. The distance between the grunt and protestor often existed because of class and racial differences, although those conditions converged as more college-educated draftees entered the front lines after 1968. Nonetheless, a chasm often developed between the grunts and the protestors that exacerbated tensions among the infantrymen about why they fought and for whom. It just intensified feelings of an unequal share of the burden falling on the young teenagers fighting in Vietnam and increased the distance between the perceived ungrateful citizen and the returning veteran who served in Vietnam, especially as the war began to wind down.

Friendly Fire

Among the many frustrations for the grunt, the problem of friendly fire carried exceptional significance. Always an obstacle in war, friendly fire increased in frequency with mechanization and new technologies. Artillery and air support amplified the chance of accidental fire falling on American troops. When combined with fighting in a tropical environment, fatigue, and poor training, the odds of friendly fire accidents increased significantly. Some estimate between 10 and 15 percent of the casualties involved friendly fire.[97] While the military tried combating the issue, the challenges made it impossible to solve and many grunts subsequently lost their lives or suffered wounds from friendly fire.

Stories of friendly fire appear frequently in veterans' letters and memoirs. Second lieutenant Robert Ransom wrote his parents that he had lost his first man during a night ambush operation. "They had been set up in a position for a few hours," he recalled, "when the flank man crawled away to take a leak or something, and as he was crawling back to position another man mistook him for a dink and shot him. He died on the chopper that dusted him off."[98] In another case, a sergeant remembered that the NVA ambushed his patrol. Suddenly, he "felt a sharp, burning pain in my leg and swung around and saw the RTO [radio telephone operator] frozen to his rifle, which was still firing. His head was gone. A round had taken it off and blood was spurting up from his neck like a water fountain. He must have had his M-14 on automatic and his trigger finger touched it off when he was hit. It put seven bullets in my leg."[99]

Aircraft, both planes and helicopters, proved one of the most dangerous sources of friendly fire. The high speeds, difficult terrain, and lack of quality communication, combined with the reliance primarily on dumb bombs (not the more sophisticated guided ones being developed and employed elsewhere) and napalm increased the chances of mishaps. Many friendly fire deaths occurred as a result, as well as bad wounds for the unlucky bystander on the ground.

In one case, Robert Peterson watched a nighttime show as a heavily armed AC-130 "Spooky" gunship blasted a position where VC snipers had shot at Americans. He marveled at the massive amount of fire being sent into the hill by the airplane's mini-Gatling guns, thousands of rounds per minute chewing up the area. Shooting at night, the airplane sent a strange glow of the tracers, every fifth round an orange one, at the enemy, giving it a surrealistic quality that broke the monotony of settling in for the night. As the Spooky turned and began another pass, one of the soldiers suddenly shrieked, "It's too high! That's coming right at us." Peterson observed, "I could hear the sound of metal whacking into the dirt around us like hailstones." He tried to find cover, but suddenly "something hit me like a hot molten hammer in the back" and soon he lost all feeling in his legs. He lived due to the immediate evacuation, but remained a paraplegic until his death in 1994.[100]

The most famous incident of friendly fire during the Vietnam War occurred in early 1970. A young draftee named Michael Mullen from

Black Hawk County, Iowa, had been pulled out of graduate school at the University of Missouri and inducted into the U.S. Army. He arrived in Vietnam in the fall of 1969, and on February 18, 1970, fell victim to an errant artillery shell. The military listed him as a "non-battle" casualty. The first reports blamed the ARVN for the mishap, highlighting that VC sappers had infiltrated and caused confusion that led to the misfiring. Such reports heightened suspicions among the Mullen family, already disenchanted with the war. Then, a letter arrived from Lieutenant Colonel Norman Schwarzkopf Jr., the commander, who reported that a test of artillery at 3 A.M. had killed Michael.[101] The discrepancies combined with other information trickling back caused Michael's mother, Peg, to begin her own investigation.

As a result of the accident, the grief-stricken and angry Mullen family decided to stop being part of the "Silent Majority," as described by President Nixon, that quietly supported or acquiesced to the war. On April 12, 1970, Peg and Gene Mullen took part of Michael's life insurance money and bought a half-page advertisement in the Des Moines *Register*. It contained fourteen rows of forty-nine crosses with an additional row of twenty-eight for the 714 Iowans who had died so far and left space for the addition of more. In small boldfaced type, it said "We have been dying for nine, long, miserable years in Vietnam in an undeclared war. . . . How many more lives do you wish to sacrifice because of your SILENCE?" It ended with an inscription, "In memory of Vietnam War Dead whom our son joined on February 17, 1970 . . . and to those awaiting acceptable sacrifice in 1970."[102]

The advertisement and subsequent media attention made the Mullens, especially Peg, a national antiwar celebrity. She denounced what she characterized as the military's policy of secrecy and deceit. In particular, she blamed Schwarzkopf and his preoccupation with body counts for leading to her son's death. She rejected his blaming a drunken artilleryman for the accident and never received an adequate explanation of why he ordered artillery fire so late at night. Her frustrations led to a confrontation with plainclothes policemen in February 1971 when President Nixon visited Des Moines. Police beat her when she refused to surrender her large 4′ x 6′ sign that read: "55,000 dead, 300,000 wounded, my son, just one."[103]

For many years afterward, Peg and Gene Mullen continued their quest for the truth. They received national attention after Courty Bryan published *Friendly Fire* in 1976 and the movie version starring Carol

Burnett and Ned Beatty that followed in 1979 won six Emmys. Bryan's book disappointed them after he repeated the Pentagon's official explanation, which a member of the firing crew discredited later in a phone call to the Mullens.

For many years, the Mullens remained outspoken critics of the Pentagon. Gene died in 1986, but Peg continued her activism. In the early 1990s, she spoke out against the impending war in Kuwait, receiving some interest when American aircraft bombed and killed eleven American Marines under the command of now General Norman Schwarzkopf Jr.[104] As late as 2005, she earned attention as the forerunner of Cindy Sheehan, who became a leading antiwar activist against the Iraq War when she lost her son, Casey. Unable to join Sheehan in Crawford, Texas, to protest the war due to poor health, the eighty-eight year old emphasized: "I would give my right arm to be there [with Sheehan]. I mean, somebody's got to stop this thing. I was wondering how I could get in touch with her, I really was. . . . Oh, I think it would be the most fun, to upset Bush like that."[105]

Peg and Gene Mullen's plight highlighted the frustrations with friendly fire. The thought of a non-battle death, the senseless loss of American soldiers, numbering in thousands, to American shells and bombs, angered everyone. While accidents have occurred in all conflicts, the new technology seemed to increase the intensity and frequency. For some like the Mullens, the grief and anger turned into political action. They joined with millions of other Americans who had at various stages begun opposing the war.

The Soldier as Protestor

The divisions in the country mirrored those that developed in the military as soldiers, especially after 1968, increasingly opposed the war and some became protestors both within the military and after they left it. The protests took multiple forms, from the most extreme of desertion in a combat zone to random acts of disobedience such as drawing peace signs on helmets in a combat zone.[106] For the military protestor, unlike the civilian, the act required more courage and willingness to accept harsher punishments. The acts began early on, but intensified as the war escalated and the military drafted more young men who questioned their service. Ultimately, the dissent within the military helped undermine morale and discipline.

An early example of protestors in the military occurred in July 1966. Three privates at Fort Dix, New Jersey—James Johnson, Dennis Mora, and David Samas—refused to ship out to Vietnam, calling the war "immoral, illegal, and unjust." The Army wavered as an investigation found grounds for court-martial for "uttering disloyal statements with intent to cause disaffection and disloyalty among members of the military service and civilian population." Yet, the commandant of Fort Dix, Major General John M. Hightower, decided not to court-martial them and instead confined them to the stockade while the Army considered other charges including a failure to obey the orders of a superior officer.[107]

Others followed the example of the young men at Fort Dix, often splitting families. Douglas MacArthur Herrera, whose father was a World War II veteran and leader of the Texas League of United Latin American Citizens (LULAC), also refused orders to ship out to Vietnam. His father implored him to go, stressing that his failure to do his duty would ensure that "your family will never live it down and your life will be ruined. You should not question your country's motives and its foreign policy." He added that "your objections will be widely publicized in Texas and your family will probably have to move out of Texas to get over the embarrassment and humiliation of what you are doing." He concluded with "please call us and tell us that you are going to do the right thing to your country and to your family."[108]

The most extreme form of dissent, desertion, has plagued the U.S. military throughout American history. Yet, in a comparative sense, the number of desertions in Vietnam remained low through 1970, as most occurred during leaves or when a soldier received his orders for Vietnam. During World War II, the U.S. military found more than 20,000 Americans guilty of desertion and executed one, Private Eddie Slovik. The majority of the 5,000 who deserted while serving in Vietnam remained rear echelon troops, many taking advantage of their mid-tour leaves to take off from Hawaii or Thailand with the assistance of sympathetic antiwar activists or concerned family members. Still, the numbers were comparatively small given the unpopularity of the war.[109]

The most common form of desertion occurred when a GI decided to leave before having to ship out to Vietnam or after having returned home after a tour, chafing under the restraints of spit-and-polish garrison duty.[110] Dick Perrin is a good example. A small town boy from Vermont, he joined the Army in 1967 when he lost his draft deferment and a recruiter promised him that he would avoid the infantry and become a mechanic.

The son of a patriotic father who consistently told him, "You should just mind your own business and do as you're told, because the President knows a lot more than you do—if you had the information he has, then you'd have a right to judge the issue," Perrin marched off with some doubts.[111] Once in the Army, his antiwar activist older brother and others made him question whether he could fight in Vietnam. A particularly bad confrontation at Fort Sill, Oklahoma, where he met with antiwar activists and was incarcerated on trumped up charges, turned him into a determined opponent of the war.[112]

When released from hard time, the military transferred Perrin to Germany. There, he decided to desert. Instead of going to Sweden like many others, he chose France, where some sympathetic antiwar activists, both French and expatriate Americans, helped him escape, secured employment and housing, and provided a support network. Perrin ultimately caused a stir when he stood alongside Black Power activist Stokley Carmichael and supported the position of Resistance In the Armed Forces (RITA) in front of interviewers for CBS and the *New York Times*. His decision to desert and outspoken condemnation of the United States in Vietnam opened a chasm with his parents, although he became something of a celebrity and interacted with antiwar activists, including Jane Fonda.[113]

Ultimately, after the upheavals of 1968 and due in part to homesickness, Perrin left France. He settled in Saskatchewan and worked as an auto mechanic and house renovator, as well as political activist. At the same time, his parents soured on the war and became active in the efforts to have the deserters return home. Ultimately, in 1977, he traveled to Fort Benjamin Harrison in Indiana where he secured an undesirable discharge from the U.S. Army and a pardon for his desertion. While he could have remained in the United States, he chose to return to Canada and continue the life that he carved out there as a Canadian citizen, rarely venturing into the United States except to visit friends and family.[114]

Unlike Perrin, who represented the norm, some deserted from a combat posting, although only rarely. In one case, Mark Gilman left after an ambush. "I saw my buddy shot beside me. That's what made me desert. I could think of no good reason why he should die, why I should die, why any GIs should die in Vietnam." With some assistance from sympathetic antiwar activists, he traveled to Sweden where he went into exile.[115]

Like deserters in previous wars, the ones in Vietnam aroused a great deal of animosity, especially after presidents Gerald Ford (1974–77) and

During an operation, U.S. soldiers use a flamethrower to destroy an enemy hooch. *(National Archives)*

Jimmy Carter (1977–81) put in place systems for clemency and pardons for draft evaders and deserters. A Mississippi Marine spoke for many veterans when he emphasized, "It's certainly not fair to the ones who lost their lives for the deserters to just be able to come back to the States and start *their* lives over again."[116] A platoon leader added:

> There is something that continues to trouble me: I can't fully forgive the guys who got out of it. What right did they have to decide not to go over there? On the other hand, if the war was a wasted effort, and if the American people were not behind it, you've got to wonder, are the guys who went to Canada the smart ones? Jimmy Carter may have had a point when he pardoned them. He said he was trying to put the bitterness of Vietnam behind us and heal the nation. Still, it galls me that they got off scot-free, even though in retrospect they may look like they made the right moral decision because of the way we conducted the war and let it be lost. They're not noble by any definition.[117]

The problems of the U.S. military in Vietnam, including desertion, reflected a breakdown of discipline that often related to a lack of leadership and support from home. By late 1970 commanders reported problems throughout the country including refusals by some platoons to follow direct commands, continued reports of fraggings, and increased drug use and racial problems.[118] In many ways, the military reflected American society where challenges to authority dominated the political and social landscape. With the war winding down, the challenges heightened, and many U.S. soldiers, both grunts and officers, fought to maintain the integrity of the military while responding to the calls for reform amid congressional investigations and terrible public relations fiascos such as the My Lai massacre.

The Baby Killer: The Realities and Myths of Atrocities in Vietnam

Military atrocities have occurred since the beginning of time. While political leaders and human rights advocates have attempted to limit the impact of conflicts on non-combatants, they have failed, especially in guerrilla wars. In particular, America encountered such challenges in its wars with the Native Americans in the nineteenth century, the Philippine insurrection (1899–1902), and military interventions in Haiti (1915–34), the Dominican Republic (1916–24), and Nicaragua (1925–33). Congressional investigations uncovered atrocities, including torture, crude forms of biological warfare, and mass killings of civilians during these conflicts as well as other larger ones.[119] In every conflict, the natural state of war has turned some men into cold-blooded killers who fail to differentiate between friend and foe, especially in relation to civilian populations.

Atrocities occurred in Vietnam as in previous U.S. interventions in the Third World, especially those fought as guerrilla wars where large numbers of civilians interacted on a daily basis with the enemy and the Americans. The scope differed, however. In other U.S. interventions, the numbers of Americans committed rarely exceeded tens of thousands while the numbers ballooned to more than 550,000 at the height of the Vietnam conflict. Also, Vietnam differed because of the new technology. The sheer firepower of the American soldier in Vietnam, both personally and from support of artillery and aerial bombing, separated this particular intervention from those of the early twentieth century. Predominantly small-scale atrocities occurred, although some larger ones unfolded also against the enemy and the civilian population. The vast majority of Americans, however, performed their duties within the established norms of modern warfare. Still, atrocities were committed that shocked the American public and undermined the rationale given by American leaders for fighting to save the South Vietnamese from the Communists.

On the front lines, the brutality of the war created tensions that sometimes transferred to the Vietnamese civilians. Americans often shot the wounded VC and NVA as neither side gave any quarter. One soldier wrote his father in March 1966 that "this war isn't by the Geneva Convention. Charlie doesn't take any prisoners nor do we. Only when the CO (Commanding Officer) sees them first. We shoot the wounded. We only keep a prisoner if there is an LZ (landing zone) near where a chopper can come in and get him out. Charlie has no facilities for keeping prisoners nor any use for them." He complained about the mutilations of several of his comrades: "We found two of them that had their privates in their mouths, sewn shut, hanging by their ankles from a tree." In response "they gave us hatchets and we lifted a couple heads. Also tied bodies on the fenders of 2½ ton trucks and drove through the village as a warning. We haven't had any mutilations since then that we know about."[120]

Soldiers often directed their hostility not toward the enemy, but toward civilians. The training that deemphasized the humanity of the Vietnamese, making them less than humans by comparing them to animals and insects combined with existing racist perceptions to create problems for some young grunts whose moral compass lacked much guidance. As one U.S. officer concluded, "You put those kids in the jungle for a while, get them real scared, deprive them of sleep, and let a few incidents change some of their fears to hate. Give them a sergeant who has seen too many of his men killed by booby traps and by lack of distrust, and who feels that the Vietnamese are dumb, dirty and weak, because they are not like him. Add a little mob pressure, and those nice kids . . . would rape like champions. Kill, rape and steal is the name of the game."[121]

While premeditated acts of violence occurred, more often young Americans found themselves enveloped by the "fog of war," where often civilians ended up caught in the cross-fire, leading to many deaths. One journalist noted that the methods of fighting explained some of the problems the soldiers faced in Vietnam. "The overriding, fantastic fact that we are destroying seemingly by inadvertence, the very country we are supposedly protecting" seemed tragic and undermined efforts to win the support of the South Vietnamese peasants, and often contradicted the grunts' understanding of why they fought.[122]

Some grunts reflexively defended American atrocities as less heinous than those perpetrated by the NVA and VC. One veteran noted that a NVA regiment entered a village and herded the people including children into bunkers and then turned flamethrowers on them. His group discovered the people he characterized as "scaly, crusty, black, like charred hotdogs." In another case, he saw pregnant women in a Montagnard village hung from the houses by the ankles and gutted. "I think that the only media that ever reported on it was probably *Stars and Stripes*," he complained.[123]

No matter the rationalization or explanation, atrocities occurred in the Vietnam War. Many went unreported for fear of continuing to serve in a unit with the perpetrators and the physical threats against snitches. Officers wanting to protect their leadership records threatened those willing to give details of the acts. In addition, the military lacked the resources, including trained lawyers, to prosecute the guilty, and the volume of paperwork undermined their efforts. Witnesses rotated out of Vietnam or died in combat, and some of the accused left the military before the trials. The Vietnamese witnesses also disappeared or proved unwilling to testify. Lieutenant General Phillip Davison stressed that "military justice was neither swift nor certain and transgressors have been free to repeat their acts with impunity."[124] As a result, very few faced prosecution. In 1968, the Army prosecuted only thirty-six cases of war crimes, resulting in twenty convictions.[125]

The My Lai Incident

Despite the lack of prosecutions, the American public, especially those in the radical elements of the antiwar movement, associated the grunt with atrocities and threw about names such as "baby-killer" at the returning soldiers. Unfortunately, some grunts reinforced these stereotypes in incidents such as the most notorious wartime atrocity in Vietnam. On the morning of March 16, 1968, Charlie Company of the 1st Battalion of the 20th Infantry entered the hamlets of My Lai. Expecting heavy resistance from a Viet Cong battalion reported in the area and having been told that all the friendlies would be gone, the unit landed. Already incensed by the loss of several of its men to snipers and booby traps, a platoon, led on the ground by Lieutenant William Calley, began slaughtering the locals just beginning their daily routines.

For four hours, the Americans murdered, raped, pillaged, and burned the hamlets, ultimately killing more than 500 civilians. Calley led the mass executions, in one case shooting point blank a child that had escaped the first volley. While some refused to participate and refused direct orders to fire on the unarmed civilians, the majority simply went along, later telling investigators that they only followed orders. At one point, a group of men decided to have lunch. As they sat and ate, they heard some Vietnamese crying out for help. They put down their meals momentarily, walked over, and shot them. In fact, the massacre would have been worse if not for a helicopter pilot, Hugh Thompson Jr. Flying overhead, he saw no resistance and the indiscriminate killings. He landed his ship between some fleeing civilians and U.S. troops, ordering his door gunner to fire on his fellow Americans if they tried to harm the Vietnamese.[126]

In the final report, the unit listed 128 enemy killed and three weapons confiscated. The only American casualty resulted from a self-inflicted accidental gun discharge. To many critics, the officers in command should have recognized the discrepancy. Also, when he returned, Thompson reported the atrocity to the commander of the 11th Infantry Brigade, Colonel Oran K. Henderson. Yet, a massive cover-up followed, facilitated by company commander Captain Ernest Medina, who told one of the soldiers "not to do anything stupid like write [his] congressman." Lieutenant Colonel Frank Barker and Major General Samuel Koster, commander of the Americal Division, also participated in the cover-up.[127] There were clear indications that something tragic had unfolded, but after a short initial investigation, the commanders found no violations.

The cover-up succeeded momentarily. However, a young grunt from Phoenix, Arizona, Ron Ridenhour, had a beer one night in April 1968 with Pfc. Charles Gruver from Charlie Company who bragged, "we went in there and killed everyone." Thinking that Gruver's drunkenness caused him to exaggerate, Ridenhour followed up by asking other company members for details. They simply confirmed the events and added particulars, leading Ridenhour to write a letter to his congressman, Morris Udall, as well as others, including President Nixon, Secretary of Defense Melvin Laird, and prominent antiwar senators J. William Fulbright and Eugene McCarthy. After outlining the charges, he stressed, "I remain irrevocably persuaded that if you and I do truly believe in the principles, of justice and equality of every man, . . . then we must press forward a widespread and public investigation of this matter."[128]

Soon after, the Army assigned Lieutenant General William Peers to begin the investigation that uncovered 224 serious violations of military codes.[129] In addition, a young journalist, Seymour Hersh, received some tips from a friendly congressional aide about the story and began looking into it.[130] In November 1969 he broke the story, and *Life* soon followed by printing horrific photos taken by a combat photographer who accompanied Charlie Company. A national debate began, with many blaming Washington for the war and its choice of how to prosecute it, while many in the military characterized it as an isolated incident and blamed Calley's incompetence. One officer emphasized, "Most professional military men are more critical of Calley than any civilian would be, because it's such an insult to a professional's ability to handle the combat situation. It's a travesty. With adequate leadership, those things don't happen. They're not part of war, and they don't have to be."[131]

The trials of Calley and Medina, the latter represented by F. Lee Bailey, garnered national attention. In the end, the military jury only found Calley guilty of the murder of twenty-two citizens in 1971. The majority of soldiers had left the Army, making it impossible to prosecute them in the military justice system, and no civilian authority stepped up to exert any oversight. Calley received a life sentence with hard labor, although he only served a few days in Fort Leavenworth and until 1974 he lived under house arrest at Fort Benning when President Nixon pardoned him. Then, he married and became the manager of his father-in-law's jewelry store in Columbus, Georgia.

Those accused of the cover-up also merited some punishment. The Army demoted General Koster, then serving as superintendent of West Point, from major general to brigadier general and his immediate subordinate Brigadier General George Young accepted a censure, but others closer to the situation, including Colonel Henderson, who received the report from Thompson, received no punishment. The leniency further fueled charges of more cover-ups and enraged many Americans, while many Vietnam veterans argued that others could not possibly understand the situation. Others, watching the U.S. forces as they withdrew, merely felt the country needed to put Vietnam behind it and look to the future.

Regardless, the My Lai massacre helped taint the Vietnam veteran. The accusations of being "baby killers" became more accepted despite the fact that most Vietnam veterans never committed any atrocities. Journalist David Halberstam, a critic of the war, reinforced this when he stated, "For every Calley, there were [large numbers of] young American officers who were brave and selfless and treated their men and the enemy with respect."[132] Of course, civilians being caught in the cross-fire in the "fog of war" occurred, but the majority of grunts never committed the acts associated with Calley, groups like the Tiger Force or the Marine "killer team" at Son Thang, or those reported by Vietnam veterans at the Howard Johnson's Hotel in Detroit during the "Winter Soldier" hearings in January and February of 1971.[133] Yet, many Americans outside of the military emerged from the Vietnam War with a very jaundiced view of soldiers. It would be many years before the military repaired its image in American society.

The Long, Hard Fall

All of the problems of the atrocities, fraggings, drugs, and racial problems reflected the challenges of the U.S. military in Vietnam, especially after the withdrawal began in 1968. As soldiers began openly expressing disapproval of fighting and going so far as to refuse to accept orders and report for service in Vietnam, the military faced severe problems of morale and cohesion. Many military leaders tried to blame society as a whole, claiming that the American soldier merely reflected the changes occurring at home regarding drug use, a lack of discipline, and questionable loyalty. That analysis failed to consider the institutional challenges plaguing the military, including training, leadership, and asking the troops to serve in an increasingly unpopular war. By the war's end, some in the military began noting these institutional failings and calling for reform.

A respected Marine, Colonel Robert D. Heinl, published a controversial article in the *Armed Forces Journal* in June 1971 that highlighted the deterioration of the U.S. military. "The morale, discipline and battleworthiness of the U.S. Armed Forces are, with a few salient exceptions, lower and worse than at any time in this century and possibly in the history of the United States." To him, the army in Vietnam appeared nearing collapse, "with individual units avoiding or having refused combat, murdering their officers and noncommissioned officers, drug-ridden, and dispirited where not near-mutinous." He found that "only the Marines—who have made the news this year by their hard line against indiscipline and general permissiveness—seem, with their expected staunchness and tough tradition, to be weathering the storm," a trend aided by the Marine's quicker withdrawal from Vietnam as well as smaller numbers and the tradition of volunteers, not draftees.[134]

After highlighting the issues of fraggings, combat refusals, "search-and-evade" tactics, race problems, and the drugs, he emphasized, "It is a truism that national armies closely reflect societies from which they have been raised. It would be strange indeed if the Armed Forces did not today mirror the agonizing divisions and social traumas of American society, and of course they do." He highlighted underground anti-military papers, GI dissent and anti-draft organizations, nationwide campaigns against ROTC on college campuses, and sabotage of military equipment, both within the military and outside. He lamented that the military's prestige had reached its lowest point and concluded that the "fall in public esteem . . . is exceeded by the fall or at least the enfeeblement of the hierarchic and disciplinary system by which they exist."[135]

Others agreed with the problems of the military as the war wound down and the withdrawal of troops escalated. In 1973, Lieutenant Colonel William L. Hauser acknowledged that a "crisis of confidence, born of an 'unwon' war, of charges of mismanagement and incompetence attendant in that war . . . is also a crisis of conscience, stemming from charges of war crimes and official cover-ups . . . embezzlement, larceny by the Army's top police official, and allegations of self-serving careerism in the professional officer corps." He concluded that it "is a crisis of adaptation," with the Army failing to "come to terms with the Age of Aquarius—a revolution in American styles, manners, and morals."[136]

Despite recognizing the deficiencies and problems of the Army in 1973, Hauser saw hope in that other armies had adapted over time to crisis, including the British and French armies at the end of their colonial adventures and the German army after World War II. The Vietnam War merely speeded up the painful process of adapting to the changes of American society. "The Army will survive," he emphasized. "It is learning how to cope with problems of racial tension, political and anti-Establishment dissent, and drugs." He called for reforms, including the creation of a "fighting Army" and "supporting Army" and a division of the military profession into commanders and specialists.[137] While Hauser remained optimistic about the ability to adapt, many others would follow his book with recommendations of their own, and the debates about the failures and successes in Vietnam would continue for three decades.

The long, hard fall of the military bottomed out by the mid-1970s. The officers, many of whom, such as Colin Powell, were veterans of multiple tours in Vietnam, returned and began rebuilding the institution to reflect the realities of the post-Vietnam period. Over time, the military evolved and reasserted itself as a major force in American politics and foreign policy. Vietnam caused a major reevaluation of the organization and its goals and procedures and created a different, although not radically altered, institution of the all-volunteer military that helped engineer an overwhelming victory in the first Persian Gulf War in 1991, although not without some road bumps along the way.

Last Goodbyes

The soldiers that continued to stream out of Vietnam after the decision to withdraw had experiences similar to those of their earlier counterparts, yelling and screaming as they left Vietnam and returned home. Yet, as the war continued and by March 1973 the last major group of U.S. forces left, sadness often accompanied by anger and disillusionment characterized the final memories. These included the realization in 1975 when the North Vietnamese and Viet Cong flooded into Saigon and raised their flags as American helicopters quickly evacuated Americans and some South Vietnamese allies that the conflict had ended in defeat for the United States. At that moment, the reality of fighting for what some perceived as ultimately a "lost cause" fully sank in for many veterans.

One American succinctly summed up the feelings of many when on his third tour of duty in 1971 he emphasized that "the significance of my final day of combat in Vietnam was not lost on me. The Warriors, who swept the battered jungles around me, were long gone. It was no longer their war. Only the ghosts of the fallen remained. Yet, the same determined enemy continued to hold this ground. They were prepared to fight on forever. For me, the war had come full circle. It was time to go home."[138]

The fall of Saigon proved especially traumatic and many veterans remembered it very vividly. Philip Caputo, a Marine veteran who had served in Vietnam in 1965–66, watched firsthand the fall of Saigon in 1975 and the accompanying sadness, bitterness, and sense of loss. He had returned as a journalist for the *Chicago Tribune* to cover the fighting of the last major offensive, his first visit since completing his tour. As he fled in a U.S. helicopter over the Mekong Delta toward a waiting ship, he lamented that he had landed in Vietnam in 1965, "swaggering, confident, full of idealism. We believed we were there for a high moral purpose. But somehow our idealism was lost, our morals corrupted, and the purpose forgotten." Landing on the U.S.S. *Denver*, he reported that one Marine looked out at Vietnam and said, "Well, that's one country we don't have to give billions of dollars to anymore." A cynicism blended with sadness summed up the feeling of many Americans, including Vietnam combat veterans.

Others proved more defiant in the face of the South Vietnamese surrender. One veteran commented on the end that "in any event, the American fighting man didn't lose the war. The last Americans were pulled out of Vietnam in 1973. The NVA overran the south in a final push in 1975. How could we lose, when we weren't even there?"[139]

No matter what their last thoughts on Vietnam were upon leaving the country or watching Saigon fall, many grunts returned home with strong feelings about the war, their sacrifice, and the ultimate result. Coming home for many proved as much of a challenge as fighting as they struggled to readjust to civilian life, just like millions of veterans of wars from other American conflicts. Others buried the memories of Vietnam deep into the recesses of their minds, longing for some sort of normalcy. The end in 1973 of U.S. combat operations and the fall of Saigon marked the end of the war, but only the beginning of making sense of it for many Vietnam veterans. It became a very long process that continues relatively unabated.

5

Coming Home

Reintegrating Into Society and Memory of the
American Infantryman in Vietnam

One grunt observed, "Most of the veterans returned home reasonably whole, as whole as returning veterans from earlier wars. The majority were not dopers, did not beat their wives or children, did not commit suicide, did not haunt the unemployment offices, and did not boozily sink into despair and futility."Author Tim O'Brien worried in the early 1980s that "we've all adjusted. The whole country. And I fear that we are back where we started. I wish we were more troubled." Yet, he noted that "some prisons are still populated with black vets; the VA hospitals still do their bureaucratic thing too often and fail to help. Some vets, more than a decade later, have not yet recovered, and some never will. . . . The vets had to build their own monument."[1]

The two men correctly underscored several important trends regarding Vietnam veterans and their journey back into American society. Many returned home and reintegrated into civilian life with few visible difficulties, becoming lawyers, bankers, politicians, doctors, businessmen, teachers, farmers, and truckers. Like veterans from previous wars, they rarely discussed their experiences with others, choosing to bury deeply most memories. Not until much later would many begin to write about their experiences and talk with others about them.

However, as O'Brien notes, unlike the World War II veterans, who marched home to ticker-tape parades and had numerous memorials erected in their honor, the Vietnam veteran returned, in the words of historian George Herring, to a nation that "experienced a self-conscious, collective amnesia."[2] For many years, Americans often ignored the sacrifices of the millions who fought in Southeast Asia, denying psychological and physical assistance to those desperately in need of it. While Vietnam remains a contested memory, Americans slowly came to grips with the war and its impact on its citizen soldiers.

The Long, Lonely Trip Home

The efforts to readjust began immediately when the grunts landed in the United States. Some found themselves assimilating back into a society that appeared frozen in time, seemingly unaware that they had left for a year to experience the horrors of combat in a strange land with the specter of death hovering over them twenty-four hours a day. Others encountered a vastly different world than that they left a year earlier. In either case, they departed a combat zone with snipers and booby traps and suddenly returned to a place where they lit cigarettes at night without fear, slept in beds with linens, and ate hot meals. The initial steps back into society sometimes proved hard and disorienting, but the majority of combat veterans ultimately overcame the difficulties.

Stepping off the plane often provided an almost surreal experience. In one case, James Seddon returned from Vietnam a day before his birthday in July 1968. After disembarking at Travis Air Force Base just outside San Francisco, he emphasized that "everything was clean; everything was new; everything glittered and sparkled. There were so many bright colors that surely rainbows could no longer exist."[3] As he entered the terminal, he received an order to change out of his jungle fatigues, "wrinkled from three days' wear," so they "were out of place in this neat, clean world." "I slowly unbuttoned my fatigue shirt," he remembered, "each stain and tattered edge reminding me of some no-name place I had been or of some horror I had seen." In the mirror, he saw "bloodshot eyes, sunburned face, hair that no longer knew how to be combed." Soon, he observed "a frog changed into a prince." As he finished changing, a man walked by with a huge trash bag and told him: "You won't be needing this anymore, young man. You're back in the world."[4]

Seddon and others commonly complained that, unlike their fathers and uncles returning from World War II, the Vietnam veteran merely arrived, often alone and with little fanfare without any time for decompression. Military parades down major thoroughfares of the big cities like New York or Washington such as those given their fathers were rare. They often received little of the respect afforded other generations of veterans. No talk of memorials was heard though thousands had cropped up around the country for the World War II veteran. The nation only appeared to want to move past this ugly chapter in American history.

Some exceptions existed. One veteran remembered being stationed at Fort Lewis and being given a leave with orders to return for a morning march through downtown Seattle on July 10, 1969. "There were about one hundred thousand people at the parade. It was an exhilarating experience." He recalled marching in fatigues, side by side with his fellow Army veterans and the 9th Marine Regiment.[5]

The majority of veterans, however, had experiences similar to those of a grunt who recalled, "I thought everybody was going to know that I was coming home. When I got home, nobody even knew I had gotten home, nobody even knew I was gone in the first place." Disappointed, he added: "I was expecting a band to be waiting for me. The only ones who really knew I had left was my family."[6]

While many people seemed unconcerned, sometimes antiwar activists acted out toward the grunt just off the plane from Vietnam. A common stereotype, one perpetuated by government outlets such as the GI-centered magazine *Stars and Stripes*, evolved of the "spitting image," one where typically a long-haired, scruffy hippie or wild-eyed woman ran up and spat on the veteran. In one case, a Mexican American veteran arrived at Travis Air Force Base in 1969 and then transferred to the San Francisco airport. There, a comrade who had taken shrapnel in his leg walked on crutches with him. After the two returnees had endured strange looks from many people in the terminal, suddenly "someone spit on the guy that was on crutches."[7] While research has shown that the actual number of such incidents remained small, it became a symbol embedded in the shared consciousness of veterans that highlighted the lack of respect accorded them by their fellow citizens.[8]

Beyond the spitting incidents, other despicable actions characterized the activities of some radical antiwar activists. George S. Patton III recalled his arrival back in April 1969. As he handled some affairs, a sergeant major reported a disturbance. "I asked what it was and he said there were some dissidents out there throwing mud and human waste on the three coffins that had been with us on the aircraft . . . I was absolutely shocked."[9] Another veteran remembered that "I came out on a stretcher at Travis Air Force Base in California, and I got stuff thrown at me, rotten eggs, tomatoes. All of us coming off that airplane were wounded, and they were throwing stuff at us."[10] In another case, a Vietnam veteran who lost his arm in combat walked across the campus of the University of Denver. While standing at a traffic light, a young man asked, "Get that in Vietnam?" When the former grunt responded affirmatively, the man responded: "Serves you right."[11]

While the general perception of the returning warrior facing antiwar activists dominated, the reception somewhat depended on the location and reflected that many Americans differentiated between the individual Vietnam veteran and the collective unit. One veteran recalled being greeted by "these long haired pukes out there waving signs about baby killers." Yet, when he landed in South Dakota, his father took him to a local bar. "It was like I won the Medal of Honor or something. People really treated me good."[12] In another case, a Mississippi Marine who lost part of his leg arrived home and recalled that it "was real nice. The people of Petal gave me a big ol' welcome home party as soon as I got here. Some of the merchants and the people that I had gone to school with put the party together at the Petal High gym. After that, we went over to my mother's house for coffee. We just had a real good time."[13]

More than a few brawls erupted between protestors and grunts that exacerbated already existing class antagonisms and anger over the uneven sacrifices. While some veterans may have exaggerated the spitting image, citizens demeaned the grunts in other ways. People turned their eyes away from them, they refused to engage in conversation, or they pretended not to know that they had served, thus symbolically they too spit upon them. This often ensured that veterans tried to avoid calling attention to themselves, in significant contrast to others who preceded them and proudly claimed the title "veteran." Much depended on location and timing, but the overall experience of a returning warrior, already difficult as most returned as individuals not units, made the transition more difficult.

The Isolation

The confrontations with antiwar protestors, lack of recognition, and rapidness of the immersion back into society made the changeover to a normal way of life extremely challenging for some veterans. A Marine,

William Jayne, summed up the feelings of many when he wrote: "We went to Vietnam as frightened, lonely young men. We came back, alone again, as immigrants to a new world. For the culture we had known dissolved while we were in Vietnam, and the culture of combat we lived in so intensely for a year made us aliens when we returned."[14]

As for numerous other veterans from previous wars, the challenge included dealing with isolation from everyone except other Vietnam combat veterans. It took awhile for many to make the transition, but ultimately most accomplished the integration into society and moved on with their lives. One veteran emphasized that upon return "families were glad to see a guy, but the general public seemed like, 'Hi, where ya been?' Just like you'd been gone a week or so."[15]

Others shared similar feelings. One veteran remembered returning home to Providence, Rhode Island, which seemed like another planet from "an episode out of *The Twilight Zone*. All these people had changed. All these sons of bitches care about was going to the beach or who was dating who. I had just left people who were fighting and dying. It was unbelievable. I hated America. I hated our materialistic superficiality and our indifference." Some of his friends gave him a surprise party that "was really a disaster." After a few moments, he locked himself in the bathroom and thought, "I couldn't wait to go back to Vietnam. I could not explain what I was feeling. I was in deep pain."[16]

When another veteran arrived home, he also faced deep isolation, even from his family. His sister asked him "Who are you fighting for, the North Vietnamese or the other guys?" His mother served a rice dish for his first meal. "Now I'd been in the rice paddies with buffalo shit. I burned rice. . . . I ate at least fifty tons of rice while I was there. . . . That's what the war was about, it was about food. The North Vietnamese needed that rice basin in the South. Rice." He complained bitterly. "I knew that nobody back here understood what was happening. Because if my own family didn't know, what hope did I have with somebody who didn't even know me?"[17]

Even other veterans contributed to the sense of isolation. One grunt remembered that "as soon as I came back in '72, got back in Lubbock, I was going to the VFW here and got run off because they said that Vietnam was not a war and never would be and we didn't know what it was like to be in a war." Disillusioned, he thought, "Well, you don't need me," so he left and never revisited.[18]

The reception created anger and frustration among veterans, some short term and some long term. This exacerbated the feelings of isolation.

Writer Tim O'Brien encapsulated the resulting feeling of many grunts. "In a general sense, all of my books are about betrayal and loss of faith. . . . I mean you go over there (Vietnam) with all these naive ideas, believing in country and your president and your fellow man, and you find yourself disillusioned in important ways . . . And that's my terrain as a writer, that sense of loss . . . Every book I've written is about that."[19]

Many others echoed that sense of betrayal and accompanying anger. A wounded Marine recalled being in the hospital with "guys that will never ever move anything except their fucking head." "They got nowhere to go and nothing coming down the road except more staring at the ceiling. And what do they do? They console themselves by the thought that goddamnit, it's a bitch but that's what you go to do to fight for freedom, for democracy. They wrap themselves up in that they paid the price for America and what we all believe in." He bitterly observed, "When you go to that guy and say, 'Hey, pal, guess what? You lost what you did for nothing. There was no purpose, no reason, and what happened to you is a total, fucking waste,' well, that's a bitter pill to swallow."[20]

One veteran Swift boat commander admitted that the combat experiences of the Vietnam veteran "were not any more searing" than those of other wars, but "in other wars, the sacrifices of the returning veterans were rightly recognized and applauded. I think that helped validate what they had been through" and made them proud of their accomplishments and helped repair some of their wounds. "The Vietnam veteran was given no support from his countrymen. Significant numbers of Americans actively supported the enemy, which made what we went through in Vietnam all the more wrenching. When we were not shunned, we were reviled as war criminals or baby killers."[21]

For many, it took years to overcome the isolation, and sometimes adjustment resulted only after years of interaction with other veterans or intense therapy. Out of the frustration often came distrust, both of government and its leaders as well as other traditional institutions. Different veterans coped in many varied ways. While it proved hard for some and the bitterness and anger remained for many years, other grunts made a quick conversion back into society.

Quick Transitions

For many Vietnam veterans, the transition back into regular life occurred quickly and often with minimal adjustment problems apparent to the outside world. Like their predecessors in World War II and Korea, Vietnam veterans returned to everyday activities including work and church, showing limited outward manifestations of their combat experience. While some battled the memories, often burying them in self-medication with alcohol like their fathers, the majority pushed themselves to restart their lives.

Chuck Hagel, future senator from Nebraska, who returned to his home state where "people in our town welcomed you with open arms," exemplifies the relatively easy transition pattern. He characterized his readjustment as minimal. He rented a small house in the woods and "just holed up there. I barely saw anybody for a year, except in my classes. I maybe had two, three dates in the whole year. Then I woke up one morning and said, 'Okay, enough of this. It's time to get back into society.' It was my way to do it. I have tremendous sympathy and understanding for veterans who seek help in the Vet Centers today. I just happened to be more disciplined."[22]

In another case, a young teacher pulled from the classroom in 1968 and sent to Vietnam, returned to his job two years later. "I stood at the door of Room 601. I was back. I was back from the jungles of Vietnam. Now the room in which I had taught history and English seemed as foreign as the Viet Cong bunker complexes of Southeast Asia. . . . But Room 601 was still a dream world, a classroom that should have been familiar was strange and alien." Over time, he adjusted with the assistance of several colleagues who also had served in Vietnam.[23]

Sometimes, events unfolded that allowed the grunt little time to do anything but respond quickly. A young Texan remembered being at his forward firebase near the Cambodian border when he received orders for home. In less than twenty-four hours, he landed in Oakland. Then he hopped a plane to Dallas and finally drove to his home just outside of Abilene. The next day, while playing tennis, a friend approached him about a job in the small town of Seminole. He told him he had to report by Monday. Within less than a week after being in the bush, he began teaching students thousands of miles away from the jungles of Vietnam.[24]

Many Vietnam veterans quickly transitioned into society. Timing and experience affected the process as many, like the latter two examples, moved quickly from the fighting into life as the military promptly processed people out as the war deescalated. Many returned to their jobs and others took advantage of the GI Bill and enrolled in college. Most buried their experiences in the darkest recesses of their brains, determined to

On April 6, 1973, two Vietnam veterans in wheelchairs parade through Times Square in New York City to commemorate the U.S. withdrawal from Vietnam and to honor those who served. *(Getty Images)*

move on with their lives and put the military experience behind them. Nonetheless, many others had significant challenges to overcome, some physical, others mental, as the fighting exacted a terrible toll.

The Hardest Road Home

During the Vietnam War, the military significantly improved its ability to save the lives of its wounded soldiers. Advances in medical procedures and new drugs combined with the speedy evacuation from the fighting by helicopter significantly reduced deaths. As a point of comparison, 22 percent of all the wounded died in Korea while the number fell to 13 percent in Vietnam, and deaths while in the hospital declined from 4.5 percent in Korea to 2.5 percent in Vietnam.[25]

Keeping more alive meant more returned home severely wounded. Tens of thousands experienced the hard trip home. One Marine went from 190 pounds to less than 100. For thirty-nine months, he stayed in a VA hospital as doctors battled to find the right medications to help him dissolve blood clots that threatened to go to his heart and kill him. He stressed that "you become just like a plant over in the corner and they come in and water you every now and then. There was no program to really get you going." Finally, after taking seventy or eighty pills a day, he left for home where he recovered by eating good food and getting off the medicine. He started walking with the help of leg braces. Ultimately, he married and had children, but only after years of suffering.[26]

Caretakers watched the process daily as the wounded poured back from Vietnam. One nurse in the orthopedic ward at Fort Gordon, Georgia, talked about caring for them, many "with amputations—both of body and soul." "I loved those guys with all my heart. They reciprocated. They broke the rules, and I covered for them. They went home on pass and came back brokenhearted—I listened. They tried to kill themselves while I was on duty—I helped revive them. . . . And they tried to talk me out of going to Vietnam. They had that in common with my daddy. I didn't listen to either of them."[27]

Captain Max Cleland provided a compelling story of a wounded Vietnam veteran who overcame substantial obstacles. Raised in the small town of Lithonia, Georgia, he volunteered for duty in Vietnam. A communications officer, he avoided the heavy fighting when he arrived in 1967, but he kept requesting more experience in the combat zone. Ultimately, during the Tet Offensive, he found himself in the operation designed to relieve Khe Sanh. One day, while dismounting a helicopter, a grenade became dislodged and as he reached for the explosive, not knowing the pin had dropped out, it detonated. In an instant, he lost one leg, most of the other, and an arm. Only the quick work of medics kept him alive long enough for evacuation.[28]

He fought for his life, surviving a five-hour surgery and the infusion of forty-one pints of blood. At a poorly maintained hospital in Thuy Hoa, he found himself on a bed flanked by wounded enemy. Only the drugs and some luck kept him alive until he boarded a plane for Japan. During his time there, he lamented that "one minute I would be utterly grateful that I was still able to see, breathe, feel and think. The next minute I would sink into despair knowing that I would never again walk on my own legs, that I would never again be the man I once was."[29] From Japan, he traveled over the polar ice cap to arrive at Walter Reed Hospital in Washington, DC, where he began a long ordeal of rehab.[30]

Fortunately for Cleland, he met some very supportive veterans at the hospital. He endured learning to use a wheelchair, to dress himself, and to go to the restroom without assistance, as well as several surgeries to repair the stumps and other injuries. Constantly, he battled depression and fear, especially facing life outside, which according to one friend constituted "the enemy."[31]

Time inside the hospital sometimes had light moments. One night, one of Cleland's roommates, Captain Jack Lawton, also known as "Nasty Jack" because of a profanity-laced tirade on national television, slipped out to a bar on 14th Street in Washington, DC. He conned a stripper into returning with him to the hospital where he slipped her past the nurses. The robust blond made the rounds to kiss each guy, but then Lawton requested a table dance. When she protested that she needed music, the rowdy group produced an old phonograph. However, they only had one record, a version of the "Star Spangled Banner." They turned it on and watched the surreal experience of a stripper dancing to the national anthem in the middle of a paraplegic ward at Walter Reed.[32]

The pain of learning to deal with no legs and only one functioning arm challenged Cleland daily. He fluctuated between loneliness and despair and hope that he would walk with the aid of artificial limbs. Numerous obstacles arose. In one case, an old girlfriend took him on a walk through Lafayette Park, across from the White House. The young woman heartily pushed his wheelchair on the bright, brisk summer night in the nation's capital. Still not familiar with the wheelchair, Cleland forgot to tell her to take him off the sidewalk backward. "Suddenly I pitched forward into the gutter of Pennsylvania Avenue. . . . For several moments I lay in the dirt and cigarette butts, frantically scrambling about, one-armed and legless, like a fish hopping on a riverbank." Horrified and embarrassed, he admitted that "the hot shame of the spill seared me like a burn that continued to throb" and he worried, "is this all that was left for me? To be hauled around like a sack of grain for the rest of my life?"[33]

Cleland continued fighting for a long time, especially after being discharged from Walter Reed and placed into the Veterans Administration (VA) program. The latter organization faced the enormous difficulty of dealing not only with the large number veterans of Vietnam, but also of other wars. The overwhelming demands ensured an extremely impersonal system that added to the disabled veteran's burden. Cleland had to fight to obtain artificial limbs, even the "stubbies" that allowed the former six-foot-tall Cleland to stand only four feet. With those at least he could begin relearning to walk.[34]

The frustrations often overwhelmed him, and he sometimes drank excessively to numb the pain. In one case, he recalled convalescing from flu in a VA hospital on Easter. "I sank into a dark depression. In a deep wrenching of the soul, I lay in bed, convulsed with agonizing, gut-wracking sobs. I was bitter over the past. I was afraid of the future. And the tortuous present seemed unbearable. I wanted to die." Ultimately, he resumed the long process that culminated in him walking erect across his parents' green Georgia lawn in June 1969, fourteen months from the day that a grenade shattered his body.[35]

Many obstacles remained ahead for Cleland, ones that he struggled to overcome. He learned how to drive a specially outfitted car and began swimming and playing basketball, admitting that "I was getting strong at the broken places," to borrow a Shakespearean line. He decided to enter politics and won his first race for state senator. Not long after, he followed President Jimmy Carter to Washington, where he worked as the administrator for the VA. He won recognition for his abilities as prominent journalist David Broder wrote in the early 1980s that Cleland "embodies, as much as any one person in public life can, the agonies and the hopes of the past twenty years."[36] Ultimately, he became a U.S. senator from Georgia, rising to demonstrate along with others like Senator Bob Kerrey that the wounds of Vietnam could not keep good men down.

Cleland's story highlights the fears and frustrations that many young Americans faced when they returned home severely wounded. Many dealt with not having proper medical care, especially after being discharged into the overwhelmed VA system. They organized in groups such as the Paralyzed American Veterans and fought for changes, often benefiting from the movement sweeping America that recognized the needs of all disabled Americans for access to facilities and respect for their efforts. Nonetheless, prejudices remained. Bitterness could lead the veteran into many problems including alcoholism and drug use, but the majority integrated into society, although rarely at the levels of Cleland. However, most never returned to their prewar physical or psychological status.

The Racial Divide Remains

While the disabled veteran faced many obstacles, perfectly able-bodied people of color also encountered significant challenges upon return. Despite their heroic service, many minorities continued to face discrimination, both outside and inside the military. Being a Vietnam veteran often added to the isolation as people, even within their own communities, ostracized them. They waged many battles, oftentimes emboldened by their military service and sacrifice.

Institutionalized racism worsened the plight of the returning veterans of color. An African American veteran from Muskogee, Oklahoma, remembered: "When first back, I flew into Dallas. I had on my uniform with my medals, feeling good about myself. Proud, too. I'd done something. I had served thirteen months in Vietnam for my country. I don't know, maybe I was looking for special treatment." Yet, when he entered a restaurant, "I sat and sat and sat. A long time. Finally a waitress came over, and the look in her eyes was, 'what are you doing in here?' It really hurt me. Tears came into my eyes. I had been looking for something that wasn't there."[37]

In another case, African American Marine Sergeant Major Edgar Huff, one of the first African American Marines in 1942, and recipient of a Bronze Star for heroism, retired in October 1972 as the senior enlisted man in the U.S. military. Just a short time after leaving, he sat down at dinner with several other African Americans at his home just down the road from Camp Lejeune. Suddenly, four white Marines drove up and threw some white phosphorous grenades into his car and home. A friend chased and apprehended them. None, however, received punishment. Instead, the Corps transferred or discharged them, although one from Tennessee eventually paid restitution for the damages. A naval investigator told

Huff that they resented a "nigger" being able to have a nice home under the American flag that he flew every day. The whole incident left Huff "pissed off" that the Marines had not done more to the thugs, especially after thirty years of his exemplary service in the Corps.[38]

Even the dead could not escape racial insults. In one case, when the family of an African American Green Beret who died in combat in 1966 asked that he be buried in the public cemetery in Wetumpka, Alabama, officials refused because the African American section had no additional plots. Instead, they encouraged the family to settle on a pauper's grave. Angry, his mother announced that he had not died a "second-class death" and "he didn't die a segregated death and would not be buried in a segregated cemetery." The family instead buried him in the Andersonville National Military Cemetery in Georgia.[39] Other deceased African Americans experienced similar disrespect. Finally, in 1970 a judge ruled for the plaintiffs representing an African American soldier killed in Vietnam in *Margaret Faye Terry, etc., et al. v. the Elmwod Cemetery, et al.* He ordered that African Americans in Alabama had the right to be buried in cemeteries alongside whites.[40]

Minority veterans often faced challenges even within their own community. One Native American veteran stressed that "at that time I hadn't developed any particular philosophy on the politics of the American Indian Movement (AIM) or really dealt with the issue of my being Indian. I was a soldier." Yet, he returned home and discovered that the FBI and Bureau of Indian Affairs (BIA) had harassed his wife, which angered him. In contrast, young radicals called him a "turncoat" and "sellout," to which he responded "anybody could put on a red bandana and wear long hair. They considered themselves AIM, but I considered myself a warrior."[41]

Whether in their own community or from whites, veterans of color encountered long-standing prejudices exacerbated by the country's negative views toward Vietnam veterans, despite their heroic service in an unpopular war. Often, more and deeper disillusionment developed among some minority veterans, leading to confrontations with establishment figures such as the police and other government officials.

The Activist Vietnam Veteran

Many Vietnam veterans returned home and tried to forget the war and regain some semblance of a normal life, although many battled guilt over leaving their comrades behind.[42] Others, however, returned and began new battles. Some veterans campaigned to end the war, to secure compensation for veterans exposed to chemicals, and to ensure better medical care for the wounded. Like many others in their generation emboldened by the civil rights and antiwar movement, they became activists, although most returned home to reintegrate and put the war behind them.

The most visible and controversial group remained the Vietnam Veterans Against the War (VVAW). Formed in 1967 by Vietnam combat veterans led by Jan Barry, its numbers peaked at more than 20,000 in the early 1970s as more disenchanted veterans returned from Vietnam. The efforts of the VVAW, primarily to end the war, earned it the wrath of the White House. The Nixon administration expended a great deal of energy trying to discredit the movement.[43]

The most memorable VVAW action occurred in April 1971. More than 1,000 veterans, perhaps 2,000, descended on Washington, DC, to participate in Operation "Dewey Canyon III." Veterans, some wearing their old uniforms, demonstrated in the streets, staging mock search-and-destroy missions and marching into the offices of Congress to lobby to end the war. On April 23 more than 500 stood in front of the Capitol and threw their medals and ribbons over a fence. The media covering the event provided a forum for many of the veterans, some in wheelchairs and missing limbs, to tell their stories on why they chose to protest. Their efforts culminated in a massive march on April 24 in which more than 300,000 Americans crowded the streets of Washington to denounce the war and its costs for Americans, in particular veterans.[44]

The VVAW remained active afterward. On December 26, 1971, VVAW members seized the Statue of Liberty and demanded an end to the fighting in Southeast Asia, and launched similar actions against the Lincoln Memorial and the Betsy Ross House in Philadelphia.[45] In New York harbor, protestors unfurled the American flag upside down (the symbol of distress) from the face of the statue, a powerful visual image that reached major media outlets across the world including *Stars and Stripes*. One protestor in Washington proudly declared, "Patriotism is not solely the property of the powerful."[46]

As the VVAW grabbed headlines, a media star developed in the form of John Forbes Kerry, a scion of a wealthy New England family. He graduated from Yale in 1966 after giving a final oration to his class in which he questioned the wisdom of U.S. involvement in Vietnam. Nonetheless, despite fitting the stereotype of the popular slogan at the time of "if you got the dough, you don't have to go," he volunteered for the Navy and followed in the footsteps of his hero, John F. Kennedy.[47]

Once in the service, Kerry volunteered for extremely dangerous duty on "Swift boats," small vessels that patrolled the waterways of South Vietnam seeking to disrupt enemy supply lines. Kerry and his shipmates fought during the very heavy offensives of 1968 and 1969. During his short tour in Vietnam, he won a Silver Star, a Bronze Star, and three Purple Hearts. His crewmates praised his courage under fire and his devotion to them, although Kerry had grown more disenchanted with the war during his time in country.[48]

Kerry mustered out of the military in early 1970. He emphasized, "I thought it was time to tell the story of what was happening over there. I was angry about what happened over there. I had clearly concluded how wrong it was."[49] He joined the VVAW after a failed attempt at Congress in Massachusetts and attended the "Winter Soldier" hearings, becoming increasingly visible at antiwar rallies. His media star rose with an appearance on *Meet the Press* in April 1971 at the height of the debate on the My Lai Massacre when he talked about firing indiscriminately in free-fire zones and burning villages during search-and-destroy missions.[50]

The future senator's most memorable public comment occurred on April 23, 1971, in front of the Senate Foreign Relations Committee. He opened with, "There is nothing in South Vietnam, nothing which could happen that realistically threatens the United States of America." He told the senators that he found a civil war where few people could differentiate between democracy and communism, and that My Lai underscored that the United States had lost "her sense of morality." He demanded Congress extricate the nation from Vietnam, and at one point, Kerry asked a particularly poignant question: "How do you ask a man to be the last man to die in Vietnam? How do you ask a man to be the last man to die for a mistake?" He concluded that he wanted thirty years from then to "be able to say 'Vietnam' and not mean a desert, not a filthy obscene memory, but mean instead where America finally turned and where soldiers like us helped in the turning."[51]

Because of his visibility and pedigree, the Nixon White House focused a great deal of attention on Kerry, believing that he provided the VVAW with a powerful and legitimate spokesman. Highlighting Kerry's brief four-month tour in the country, presidential adviser Charles Colson told the president, "He is sort of a phony, isn't he?" Publicly, administration officials tried to discredit him and his colleagues in the VVAW, but after

Kerry's testimony, Nixon acknowledged, "he was extremely effective." They would continue to denounce him as Nixon complained bitterly "the only good one of the damn veterans group, only good from a PR standpoint, is Kerry." The White House employed a former Swift boat commander, John O'Neill, to "destroy this young demagogue before he becomes another Ralph Nader." Kerry and O'Neill eventually debated on the Dick Cavett show, which led one Nixon confidant to crow, "I hear he (O'Neill) did very well." This would not be the last time that the two tangled on the national stage.[52]

The VVAW continued to work through the withdrawal of most U.S. troops in 1973 and the final collapse of the Saigon government in 1975, although Kerry had left not long after 1971 to pursue politics. The impact of the VVAW, like so many of the protest groups, remains difficult to fully ascertain. The fact that the White House devoted so much time to discrediting it demonstrates its power relative to other groups and its perceived credibility. Yet, many members remained extremely frustrated at their inability to end the war. While many sustained their activism through the years on issues such as Agent Orange and health benefits, others became disillusioned and left the organization to focus on individual problems and challenges. For some, participation in the group became an albatross later in their lives, including John Kerry, who paid a significant price in 2004.

Before and after the fall of Saigon in 1975, veterans outside of the VVAW remained active at many levels as advocates for their comrades. Particularly prominent was the Vietnam Veterans of America (VVA), founded in 1978 and led by disabled veteran activist Bobby Muller.[53] Other organizations joined the efforts to push to reconceptualize the Vietnam veterans and their service; among these was the Vietnam Veterans Leadership Program (VVLP). Created in 1981 with the support of the Reagan administration, the VVLP sought to challenge, according to its first director John Wheeler, the perception of the "Vietnam veteran portrayed as either an emasculated misfit or a supercharged sexual symbol." He called for assistance in creating a new image of a "healthy masculinity."[54]

In 1981, President Reagan recognized the VVLP at a Rose Garden ceremony where he emphasized that most veterans reintegrated into society quickly but that some veterans "found it difficult to come to grips with the problems that can be traced to their wartime experiences." In response, the founders of the VVLP committed themselves to repairing "the image of the Vietnam veteran portrayed as losers, fools, or dope addicts . . . [and other] guilt-ridden victims, ashamed of their service." They fit well into the efforts of the Reagan administration to characterize the struggle as a "noble cause." Some observers, including Vietnam veterans, argued that this had more to do with wanting to put the war behind them so that they could justify new foreign interventions than the veteran issue itself, but the VVLP welcomed the presidential recognition nonetheless.[55]

The VVLP established offices throughout the country to create "a self-sufficient attitude" among troubled veterans. It recruited successful Vietnam veterans as mentors and pushed employers to provide opportunities. James Webb, future secretary of the Navy and U.S. senator, urged people to "buy him (Vietnam veteran) the beer you owed him ten years ago. . . . You'll find out he is by and large a class act, much tougher than his nonveteran peers, much more used to hassle and disappointment. . . . And you may end up offering him a job, or at least another beer."[56]

Within three years, the VVLP had built up services including job placement and mentoring to help struggling veterans. In addition, it produced more than 700 articles in newspapers and magazines promoting favorable views of Vietnam veterans, especially battling the often-negative stereotypes that continued to evolve in movies and other popular culture throughout the 1980s.[57] Its efforts correlated with the changing mood in the country toward veterans as evidenced by the Vietnam Memorial and even parades in places like New York City and Houston. By 1988, John Wheeler crowed, "Veterans' benefits are merely outward and visible signs of an inward and invisible grace that has come to our land. Vietnam service is once more universally recognized as a badge of pride."[58]

In addition to the VVLP and other Vietnam-specific groups, many other organizations, including traditional ones such as the Veterans of Foreign Wars (VFW) and American Legion, attracted veterans who pushed for support for their causes. Others joined specialty groups such as the Disabled American Veterans or groups focusing on issues such as the missing-in-action (MIA) or taking care of Amerasian children left behind.[59] Others focused on reforming the military devastated by the conflict.[60] Perhaps no other group mobilized so quickly and effectively as the Vietnam generation, largely because of the lack of support provided by the country and the fact that many came into political consciousness during the turbulent and politically charged 1960s. Unfortunately for them, they faced significant obstacles in the postwar period, which

"Viet Nam Veterans II"; a painting by Sandow Birk.
(Photo courtesy of the artist)

included securing physical and psychological assistance for themselves
and their comrades.

"A Genie of Anguish"

Marine Bernard Trainor wrote that the war for him produced a "genie
of anguish" that remained bottled up inside him. He talked about the
58,000 lost lives, "good kids" and "deep down there's a hurt and I don't
know what it is. I can't control it. It's always there and I think I'll just
live with it for the rest of my life."[61] For many Vietnam veterans like
Trainor, their experiences in combat exacted a significant physical and
especially psychological toll. The "genie of anguish" sometimes spilled
out in negative ways, including violence, drug abuse, and suicide. After
their advocates expended much energy and effort, Vietnam veterans
received recognition for suffering from a series of maladies including
post–traumatic stress disorder (PTSD).

Health care professionals struggled with defining PTSD and its
symptoms, although many veterans such as World War II veteran Audie

Murphy had dealt with it before Vietnam, although Murphy's illness went undiagnosed and untreated for many years. The response to a catastrophic event and experience included a hostile and mistrustful attitude toward the outside world, depression, and anxiety that led to withdrawal from society and estrangement from families and friends. Chronic health problems related to stress and alcohol and drug abuse often developed. Many veterans experienced varying degrees of PTSD, with the severity often depending on the intensity of their own experiences. While the exact numbers affected remain unknown as other psychiatric problems intermeshed with PTSD, several hundred thousand Vietnam veterans dealt with the disorder.[62]

Many advocated for veterans suffering from PTSD, including a New York psychiatrist, Chaim Shatan, who wrote about the "post–Vietnam syndrome." He argued it represented the "unconsummated grief of soldiers—impacted grief in which an encapsulated, never-ending past deprives the present of meaning." When he wrote an op-ed in the *New York Times* in May 1972 entitled "The Grief of Soldiers," people across the country began calling him, which contributed to the founding of the National Vietnam Resources Project (NVRP) to assist struggling veterans.[63]

Many soldiers suffered from diagnosed and undiagnosed PTSD, often with severe consequences. One Marine admitted that he drank heavily when he returned from Vietnam. "You get drunk and you don't dream, at least I don't."[64] Another emphasized, "I started getting drunk when I got out of there. I needed medicine, and I prescribed it for myself. Looking for a way to forget. It's stupid, because you're never going to forget. The past is a sickness you can't cure."[65]

A young Apache Indian from the San Carlos Reservation of Arizona, Sam Ybarra, represented a particularly tragic, grotesque figure shaped in Vietnam. A member of the infamous Tiger Force, Ybarra had many years of pent up frustrations from the racism that plagued society in the small town of Globe. The Army offered him a way out of the copper mines and channeled his deep reservoir of anger toward the enemy once he arrived in Vietnam, although his commanders lost control of him after the death of a close high school friend in his unit, Kenneth Green. He took enemy ears, strung them to make a necklace, and wore the gruesome keepsake. His thirst for blood included the ghastly decapitation of an infant. Ultimately, the Army gave him a dishonorable discharge, not for the atrocities, but for insubordination.[66]

Shattered by his experiences in Vietnam, Ybarra returned to the reservation. He drank heavily and used drugs, seeking to bury his memories. Ultimately, he married, although his wife and mother feared him when he had flashbacks and started talking about his experiences in Vietnam. Over time, he ballooned to over 300 pounds, rarely working and sleeping much of the day before drinking heavily to fall back to sleep. Near his death in 1982, he began talking about wanting to go to Vietnam to try and help the people whose lives he destroyed. At the age of thirty-six, he died weighing less than 100 pounds because of complications from alcohol abuse.[67]

Another extreme case of a Vietnam veteran who most likely suffered from PTSD was Wayne Felde, who landed in Vietnam in March 1968 on his nineteenth birthday. He witnessed unspeakable horrors of war that included watching friends napalmed and a "gook abortion" where a GI sliced open a pregnant Vietnamese woman with a machete. Upon returning home, he suffered nightmares and flashbacks and developed drug and alcohol addictions. In the two years after returning, he held fifteen different jobs and his marriage to a high school sweetheart lasted only six months. In 1972, he got into a fight with a coworker and killed him during a struggle for a gun. As the police arrived, he freaked out, yelling, "Vietnam, Vietnam, come and get me!" He went to jail only to escape three years later and hid out for two years until he resurfaced to visit his dying mother in Shreveport, Louisiana.[68]

The situation only deteriorated thereafter. Police arrested him a few weeks after his mother's death. Felde tried to kill himself with a concealed .357 Magnum, but in the ensuing struggle, the gun discharged and caused him to lose a kidney and part of his liver. It also crippled his right leg. Another errant shot killed an officer sitting in the front of the patrol car. Within a short time, a jury convicted him of first-degree murder, and he received the death penalty. Vietnam veteran and journalist Philip Caputo covered the story, writing: "Felde was not at the scene of either crime. He was where he has been for nearly 14 years, at a place called Fire Base Polly Ann." Felde, only a week before his death by electrocution on March 14, 1988, stressed "They can kill the messenger but they can't kill the message of what the Vietnam War did to people like me." He died nearly twenty years to the day after he had landed in Vietnam. Afterward, one commentator suggested that a special section of the Vietnam Memorial be dedicated to people like Felde who carried the scars of the war.[69]

While Ybarra and Felde represent extreme cases of those suffering from the Vietnam experience who never received the help they needed, many others did get help despite battling some significant obstacles, often thrown up by fellow veterans. A major one revolved around the perception of what PTSD reflected in relation to masculinity. One author emphasized: "Men, especially the machine men of the military, are not supposed to be helpless, depressed, or unable to handle life. The masculine mystique causes the ostracism of men who ask for help, who experience fright, horror, and worst of all, who have become dependent on people or the government." He concluded: "After all, real men pull themselves up by their bootstraps and don't go 'cry babying' about jitters or bad dreams."[70]

Fellow Vietnam veterans often proved the most critical of their comrades. One Vietnam vet wrote in a *Wall Street Journal* opinion piece that "the vast majority of men who fought in the war . . . simply do not fit these images. Many of us are embarrassed by them."[71] One Green Beret expressed skepticism of the PTSD claims. "I believe that there is such a thing as this post–traumatic stress syndrome, but I don't believe all of the cases of it that I hear about. I think there are a lot of people who use Vietnam as a scapegoat for other personal problems in life."[72] Of course, when people falsely claimed that they had served in Vietnam and had symptoms of PTSD, critics seized on the acts to discredit others.[73]

With such attitudes, advocates faced significant challenges in securing assistance for Vietnam veterans at all levels, including Congress. Powerful Chairman of the House Committee on Veterans Affairs Olin "Tiger" Teague (D-TX) proved especially intransigent. Although a decorated World War II veteran, he joined others in expressing skepticism of the Vietnam veterans' claims. As one congressional staffer observed, Teague believed "Well, you know, this is tough, but we [World War II veterans] sucked it up and we didn't need to go into . . . counseling." At one point, Teague opined, "How can you little wimps be sick? A tour of duty lasted only twelve months. In World War II, soldiers fought in the war for years. How can you be traumatized?"[74]

Despite such criticisms, changes occurred over time as Vietnam veterans and their advocates mobilized. They found willing allies in leaders such as Senator Alan Cranston (D-CA), who pushed for increased drug and alcohol treatment at the VA. Others, such as the NVRP, helped create networks of treatment centers that provided counseling and an opportunity for veterans to join "rap groups" where they talked about their experiences with comrades. The VA under the leadership of veterans like Max Cleland pushed for new programs that helped identify and treat PTSD throughout the country. Some sufferers began receiving disability payments, depending on the severity of the condition.[75]

Despite the efforts to cope with the debilitating effects of PTSD, many people remained untreated. Too often they suffered in silence, receiving little help or never seeking it out due to their own pride and belief in their own ability to overcome the nightmares and depression. Many turned to alcohol and drugs, losing jobs and families, and well into the twenty-first century homeless shelters and other community aid programs continued seeing a disproportionate number of Vietnam veterans in relation to their overall numbers. Others chose suicide, thousands dying by their own hand. While there were significant efforts to address the problem, overall the country failed many veterans terribly as well as others battling different afflictions.

The Long-Suffering Wives and Families

The veteran's family, whether he/she suffered from PTSD or not, often faced huge obstacles in dealing with a spouse, parent, son, or daughter who had seen the horrors of war. Some lamented the loss of the innocence of their loved one, how they had changed after Vietnam, and too often the challenges of handling a wounded soldier, both physically and psychologically. The conflict affected everyone around the veteran, but especially family members.

A Tennessee veteran stressed that his wife had "gone through a lot of counseling herself at the Vet Center in Johnson City and she's learned that she's not the only woman trying to live with a Vietnam veteran." He expressed grief that it also had been difficult for his children. "I think my stepson Franklin understands me now more than he did, even though he lived away from home for three years because the courts said it was a bad idea for him to live under the same roof with me. I have a twenty-year-old stepdaughter who lives in Florida. She won't speak to me because she considers me too unpredictable."[76]

In particular, wives carried a huge burden. One wife of a combat veteran, Laura, bemoaned, "I was eight months pregnant and sick with the flu when my husband shot the phones, barricaded the house, and threatened to kill the first person in uniform that tried to enter the door." This led the terrified postman to run down the street screaming about the "weirdo," which left the veteran's eight-year-old child under the bed crying about the "weirdo." She added that her husband suffered from all the common symptoms of flashbacks, rage, and nightmares, and that "every Fourth of July, Veteran's Day, or anniversary date of the death of certain buddies, I could expect smashed records, broken windows, or another hole in the wall. I could also expect that sooner or later, I would be up all night holding him."[77]

For the wife, loneliness also became a constant companion. Laura lost contact with her family, upset over the fact that she married a vet from "that war." Her husband's anger and distance alienated friends and family and hindered his efforts to find employment as he went through twenty jobs in fifteen years. "I've also lost myself. All I know is that I must keep on functioning. My family depends on me. I'm constantly running, from one job to the next, one chore to the next. . . . I never know when Dave is going to act up again. I wish he would go get help, but he won't hear of it."[78] So, she settled into a life where "I guess I'm Dave's therapist and most of my life is organized around arranging his life to be as comfortable and stress free as possible. He simply can't handle pressures and if he goes off, I'll have yet another problem. I am the buffer between him and the world, and at times, his only link to sanity."[79]

Every day she struggled, watching every sentence, never sure what would set him off. At times, he simply walled himself off, rarely talking or making physical contact for days at a time. "Don't ask me what it means to be a woman anymore. My life is too hard, and I'm bitter, and too afraid of the anger and the pain inside me. I'm also afraid that someday my husband's depression will engulf him—that I will lose him entirely to that sad far-away look in his eyes, to that 'other woman'— Vietnam."[80]

Children also bore a great burden of dealing with fathers and some mothers who suffered from PTSD. One child remembered her father leaving for Vietnam as "I cried terribly when he left, and emptiness and fear flooded my body and mind." Her father returned partially deaf and often had nightmares or sometimes dove into bushes when he heard a loud noise. He drank heavily and physically and verbally abused the entire family. "I never, never knew what to expect. . . . Him being so unpredictable aroused a tremendous amount of paranoia in my daily living."[81]

This child acted out against both parents as she admitted, "my resentment toward my mother grew also. I felt she didn't care for the kids or else she would protect us from this insane man. It was a terrible, horrid fear in her eyes and face when Dad would lash out and attack us as if we were the enemy." As a result, "a lot of bitterness, hatred, anger, resentment, and absolutely no pity for him was all I felt for quite a few years." She lamented the fact that she had no one to talk with or understand what happened in the house, and admitted: "I became an extremist for destruction and hate and blame toward myself. I held myself responsible for my father's behavior, because I felt I was unacceptable and hated in his eyes."[82]

Finally, after more than a decade, the anger and resentment dissipated as she came to realize that the war caused his anger. "I was ashamed of myself and felt extremely guilty for all the years of condemning my father to hell when he was already in a living hell of guilt, remorse, and hatred toward himself." She talked about trying to learn about and understand the destruction of the war and stressed, "It tears me up inside to see their unmistakable misery within." Refusing to ever forget the "craziness" of her father and in turn herself, she emphasized "My awareness and acceptance is the biggest asset I have today . . . to keep trying and keep loving him for who he is and where he's been."[83]

The veteran dealing with PTSD affected everyone around him, but especially himself. Many struggled to hold jobs and sustain relationships, often relying on self-medication to combat the nightmares and feelings of isolation. It extracted a significant physical and psychological toll, often causing illness and for probably many, a premature death. PTSD also affected everyone around the veteran, particularly the wife or children who daily dealt with its damaging effects. While previous generations of American warriors grappled with war in silence, the Vietnam generation fought and overcame huge obstacles in securing recognition and assistance for addressing the damage.[84]

Death From Above: The Agent Orange Question

In addition to the psychological and physical damage related to combat, a new ugly reality surfaced for some veterans exposed to toxic chemicals that literally rained down on them during the war. While Americans had employed biological and chemical weapons for nearly a century, first in crude forms against the Native Americans and Filipinos and continuing through the world wars, the sheer volume of the arsenal in Vietnam trumped previous conflicts. From napalm to herbicides, American soldiers faced new and sometimes prolonged threats to their health.

The most widely used chemical weapon in Vietnam remained herbicides used to clear the jungle and thick grasses that hid the enemy. In 1961, American forces began spraying defoliants throughout Vietnam in what became known as Operation Ranch Hand. The primary concoction, a mixture of 2,4,5-trichlorophenoxy acetic acid and 2,4-dichlorophenoxyacetic acid, became known as "Agent Orange." While there were other variations including Agents Purple, Pink, Blue, and White, Agent Orange became the herbicide of choice as U.S. forces sprayed more than 13 million gallons from the special systems developed for C-123 transport planes and helicopters.[85]

While questions regarding the effects surfaced early on, often from villages underneath the dense spray where miscarriages among women and animals increased, the U.S. military continued the defoliation through 1971. That year, a leaked government report and congressional investigations led to the suspension of its use. However, by that time, the military had dumped nearly 20 million pounds of herbicides on approximately 6 million acres of land. The mist fell on American troops and found its way into the water they waded and bathed in, and the food they often bought from locals.[86]

The effects of Agent Orange on veterans became well documented. A Mexican American veteran admitted that "Agent Orange is a dioxin, it's fatal. I mean, I know I'm dying. You have to remember that while you were in Vietnam, regardless of where you were, you had to drink water. You had to wash up." In other cases, someone told soldiers that the yellow substance worked as a bug killer so people rubbed it on themselves to fend off gnats and mosquitoes. "I have proof of what happened to me because I shot a film when I was in Vietnam." He would suffer from rashes and sometimes "I also got things in my head and I was going crazy."[87]

Some of the afflicted became activists pushing for support for fellow sufferers, whether American or Vietnamese.[88] Paul Reutershan formed an organization, Agent Orange Victims International, to fight for compensation and medical support for victims worldwide. A helicopter pilot in Vietnam, he often flew through the mists of Agent Orange on his way to missions. In 1978, at the age of twenty-eight, he died of cancer. He lamented just before he died: "I got killed in Vietnam. I just didn't know it at the time."[89]

Perhaps the most memorable story of the effects of the chemicals on people occurred with the Zumwalt family. In 1968, Admiral Elmo Zumwalt Jr. assumed command of U.S. naval forces in Vietnam. The Navy primarily fought on the rivers and canals in Swift boats, small and fast gunboats that easily circumnavigated the often-shallow waters to interdict VC and NVA supplies floating down from Cambodia. Soon after, he ordered intensified spraying of Agent Orange and other defoliants along the riverbanks to remove cover for the VC who liked to ambush the sailors.

Ironically, one of the sailors plowing through the waters near where the chemicals fell was Zumwalt's young son, Elmo III. A Swift boat commander, he spent a year in Vietnam where he observed that "dramatic changes took place before our eyes in many areas we patrolled. One week, there would be thick, green foliage, and the next we would see leaves and grass eaten away from the devastating effects of Agent Orange." He admitted that his boat traversed these areas often, and he suspected that they went through a chemical mist on several occasions. He also noted, "I had often walked through and washed and waded in the rivers and canals" where the planes sprayed the chemicals.[90] Like many others exposed to Agent Orange, he began developing rashes, but he initially blamed them on too much sun.

Problems escalated for Elmo III when he returned home. He studied law at the University of North Carolina-Chapel Hill, and then started a practice in Fayetteville, North Carolina. The first difficulty occurred with his son, Russell, who had significant learning disabilities, a trait linked to other children whose parents endured exposure to Agent Orange in Vietnam. More importantly, in early 1983, Elmo developed cancer, which disproportionately afflicted Vietnam veterans exposed to Agent Orange.

Nonetheless, the younger Zumwalt refused to participate in the class action suit brought by Vietnam veterans in the early 1980s, arguing that as a high profile victim he would have been required often to testify and provide depositions, taking his limited time away from his family. Still, he acknowledged, "I do not think I could prove in court, by the weight of the existing scientific evidence, that Agent Orange is the cause of all these medical problems. But I am convinced that it is. I believe Agent Orange is responsible for my cancers, for Russell's learning disorder, and for illness suffered by many Vietnam veterans."[91]

He fought the cancer for six years, participating in several experimental programs. His father rallied to his side, collaborating on a book, *My Father, My Son*, that outlined the ordeal. The admiral remained steadfast in his decision, writing that he realized "that had I not used

"The Three Soldiers," a sculpture at the Vietnam Memorial in Washington, DC. *(Photo by Kyle Longley)*

Agent Orange, many more lives would have been lost in combat, perhaps even Elmo's. And knowing what I now know, I still would have ordered the defoliation to achieve the objectives it did." Still, he admitted that he felt anguish for his son's disease and his grandson's disability. "It is the first thing I think of when I awake in the morning, and the last thing I remember when I go to sleep."[92] Ultimately, in 1988, Elmo III died at the age of forty-two.

The battle of all of those sprayed with Agent Orange in Vietnam continued for many years. In the late 1970s, veterans began filing medical disability claims with the VA for Agent Orange–related illnesses ranging from skin rashes to cancer and birth defects. By 1982, veterans had made more than 12,000 claims, although the VA often blamed the health problems on other causes. In 1982, more than 9,000 veterans filed a class action lawsuit for more than $44 billion against the producers of Agent Orange, including multinational giant Dow Chemical. In 1984, both sides reached a settlement agreeing to $184 million in compensation. The distribution ranged from $256 to $12,500 for each disabled veteran, and families who lost their relatives received $340 to $3,400. About 39,000 veterans collected payments, although more than 28,000 obtained nothing after mediators denied their claims. Additional lawsuits continued into the modern era from those who missed the initial settlement and had illnesses develop after 1984, albeit often with few gains.[93]

Later, veterans of the First Persian Gulf War experienced similar difficulties dealing with diseases that doctors could not explain. The government again tried limiting the claims but unlike before, the Gulf veterans had no American companies to sue, although some veterans blamed shots and medicines forced on them. In many ways, some argue, both responses reflected a complete betrayal of the veteran. In the case of Vietnam, the government literally helped poison tens of thousands of veterans, many of whom probably never sought a diagnosis of their condition. The settlement proved a miniscule effort as widows received just over $3,000 for their husbands' lives. Bitterness and distrust remained and left veterans and their families searching for some other forms of recognition of their sacrifice.

The Healing of a Nation: The Vietnam Veteran's Memorial and Beyond

For many years, the Vietnam veterans, including those struggling with lasting effects, fought to redefine their service and receive recognition for it. An important effort revolved around how to memorialize their sacrifice. From the American Revolution through the Civil War, World War I, and World War II, Americans led by veterans worked to erect memorials to those who fought and died. However, starting with Korea and especially during the long, tumultuous struggle in Vietnam, Americans seemed to want to forget, not glorify the conflict. While there were some memorialization efforts, they paled in comparison to other wars outside of maybe the Korean War.[94]

Many Vietnam veterans fought to overcome prejudices and stereotypes and make sure that their sacrifices had meaning in American history. One noted that Hemingway had written that "abstract words such as glory, honor, courage, or hallow were obscene beside the concrete names of villages, the numbers of roads, the names of rivers, the number of regiments and the dates." He feared that while Vietnam veterans knew names such as Con Thien, the Arizona Territory, and Hill 881, "those concrete terms meant nothing in the new world of America in the 70s."[95]

As a result, individuals began erecting memorials on their own even before the war officially ended. A good example occurred in Angel Fire, New Mexico, only a few miles outside of the mountain resort of Taos.

On May 22, 1968, 1st Lieutenant Victor Westphall III died in combat in Vietnam. Grief stricken, his parents, Jeanne and Victor Westphall II, took the insurance money and began constructing the Vietnam Veterans Peace and Brotherhood Chapel on a windswept hill overlooking the Moreno Valley.[96] Ultimately, they built a vast, gull like structure designed by Santa Fe architect Ted Luna, who sought to achieve "simplicity without sterility."[97]

After scrimping and saving and battling the elements, the family dedicated the site on May 22, 1971, the third anniversary of Victor's death. The Westphalls invited John Kerry as the keynote speaker, and the three major television networks covered the dedications. The beautiful white building, extending fifty feet into the air, had a quarter-circle arc of a ninety-nine foot radius. Designed to promote peace and reconciliation, the chapel, Dr. Westphall explained, embodied his hope that his son's death and those of others in Vietnam would "become a symbol that will arouse all mankind and bring a rejection of the principles which defile, debase, and destroy the youth of the world."[98]

Ultimately, the Westphalls received requests to replicate the memorial, even one from Jan Scruggs, who headed the planning of the national memorial in Washington, DC, in the early 1980s. Dr. Westphall declined. Ultimately, for financial reasons, the family turned over title to the property in 1982 to the Disabled Veterans of America (DAV). It built a visitor's center, with numerous photographs ranging from one of young Vietnamese girls walking past stacked sandbags to an exploding ammunition depot at Khe Sanh. Finally, the thirty-acre site became a state park on Veterans Day in 2005.[99]

The Vietnam Veterans Peace and Brotherhood Chapel constituted an early example of the refusal to forget, and Vietnam veterans led the charge to build the most recognizable Vietnam memorial in the 1980s. The project, the brainchild of Jan Scruggs, a Vietnam vet, began after he walked away from the movie *The Deer Hunter.* Afterward, he experienced flashbacks, seeing the faces of his fallen comrades. "The names," he lamented, "the names. No one remembers their names." He decided to build a memorial that would "have the names of everyone killed."[100]

For more than three years, Scruggs worked to raise money to construct the monument through the Vietnam Veterans Memorial Fund (VVMF). The group also lobbied Congress to allocate a site on the National Lawn near the Lincoln Memorial to place the structure.

As Vietnam veteran Robert Doubek told members of Congress, the "Vietnam Veterans Memorial is conceived as a means to promote the healing and reconciliation of the country after the divisions caused by the war." With bipartisan support, construction proceeded, as one congressman stressed that it represented a "harmonious and unifying" project arising out of the ashes of a "disharmonious period of our national history."[101]

The plan never lacked critics, especially as the design selection went forward. The American Institute of Architects oversaw the competition. A twenty-one-year-old Yale University undergraduate student, Maya Lin, won the contest. She envisaged a wall built into the ground in the shape of a V with the names of the service people who died engraved in black granite. Ten feet tall at the lowest point, the memorial listed the names of the fallen according to when they died in Vietnam, tapering from right to left. To personalize the experience, the polished stone would reflect the image of the person viewing the names. Lin emphasized that her design left it "up to each individual to resolve or come to terms with this loss. For death is in the end a personal and private matter and the area containing this within the memorial is a quiet place, meant for personal reflection and private reckoning."[102]

When the VVMF unveiled the winner, some people immediately denounced the design. One of the losers in the contest and a veteran, Tom Carhart, characterized it as a "black scar . . . a black shaft of shame thrust into the earth." He condemned the choice of black as "the universal color of sorrow and shame" and bemoaned that the memorial existed "in a hole, hidden as if out of shame. . . . Can America truly mean that we are to be honored by a black pit."[103] Jim Webb called it a "wailing Wall for future anti-draft and anti-nuclear demonstrators."[104] Conservatives, feeling remasculized by Reagan's strident rhetoric, joined the chorus, and pressure for a redesign mounted from many quarters including Secretary of the Interior James Watt and Texas billionaire H. Ross Perot.[105]

The VVMF wavered and sought a compromise. They accepted a supplemental sculpture, "The Three Soliders," by Frederick Hart. His figures, a muscular white man flanked by an African American and another man of unknown ethnicity, looked very masculine and empowered. While Hart intended them to be looking for the enemy, the location 100 feet from the wall ensured different interpretations, including that they gazed at the wall, "apparently transfixed by its power," according to one observer. The compromise also added a flagpole, although away from the walls as not to change Lin's vision.[106]

Finally, on November 12, 1982, the official unveiling of the memorial occurred. One veteran carried a sign: "I am a Vietnam veteran/I like the memorial/And if it makes it difficult to send people to battle again/I like it even more."[107] Overall, people responded very favorably as visitors from all over the country arrived, making it one of the most popular memorial sites in Washington. For some, especially family members, friends, and comrades in arms, it became a source of healing. People began leaving everything from teddy bears to clothing. One particularly poignant letter left at the memorial by Glen who served in 1968–69 read: "I have seen the names of those I know, and yes, I have cried. My problem is I don't know the names of those I tried to help only to have them die in my arms. In my sleep I hear their cries and see their faces." He then attached his service medals and concluded, "These belong to you and your family and your friends. I don't need them to show I was there. I have your faces in my sleep."[108]

The overall response of the Vietnam veterans proved extremely positive. One Marine emphasized that he had been to the wall in 1984 and found the names of his friends. "I think the Vietnam Memorial has been a great thing for the Vietnam veterans. It's really focused people's attention on Vietnam veterans in a respectful way. . . . I think it's helped us 100 percent."[109] Another remembered going to the wall in 1984: "It was really overpowering. I saw the names of some guys I knew. . . . Cried real hard." "But, you know," he added, "I think it's a lot easier for Americans to feel bad about the guys that died than it is for them to think about those of us who are still around. Those guys who died, their stories died with them. I'm not sure people want to hear the kind of stories they could tell."[110]

For others, mixed emotions sometimes arose. A sister of a soldier killed in Vietnam complained, "When I walked past the Vietnam Veterans Memorial in Washington, DC, a few years ago and saw the line of people passing by and looking sad, I felt angry. What right did they have to mourn those men? What right did they have to look sad? Where were they back then? What did they do to stop the war? What did they give up to stop the killing?"[111]

Historian Kristin Ann Hass summarized the effect of the monument very well. "The Wall elicits a physical response. It has inspired visitors to represent their own grief, loss, rage, and despair. Contributing their private representations to public space, they cross the boundary between the private and public, the nation and the citizen, powerfully claiming the memorial as their own."[112]

The Vietnam veterans had to build their own memorial, and when completed, it helped alter the way Americans remember the sacrifices of their war dead and others. It personalized the event and allowed room for interpretation, oftentimes created by a person's own experiences and political leanings. Nonetheless, it remains a fundamental part of the landscape of memory in America, a position unlikely changed even as other memorials appeared to the Korean War and World War II on the National Mall.

The Vietnam veterans' sense of betrayal diminished throughout the 1980s as more memorials and events commemorated their service and sacrifice. Belatedly, they received a massive parade on May 7, 1985, in New York City where 25,000 Vietnam veterans proudly marched through the Broadway "Canyon of Heroes" in front of more than 1 million spectators who sent flying 468 tons of ticker tape. Other towns, such as Houston and Chicago, followed with similar celebrations.[113] Various organizations also erected many other memorials throughout the country to honor the service and the lives of fallen comrades. They differ in simplicity from the rustic beauty of a veteran's memorial on Mare's Bluff overlooking the small community of Clifton, Arizona, to that of a Huey helicopter and small black stones with the names of the dead in front of the San Angelo, Texas, airport.

Despite the improvement, the image of the Vietnam veteran continued to suffer at various junctures as films and other forms of popular culture insisted on perpetuating numerous negative and unflattering stereotypes. Partisan politics often played a role as evidenced in the attacks in 2000 on John McCain during the Republican primary in South Carolina. Soon after, Republican operatives launched vicious assaults on Max Cleland in Georgia during his reelection efforts in 2002, questioning his patriotism despite his sacrifices in Vietnam. Finally, the question of service in Vietnam peaked with the brutal offensive against John Kerry in the 2004 presidential race where opponents, oftentimes led by Vietnam veterans, including his old nemesis John O'Neill, questioned not only Kerry's actions upon return, but his bravery and his citations, rarely understanding that to challenge his commendations called into question the entire system and thereby all awards received by Vietnam soldiers.[114] By 2008, no Vietnam veteran other than naval aviator and POW McCain had entered the presidential race.

Conclusion

As the events that have unfolded in the twenty-first century demonstrate, the legacy of the war remains contested ground. More than forty years since the first Americans started returning home as combat veterans from Vietnam, the war remains divisive. The soldiers who fought returned home to an often-ungrateful country, causing isolation and resentment. Some responded by battling for many causes related to their service including health benefits. Others expended significant energy challenging the negative stereotypes that evolved out of their service. While progress occurred and most veterans reintegrated into society to lead extremely productive lives, battles continue as Vietnam veterans enter the autumn of their lives, forever changed by their experiences more than forty years ago on battlefields far away from their homes.

Epilogue

The voices of Vietnam echo loudly in 2008 as the United States once again finds itself bogged down in an intractable guerrilla conflict, this time in Iraq and to a lesser degree Afghanistan. While some leaders try to downplay the comparisons, fearful of provoking the ghosts of Vietnam, many people find similarities, particularly combat veterans asked to fight an increasingly unpopular war in a country thousands of miles from America's shores under a cloud of suspicion on how the leaders led the people into war. The modern grunts fight in a very hostile environment against an elusive enemy among a typically ambivalent population. The country again finds itself losing thousands and spending billions in a conflict that appears to have no end, at least a satisfactory one.

The effects, while smaller in proportion to Vietnam in terms of over-all impact on society, nonetheless trickle down throughout the country. For example, in Tucson, just a little more than 100 miles from Morenci, Arizona, is the primarily working and middle-class school district of Mountain View High School. In April 2005, a roadside bomb in Baghdad killed Sam Huff, the former drum major, who had attended her prom only a year earlier.[1] Then, another former student, Kenneth Ross, died in a helicopter crash in Afghanistan. Roadside bombs killed two others, Chad Kenyon and Budd Cote, a year later in Iraq. Most recently, in February 2007, Alan McPeek died from enemy fire on his last day of his fourteen-month tour in Iraq.[2]

Like forty years before at the height of the Vietnam conflict, f and friends in Arizona find themselves dealing with the loss of life in war. The classmates of the five bear a particularly heavy portion of the loss. As McPeek's best friend, Shaun Moreland, emphasized, "Everybody I knew who was over there is no longer with us." Another friend, Ryan Azuelo, told a reporter, "The war just keeps getting closer and closer."[3]

Many high school friends remembered their friends lost in war and argued over the conflict including those who joined before and after. Friends and family often traveled to Evergreen Cemetery where McPeek lay. They deposited mementos ranging from a GI Joe toy and small American flag to an unopened can of beer. One day, Moreland lit a Marlboro Red and smoked part of it and then buried the remainder in the grave near where McPeek's head lay. "It's the hardest thing in the world," he said. "I never thought I'd be doing this with my best friend."[4]

More than 4,000 times, people across the country have found military officials arriving at their doorsteps to deliver bad news about the loss of a loved one. Tens of thousands of others have watched their family members, both men and women, return home terribly wounded, many missing limbs, having brain damage, or suffering from PTSD. Murders and suicides around bases with returning soldiers have increased significantly. The soldiers and their families face many years of dislocation from the effects of the war, even as forty years later Vietnam veterans and their families continue to struggle with the effects of that conflict.

Many similarities exist between the Vietnam and Iraq/Afghanistan veterans. First, the fighting has fallen on only a small proportion of society, oftentimes those pushed into military service by the promise of a job and benefits such as grants for college. These people, many of whom joined the National Guard and Reserves for the extra pay, found themselves serving multiple tours in Iraq after 2003. Often poorly equipped for the insurgents' tactics such as roadside bombs, they have carried a significant burden for the war while most of their counterparts have gone about their everyday lives with little thought about their brethren in the armed services.

In Iraq especially, the young men and women, as well as some Vietnam veterans, have found themselves embroiled in a guerrilla war against an elusive enemy fighting among a civilian population that often supports the insurgents. With internal factions dividing the populace and often unreliable and poorly led allies, the Americans have faced the frustration of being caught between internal religious factions while trying to maintain the peace and promote public works projects in a struggle for the hearts and minds of the population. As a result, atrocities have occurred and led to a questioning of the combat soldiers' decisions and their effect on the mission. While the accusations of baby killer have not been bandied about like in Vietnam, more people have begun to look at the returning warriors with some suspicion about their mindset and temperament.

In addition, like their Vietnam counterparts, the returning warriors find a bureaucratic maze dominating, even as more people recognize the devastation of PTSD and its effects on families. Underfunded VA hospitals deal with severely wounded grunts in much higher numbers as advances in medical technology save lives that would have been lost in earlier contests. While the numbers remain fairly small when compared to Vietnam, nonetheless, they remain significant and will continue to put a tremendous strain on the overextended VA system for many years in the future.

Of course, differences also exist. More women have served in combat roles in Iraq than in Vietnam, dying at a much higher rate than in earlier conflicts. Also, the treatment of the Iraq veteran by the general public has changed significantly, partly in response to the shame of how the Vietnam veteran experienced the return. Iraq veterans often receive warm welcomes, even as the war has dragged on for longer than World War II and become increasingly unpopular with the majority of Americans. They return to VFW and American Legion halls dominated now by Vietnam veterans who understand the anguish of fighting a guerrilla war against an elusive enemy among civilians. Still, many challenges continue for the returning soldier.

If anything, the war in Iraq primarily has increased the debates about Vietnam. People who support President George W. Bush's decision to intervene argue that to withdraw prematurely will lead to chaos in Iraq, like that which developed in Southeast Asia more than four decades ago. They like to blame the press and antiwar movement for undermining the mission and aiding the enemy, echoing the rationales for failure given by men such as General William Westmoreland.

On the other side, members of the antiwar movement argue that staying longer only weakens the United States globally in its war against terrorism. They make the point that the United States has placed its troops in a religious civil war where conflict between the sects remains inevitable and that the U.S. presence merely exacerbates the tensions and makes U.S. soldiers the targets of nationalist resentment. Led by Vietnam veterans such as Chuck Hagel, Jim Webb, Wes Clark, John Kerry, and many others, they raise many questions about how the United States became involved and its effects in the short term and long term.

No matter what the view of the war in Iraq, the ghosts of Vietnam clearly play a role in shaping the American perspective of the conflict. Understanding the experience of the Vietnam veteran helps provide some context and comprehension of fighting in primarily guerrilla wars thousands of miles from America's shores in alien cultures among ambivalent hosts. Today, the Vietnam and Iraq veteran are two generations linked despite the separation of forty years.

Notes

Introduction

1. *Arizona Republic,* April 30, 2000.
2. Interview by the author with Mike Cranford, May 23, 2003, York, Arizona; interview by the author with Joe Sorrelman, July 20, 2003, Glendale, Arizona.
3. Ibid.
4. Interview by the author with Leroy Cisneros, June 6, 2007, Yuma, Arizona.
5. Interview by the author with Mike Cranford, May 23, 2003, York, Arizona; interview by the author with Joe Sorrelman, July 20, 2003, Glendale, Arizona; interview by the author with Leroy Cisneros, June 6, 2007, Yuma, Arizona.
6. Interview by the author with Leroy Cisneros, June 6, 2007, Yuma, Arizona.
7. Interview by the author with Joe Sorrelman, July 20, 2003, Glendale, Arizona.
8. Interview by the author with Penny King, Safford, Arizona.
9. Interview by the author with Carol Navarette, Morenci, Arizona.
10. Photo in personal possession of Julia and Clive Garcia Sr., private correspondence of Clive Garcia Jr., copy with the author.
11. Interview by the author with Danny Garcia, September 18, 2005, Benson, Arizona.
12. Lieutenant Dave Miller to Julia Garcia, February 7, 1970, South Vietnam, letters of Clive Garcia Jr.
13. Interview by the author with Danny Garcia, September 18, 2005, Benson, Arizona.
14. Edwin McDowell, "Close-Knit Community of Morenci Sags Under Weight of Vietnam Casualties," *Arizona Republic* (n.d.), Morenci Public Library, Morenci, Arizona.
15. *Arizona Republic,* December 11, 1969.
16. Ibid.
17. Ibid.
18. Interview by the author with Julia Garcia, April 23, 2004, Safford, Arizona.
19. Interview by the author with Leroy Cisneros, June 5, 2007, Yuma, Arizona.
20. Ibid.; interview by the author with Joe Sorrelman, July 20, 2003, Glendale, Arizona.
21. Interview by author with Mike Cranford, May 23, 2003, Duncan, Arizona.

22. *Arizona Republic,* April 30, 2000.

23. Vincent Okamoto, "Damn, I'm a Gook," in Christian G. Appy, *Patriots: The Vietnam War Remembered From All Sides* (New York: Penguin, 2003), 361.

24. Bob Kerrey, *When I Was a Young Man: A Memoir* (New York: Harcourt, 2002), 167.

25. Christian Appy, *Working Class War: American Combat Soldiers and Vietnam* (Chapel Hill: University of North Carolina Press, 1993); James R. Ebert, *A Life in a Year: The American Infantryman in Vietnam, 1965–1972* (Novato, CA: Presidio Press, 1993).

26. Ebert, *A Life in a Year,* xiii.

27. Charlie Earl Bodiford, "Atmore, Alabama, Marine Machinegunner, 1969–70," in James R. Wilson, ed., *Landing Zones: Southern Veterans Remember Vietnam* (Durham, NC: Duke University Press, 1990), 201.

Chapter 1

1. Tim O'Brien, *If I Die in a Combat Zone: Box Me Up and Ship Me Home* (New York: Laurel Books, 1987), 27.

2. Lawrence M. Baskir and William A. Strauss, *Chance and Circumstance: The Draft, the War, and the Vietnam Generation* (New York: Knopf, 1978), 5.

3. George Q. Flynn, *The Draft, 1940–1973* (Lawrence: University Press of Kansas), 150; James R. Ebert, *A Life in a Year: The American Infantryman in Vietnam, 1965–1972* (Novato, CA: Presidio Press, 1993), 21.

4. James W. Davis Jr. and Kenneth M. Dolbeare, *Little Groups of Neighbors: The Selective Service System* (Chicago: Markham, 1968), v.

5. Ibid., 33.

6. Ibid., 78–124.

7. Jonathan Polansky, "Shanghai'd," in Al Santoli, ed., *Everything We Had: An Oral History of the Vietnam War by Thirty-Three American Soldiers Who Fought It* (New York: Random, 1981), 102.

8. Ebert, *A Life in a Year,* 29.

9. Flynn, *The Draft,* 212.

10. Howard Bingham and Max Wallace, *Muhammad Ali's Greatest Fight: Cassius Clay vs. the United States of America* (New York: M. Evans, 2000).

11. Ebert, *A Life in a Year,* 29.

12. Mark Baker, *Nam: The Vietnam War in the Words of the Men and Women Who Fought There* (New York: Quill Books, 1982), 25.

13. Interview of Thomas Brown by Jonathan Bernstein, October 22, 2001, Vietnam Archive Oral History Project, Texas Tech University, Lubbock, Texas, 2–3.

14. Christian Appy, *Working Class War: American Combat Soldiers and Vietnam* (Chapel Hill: University of North Carolina Press, 1993), 31.

15. George Mariscal, ed., *Aztlán and Vietnam: Chicano and Chicana Experiences of the War* (Berkeley: University of California Press, 1999), 20.

16. Interview of Ted Cook by Steve Maxner, October 2, 1999, Vietnam Archive Oral History Project, Texas Tech University, Lubbock, Texas, 7.

17. Lewis B. Puller Jr., *Fortunate Son: The Autobiography of Lewis B. Puller, Jr.* (New York: Bantam, 1991), 91.

18. Thomas G. Sticht, William B. Armstrong, Daniel T. Hickey, and John S. Caylor, *Cast-off Youth: Policy and Training Methods from the Military Experience* (New York: Praeger, 1987), 46–56.

19. Appy, *Working Class War*, 33.

20. James E. Westheider, *Fighting on Two Fronts: African Americans and the Vietnam War* (New York: New York University Press, 1997), 25.

21. Davis and Dolbeare, *Little Groups of Neighbors*, 57.

22. Appy, *Working Class War*, 37.

23. Baskir and Strauss, *Chance and Circumstance*, 48–49.

24. Ibid., 49.

25. Ibid., 6.

26. Colin Powell, with Joseph Perisco, *My American Journey* (New York: Random, 1995), 148.

27. Flynn, *The Draft*, 171.

28. Davis and Dolbeare, *Little Groups of Neighbors*, 13.

29. Tom Birhanzel interview in *South Dakotans in Vietnam: Excerpts From the South Dakota Vietnam Veterans Oral History Project, Pierre Area* (Pierre: State Publishing, 1986), 3.

30. Phil Ball, *Ghosts and Shadows: A Marine in Vietnam, 1968–1969* (Jefferson, NC: McFarland, 1998), 5.

31. Baker, *Nam,* 30.

32. *Mesa Tribune,* November 11, 1993.

33. Loren Baritz, *Backfire: A History of How American Culture Led Us Into Vietnam and Made Us Fight the Way We Did*, 2nd edition (Baltimore: Johns Hopkins University Press, 1998), 14.

34. As cited in Robert D. Dean, *Imperial Brotherhood: Gender and the Making of Cold War Foreign Policy* (Amherst: University of Massachusetts Press, 2001).

35. Graham Dawson, *Soldier Heroes: British Adventure, Empire and the Imaging of Masculinities* (New York: Routledge, 1994), 1, 22–23.

36. Baker, *Nam,* 28.

37. E. Anthony Rotundo, *American Manhood: Transformations in Masculinity From the Revolution to the Modern Era* (New York: Basic Books, 1993), 234–35.

38. John M.G. Brown, *Rice Paddy Grunt: Unfading Memories of the Vietnam Generation* (Lake Bluff, IL: Regnery Books, 1986), 25.

39. Baker, *Nam,* 33–34.

40. Interview by the author with Steve Guzzo, May 23, 2003, Clifton, Arizona.

41. Interview by the author with Oscar Urrea, January 30, 2004, Mesa, Arizona.

42. Ken Moorefield, "Gathering Storm," in Al Santoli, ed., *To Bear Any Burden: The Vietnam War and Its Aftermath in the Words of Americans and Southeast Asians* (New York: Dutton, 1985), 112.

43. Bethanne Kelly Patrick, "Lt. Gen. Lewis Berwell Puller: The Legendary 'Chesty' Puller Was a True 'Marine's Marine' Who Never Forgot His Noncom Days," Military. com. www.military.com/Content/MoreContent?file=ML_puller_bkp, accessed February 25, 2005.

44. Puller, *Fortunate Son,* 1.

45. Ibid., 5–6.

46. Ibid., 23.

47. Ibid., 35.

48. Ibid., 184–89.

49. Marc Feigen Fasteau, *The Male Machine* (New York: McGraw-Hill, 1974), 101–14; Rotundo, *American Manhood,* 239–44.

50. Tom Magedanz interview in *South Dakotans in Vietnam*, 3.

51. Puller, *Fortunate Son,* 25.

52. As cited in Dean, *Imperial Brotherhood*, 3.

53. John Ketwig, . . . *And a Hard Rain Fell: A GI's True Story of the War in Vietnam* (Naperville, IL: Sourcebooks, 2002), 16.

54. Norman Summers, "A Sense of Duty," in Stanley W. Beesley, *Vietnam: The Heartland Remembers* (Norman: University of Oklahoma Press, 1987), 11–12.

55. Andrew Kimbrell, *The Masculine Mystique: The Politics of Masculinity* (New York: Ballantine, 1995), 304.

56. Rotundo, *American Manhood,* 258.

57. Ibid., 238.

58. Robert Peterson, *The Boy Scouts: An American Adventure* (New York: American Heritage, 1984), 250.

59. Ibid., 241–42. The Cub Scout Promise emphasized: "I (name) promise to do my best to do my duty to God and my country, to help other people, and to obey the Law of the Pack." The Scout Oath was: "On my honor I will do my best to do my duty to God and my country and to obey the Scout Law; to help other people at all times; to keep myself physically strong, mentally awake, and morally straight."

60. Jay Mechling, *On My Honor: Boy Scouts and the Making of American Youth* (Chicago: University of Chicago Press, 2001), 128–29.

61. Interview by the author with Oscar Urrea, January 30, 2004, Mesa, Arizona.

62. Interview by the author with George Vasquez, April 23, 2004, Morenci, Arizona.

63. Michael Kimmel, *Manhood in America: A Cultural History* (New York: Free Press, 1996), 267–69; Fasteau, *The Male Machine,* 163–65.

64. Dean, *Imperial Brotherhood,* 169–99.

65. Phone interview of Martin Brady by Richard Verrone, June 25, 2003, Vietnam Archive Oral History Project, Texas Tech University, Lubbock, Texas, 6.

66. Philip Caputo, *A Rumor of War* (New York: Henry Holt, 1977), xiv.

67. Tom Roubideaux interview in *South Dakotans in Vietnam,* 58.

68. Allen C. LoBean, "Persimmon Community, Rabun County, Georgia, Navy Swift Boat Gunner, 1966–68," in James R. Wilson, ed., *Landing Zones: Southern Veterans Remember Vietnam* (Durham, NC: Duke University Press, 1990), 56.

69. Douglas Brinkley, *Tour of Duty: John Kerry and the Vietnam War* (New York: Morrow, 2004), 35–38; Michael Kranish, Brian C. Mooney, and Nina J. Easton, *John F. Kerry: The Complete Biography by the Boston Globe Reporters Who Know Him Best* (New York: Public Affairs, 2004), 32–34.

70. Ron Kovic, *Born on the Fourth of July* (New York: Pocket Books, 1976), 55.

71. Stanley Corkin, *Cowboys as Cold Warriors: The Western and U.S. History* (Philadelphia: Temple University Press, 2004).

72. As covered in a chapter titled "The Images of the Marines and John Wayne," in Lawrence H. Suid, *Guts and Glory: The Making of the American Military Image in Film,* revised and expanded edition (Lexington: University of Kentucky Press, 2002), 116–35.

73. Frank J. Wetta and Stephen J. Curley, *Celluloid Wars: A Guide to Film and the American Experience of War* (Westport, CT: Greenwood Press, 1992), 157–83.

74. "*Combat!* Storms Back into Action with 24-Hour Memorial Day Marathon and New Original Special," www.jodavidsmeyer.com/combat/episodes/encore-action-special. htm, accessed July 11, 2005.

75. Kovic, *Born on the Fourth of July,* 55.

76. "Navy Officer (1964–1966, 1968–1969)," in William J. Brinker, ed., *A Time for Looking Back: Putnam County Veterans, Their Families, and the Vietnam War* (Cookeville: Tennessee Technological University, 1990), 59.

77. Robert Tonsetic, *Warriors: An Infantryman's Memoir of Vietnam* (New York: Ballantine, 2004), 4.

78. As cited in Ebert, *A Life in a Year*, 11.

79. *Arizona Republic,* April 30, 2000.

80. Charley Trujillo, "It Sure as Hell Wasn't 'English Only' in Vietnam," in Christian G. Appy, *Patriots: The Vietnam War Remembered From All Sides* (New York: Penguin, 2003), 367.

81. As cited in Appy, *Working Class War*, 75.

82. Bradford W. Wright, *Comic Book Nation: The Transformation of Youth Culture in America* (Baltimore: Johns Hopkins University Press, 2001), 187–99.

83. Joseph A. Fry, *Dixie Looks Abroad: The South and U.S. Foreign Relations, 1789–1973* (Baton Rouge: Louisiana State University Press, 2002), 270–71; James Perone, *Songs of the Vietnam Conflict* (Westport, CT: Greenwood Press, 2001), 86–87.

84. Charles C. Moskos Jr., *The American Enlisted Man: The Rank and File in Today's Military* (New York: Russell Sage Foundation, 1970), 23–24.

85. Michael Clodfelter, *Mad Minutes and Vietnam Months: A Soldier's Memoir* (Jefferson, NC: McFarland, 1988), 2.

86. Luis Martinez, "A Puerto Rican Marine," in Santoli, *Everything We Had*, 160.

87. For more on the topic of the importance of religion and its impact on volunteers and draftees, see James Carroll, *American Requiem: God, My Father, and the War That Came Between Us* (Boston: Houghton Mifflin, 1996), and Anne C. Loveland, *American Evangelicals and the U.S. Military, 1942–1993* (Baton Rouge: Louisiana State University Press, 1996).

88. Herman Graham III, *The Brothers' Vietnam War: Black Power, Manhood, and the Military Experience* (Gainesville: University of Florida Press, 2003), 1–14.

89. Westheider, *Fighting on Two Fronts*, 2.

90. Graham, *The Brothers' Vietnam War*, 16–21.

91. As cited in John Laffin, *Americans in Battle* (New York: Crown, 1973), 187.

92. Reginald "Malik" Edwards, "Rifleman, 9th Regiment, U.S. Marine Corps, Danang, June 1965–March 1966," in Wallace Terry, ed., *Bloods: An Oral History of the Vietnam War* (New York: Random House, 1984), 4.

93. Wayne Smith, "I Was Thanking God They Didn't Have Air Support," in Appy, *Patriots*, 362.

94. Paul Hathaway, "I'll Stick with My Country," *Washington Evening Star*, May 8, 1968.

95. The exact number of casualties at different points is the subject of debate, but clearly they exceeded the proportion of the population throughout much of the conflict. Graham, *The Brothers' War*, 21; and B.G. Burkett and Glenna Whitley, *Stolen Valor: How the Vietnam Generation Was Robbed of Its Heroes and Its History* (Dallas: Verity Press, 1998).

96. Mariscal, *Aztlán and Viet Nam*, 3.

97. Charley Trujillo, ed., *Soldados: Chicanos in Vietnam* (San Jose: Chusma House, 1990), vii; Mariscal, *Aztlán and Viet Nam*, 3; Ruben Treviso, "Hispanics and the Vietnam War," in Harrison E. Salisbury, ed., *Vietnam Reconsidered: Lessons From a War* (New York: Harper and Row, 1984), 184–86.

98. As cited in Trujillo, *Soldados*, i.

99. Appy, *Working Class War*, 15.

100. Mariscal, *Aztlán and Viet Nam*, 21.

101. Ibid., 21.

102. Trujillo, *Soldados*, 80.

103. Ibid., vii.

104. For a discussion of the Mexican American opposition to the war, see Lorena Oropeza, *¡Raza si! ¡Guerra no! Chicano Protest and Patriotism During the Viet Nam War Era* (Berkeley: University of California Press, 2005).

105. Manuel T. Valdez interview in Wilson, *Landing Zones*, 45.

106. Baker, *Nam*, 35.

107. Trujillo, "It Sure as Hell Wasn't 'English Only' in Vietnam," 367.

108. Manuel "Peanuts" Marin, "Waiting for Brother," in Trujillo, *Soldados*, 41.

109. Tom Holm, *Strong Hearts, Wounded Souls: Native American Veterans of the Vietnam War* (Austin: University of Texas Press, 1996), 11.

110. Ibid., 12.

111. Ibid., 118.

112. As cited in Ebert, *A Life in a Year*, 6.

113. As cited in Holm, *Strong Hearts, Wounded Souls*, 121.

114. William C. Meadows, *Kiowa, Apache, and Comanche Military Societies: Enduring Veterans, 1800 to the Present* (Austin: University of Texas Press, 1999); Cynthia H. Enloe, *Ethnic Soldiers: State Security in Divided Societies* (Athens: University of Georgia Press, 1980), 192–93; Kenneth W. Townsend, *World War II and the American Indian* (Albuquerque: University of New Mexico Press, 2000); Jere Bishop Franco, *Crossing the Pond: The Native American Effort in World War II* (Denton: University of North Texas Press, 1999).

115. Tom Roubideaux interview in *South Dakotans in Vietnam*, 62.

116. As cited in Holm, *Strong Hearts, Wounded Souls*, 66.

117. As an example of the influence of the 442nd legend on Japanese Americans, see Richard Halloran, *My Names Is . . . Shinseki . . . and I am a Soldier* (Honolulu: Hawaii Army Museum Society, 2004), 10–11. The work focuses on the future chief of staff of the U.S. Army and a decorated Vietnam veteran.

118. Vincent Okamoto, "Damn, I'm a Gook," in Appy, *Patriots*, 357.

119. While there is little information on the reasons for joining, some information can be found in Carina A. del Rosario, *A Different Battle: Stories of Asian Pacific American Veterans* (Seattle: University of Washington Press, 1999).

120. Kathryn Marshall, *In the Combat Zone: An Oral History of American Women in Vietnam, 1966–1975* (Boston: Little, Brown, 1987), 4.

121. Christine McGinley Schneider in Keith Walker, ed., *A Piece of My Heart: The Stories of 26 American Women Who Served in Vietnam* (San Francisco: Presidio Press, 1985), 36.

122. Judy Hartline Elbring in Ron Steinman, ed., *Women in Vietnam* (New York: TV Books, 2000), 140.

123. Baker, *Nam*, 28.

124. Becky Pietz in Marshall, *In the Combat Zone*, 103.

125. Lily Jean Adams, "Army Nurse," in Steinman, *Women in Vietnam*, 48.

126. Lynda Van Devanter, *Home Before Morning: The Story of an Army Nurse in Vietnam* (New York: Time Warner Books, 1983), 23.

127. Kathryn Marshall, *In the Combat Zone*, 12.

128. Brenda Sue Castro, "Somerville, Alabama, Army Nurse, 1967–1968," in Wilson, *Landing Zones*, 88.

129. Gayle Smith, "The Nurse With Round Eyes," in Santoli, *Everything We Had*, 141.

130. Cherie Rankin in Kathryn Marshall, *In the Combat Zone*, 62.

Chapter 2

1. Telephone interview of David Crawley by Steve Maxner, February 27, 2001, Vietnam Archive Oral History Project, Texas Tech University, Lubbock, Texas, 6.

2. Telephone interview of Michael Bradbury by Richard Burks Verrone, September 15, 2003; ibid., 6.

3. William E. Merritt, *Where the Rivers Ran Backward* (Athens: University of Georgia Press, 1989), 3–4.

4. Ibid., 4.

5. *Los Angeles Times,* June 8, 1966.

6. Tom Roubideaux interview in *South Dakotans in Vietnam: Excerpts From the South Dakota Vietnam Veterans Oral History Project, Pierre Area* (Pierre: State Publishing, 1986), 60.

7. John S. Candler Jr., interview in by James R. Wilson, ed., *Landing Zones: Southern Veterans Remember Vietnam* (Durham, NC: Duke University Press, 1990), 148.

8. Ray Raphael, *The Men From the Boys: Rites of Passage in Male America* (Lincoln: University of Nebraska Press, 1988), 21.

9. James R. Ebert, *A Life in a Year: The American Infantryman in Vietnam, 1965–1972* (Novato, CA: Presidio Press, 1993), 31–32.

10. W.D. Ehrhart, *Vietnam-Perkasie: A Combat Marine Memoir* (Jefferson, NC: McFarland, 1983), 12.

11. Telephone interview of Michael Bradbury by Richard Burks Verrone, September 15, 2003, Vietnam Archive Oral History Project, 6.

12. Telephone interview of Michael Bradbury by Richard Burks Verrone, September 15, 2003; ibid., Texas, 6–8.

13. Telephone interview of Alfred DeMailo by Steve Maxner, January 24, 2003; ibid., 9–10.

14. Jerry Morton, *Reluctant Lieutenant: From Basic to OCS in the Sixties* (College Station: Texas A&M Press, 2004), 13–22.

15. Jonathan Polansky, "Shanghai'd," in Al Santoli, ed., *Everything We Had: An Oral History of the Vietnam War by Thirty-Three American Soldiers Who Fought It* (New York: Random, 1981), 103–4.

16. Ebert, *A Life in a Year*, 38.

17. Philip Caputo, *Rumor of War* (New York: Owl Books, 1977), 18–19.

18. David Parks, *GI Diary* (Washington, DC: Howard University Press, 1984), 14.

19. Peter Barnes, *Pawns: The Plight of the Citizen-Soldier* (New York: Knopf, 1972), 77–78.

20. Ibid., 78.

21. Interview of Robert Wrinn by Wayne Johnson, Lexington, Kentucky, May 12, 19, 1989, University of Kentucky Oral History Program, University of Kentucky, Lexington, Kentucky, 6.

22. Ibid., 4.

23. Telephone interview of Gonzalo Baltazar by Steve Maxner, March 23, 2001, Vietnam Archive Oral History Project, 4.

24. Ibid., 5.

25. William U. Tant interview by Wilson, *Landing Zones*, 46.

26. Interview of William Terry Ginter by Terry L. Birdwhistell, Lexington, Kentucky, January 30, 1985, University of Kentucky Oral History Program, 3.

27. Rev. J. Houston Matthews in Wilson, *Landing Zones*, 46.

28. George D. Riels interview in ibid., 46.

29. Richard E. Marks, *The Letters of Pfc. Richard E. Marks, USMC* (Philadelphia: Lippincott, 1967), 8–11.

30. Ebert, *A Life in a Year*, 33.

31. Telephone interview of Keith Erdman by Steve Maxner, February 26, 2001, Vietnam Archive Oral History Project, 10.

32. John Ketwig, . . . *And a Hard Rain Fell: A GI's True Story of the War in Vietnam* (Naperville, IL: Sourcebooks, 2002), 21.

33. Interview of V. Dean Quillet by Terry L. Birdwhistell and George Herring, Louisville, Kentucky, March 18, 1985, University of Kentucky Oral History Program, 2.

34. Christian Appy, *Working Class War: American Combat Soldiers and Vietnam* (Chapel Hill: University of North Carolina Press, 1993), 88.

35. R. Wayne Eisenhart, "You Can't Hack It Little Girl: A Discussion of the Covert Psychological Agenda of Modern Combat Training," *Journal of Social Issues* 31 (Fall 1975): 16–17.

36. Ron Kovic, *Born on the Fourth of July* (New York: Pocket Books, 1982), 82.

37. Susan Danziger Borchert, "Masculinity and the Vietnam War," *Michigan Academician* (Winter 1983): 197.

38. Robert D. Dean, *Imperial Brotherhood: Gender and the Making of Cold War Policy* (Amherst: University of Massachusetts Press, 2001).

39. Tim O'Brien, *If I Die in a Combat Zone: Box Me Up and Ship Me Home* (New York: Laurel Books, 1969), 54.

40. Parks, *GI Diary,* 6.

41. Reginald "Malik" Edwards, "Rifleman, 9th Regiment, U.S. Marine Corps, Danang, June 1965–March 1966," in Wallace Terry, ed., *Bloods: An Oral History of the Vietnam Veteran by Black Veterans* (New York: Random, 1984), 7.

42. Mark Baker, *Nam: The Vietnam War in the Words of the Men and Women Who Fought There* (New York: Quill Books, 1982), 36.

43. Manuel T. Valdez interview in Wilson, *Landing Zones,* 46.

44. Appy, *Working Class War,* 100–1.

45. For more on the importance of race in World War II in the Pacific theater, see John Dower, *War Without Mercy: Race and Power in the Pacific War* (New York: Pantheon, 1987).

46. Appy, *Working Class War,* 101.

47. Baker, *Nam,* 38.

48. Ibid.

49. Telephone interview of David Crawley by Steve Maxner, February 27, 2001, Vietnam Archive Oral History Project, 9.

50. Appy, *Working Class War,* 54.

51. Ebert, *A Life in a Year,* 46.

52. Interview of Robert Wrinn by Wayne Johnson, May 12, 19, 1989, University of Kentucky Oral History Program, Lexington, Kentucky, 4.

53. Ebert, *A Life in a Year,* 46.

54. Lucinda Franks, *Waiting Out a War: The Exile of Private John Picciano* (New York: Coward, McCann, and Geoghegan, 1974), 57.

55. Barnes, *Pawns,* 70.

56. Ibid., 69–71; telephone interview of David Crawley by Steve Maxner, February 27, 2001, Vietnam Archive Oral History Project, 7.

57. Baker, *Nam,* 42–43.

58. Ibid., 44–45.

59. Appy, *Working Class War,* 102.

60. G. David Curry, *Sunshine Patriots: Punishment and the Vietnam Offender* (Notre Dame, IN: University of Notre Dame Press, 1985), 16.

61. Cincinnatus, *Self-Destruction: The Disintegration and Decay of the United States Army During the Vietnam Era* (New York: Norton, 1981), 150.

62. Barnes, *Pawns,* 114–15.

63. Ibid., 114–15.

64. Ibid., 105–7.

65. Telephone interview of Keith Erdman by Steve Maxner, February 26, 2001, Vietnam Archive Oral History Project, Texas Tech University, Lubbock, Texas, 5–6.

66. Ibid., 6.

67. Parks, *GI Diary*, 16.

68. Ebert, *A Life in a Year*, 41.

69. Raphael, *The Men From the Boys*, 29.

70. Caputo, *Rumor of War*, 10–11.

71. Baker, *Nam*, 40–41.

72. Herman Graham III, *The Brothers' Vietnam War: Black Power, Manhood, and the Military Experience* (Gainesville: University of Florida Press, 2003), 43.

73. Ehrhart, *Vietnam-Perkasie,* 19.

74. Gwynne Dyer, *War* (New York: Crown, 1985), 112.

75. Barnes, *Pawns*, 74–76.

76. Telephone interview of David Crawley by Steve Maxner, February 27, 2001, Vietnam Archive Oral History Project, 10.

77. Ebert, *A Life in a Year*, 29.

78. Telephone interview of David Crawley by Steve Maxner, February 27, 2001, Vietnam Archive Oral History Project, 10–11.

79. William U. Tant interview in Wilson, *Landing Zones*, 46.

80. As cited in Tom Holm, *Strong Hearts, Wounded Souls: Native American Veterans of the Vietnam War* (Austin: University of Texas Press, 1996), 127.

81. Barnes, *Pawns*, 86–88.

82. Graham, *The Brothers' Vietnam War*, 44.

83. Ebert, *A Life in a Year*, 54–55.

84. Ibid., 54.

85. Interview of Gary Franklin by Jonathan Bernstein, November 1, 2001, Vietnam Archive Oral History Project, 2.

86. Telephone interview by the author with Novice Kniffen, August 11, 2005.

87. Telephone interview of David Crawley by Steve Maxner, February 27, 2001, Vietnam Archive Oral History Project, 15.

88. Jim Raysor interview in *South Dakotans in Vietnam*, 5.

89. Edwards, "Rifleman," 5.

90. Haywood T. "The Kid" Kirkland, "Recoilless Rifleman, 25th Infantry Division, 4th Infantry Division, U.S. Army, Duc Pho, May 1967–April 1968," in ibid., 86.

91. Ebert, *A Life in a Year*, 63.

92. Ibid., 59.

93. Interview of Gary Franklin by Jonathan Bernstein, November 1, 2001, Vietnam Archive Oral History Project, 3.

94. Interview of Robert Wrinn by Wayne Johnson, May 12, 19, 1989, University of Kentucky Oral History Program, Lexington, Kentucky, 8.

95. Lewis B. Puller Jr., *Fortunate Son: The Autobiography of Lewis B. Puller, Jr.* (New York: Bantam, 1991), 46.

96. Jim Raysor interview in *South Dakotans in Vietnam*, 5.

97. Interview of David Brown by Terry L. Birdwhistell and George Herring, Olive Hill, Kentucky, May 19, 1985, University of Kentucky Oral History Program, 2.

98. Candler, interview in Wilson, *Landing Zones*, 149.

99. Rick Atkinson, *The Long Gray Line* (New York: Owl Books, 1989), 129.

100. Ebert, *A Life in a Year*, 73. Another critique is provided in Joseph W. Callaway Jr., *Mekong First Light* (New York: Ballantine, 2004), 75.

101. Telephone interview of David Crawley by Steve Maxner, February 27, 2001, Vietnam Archive Oral History Project, 15.

102. Telephone interview of Michael Cisco by Mark Taylor, March 21, 1990, ibid., 9.

103. Andrew F. Krepinevich Jr., *The Army and Vietnam* (Baltimore: Johns Hopkins University Press, 1986), 5, 53–55.

104. David H. Hackworth, with Julie Sherman, *About Face: The Odyssey of an American Warrior* (New York: Touchstone, 1989), 623–24.

105. Ibid., 625–31.

106. Ibid., 775–76, 784.

107. For more on specialized training such as the SEALs, see Rad Miller Jr., *Whattaya Mean I Can't Kill 'Em* (New York: Ivy Books, 1998), 87–112.

Chapter 3

1. Philip Caputo, *A Rumor of War* (New York: Holt, 1996), xiv.

2. Lewis B. Puller Jr., *Fortunate Son: The Autobiography of Lewis B. Puller, Jr.* (New York: Bantam, 1991), 69.

3. Terry Topple interview in *South Dakotans in Vietnam: Excerpts From the South Dakota Vietnam Veterans Oral History Project, Pierre Area* (Pierre: State Publishing, 1986), 7.

4. James R. McDonough, *Platoon Leader: A Memoir of Command in Combat* (New York: Ballantine, 1985), 14.

5. Kathryn Fanning interview in Stanley W. Beesley, *Vietnam: The Heartland Remembers* (Norman: University of Oklahoma Press, 1987), 27–28.

6. Donna Moreau, *Waiting Wives: The Story of Schilling Manor, Home Front to the Vietnam War* (New York: Atria Books, 2005).

7. David Parks, *GI Diary* (Washington, DC: Howard University Press, 1984), 45.

8. Ibid., 47.

9. Ibid., 47–49.

10. Micki Voisard, "Civilian Flight Attendant," in Keith Walker, ed., *A Piece of My Heart: The Stories of 26 American Women Who Served in Vietnam* (San Francisco: Presidio Press, 1985), 241–42.

11. Interview of V. Dean Quillet by Terry L. Birdwhistell and George Herring, Louisville, Kentucky, March 18, 1985, University of Kentucky Oral History Program, University of Kentucky, Lexington, Kentucky, 5.

12. Franklin D. Miller, with Elwood J.C. Kureth, *Reflections of a Warrior: Six Years as a Green Beret in Vietnam* (New York: Pocket Books, 1991), 3.

13. John Ketwig, . . . *And a Hard Rain Fell: A GI's True Story of the War in Vietnam* (Naperville, IL: Sourcebooks, 2002), 8.

14. Robert Peterson, *Rites of Passage: Odyssey of a Grunt* (New York: Ballantine, 1997), 9.

15. Ches Schneider, *From Classrooms to Claymores: A Teacher at War in Vietnam* (New York: Ivy Books, 1999), 18.

16. Interview of Thomas Brown by Jonathan Bernstein, October 22, 2001, Vietnam Archive Oral History Project, Texas Tech University, Lubbock, Texas, 2–3.

17. Peterson, *Rites of Passage*, 9.

18. Gayle Smith, "The Nurse with Round Eyes," in Al Santoli, ed., *Everything We Had: An Oral History of the Vietnam War by Thirty-Three America Soldiers Who Fought It* (New York: Random, 1981), 142.

19. Letter from George Williams to his Mother, April 1967, in Bernard Edelman, ed., *Dear America: Letters Home From Vietnam* (New York: Norton, 1985), 105.

20. Schneider, *From Classrooms to Claymores*, 22.

21. Richard C. Ensminger, "Blowing Rock, North Carolina, Marine Forward Observer," in James R. Wilson, ed., *Landing Zones: Southern Veterans Remember Vietnam* (Durham, NC: Duke University Press, 1990), 25.

22. Miller, *Reflections of a Warrior*, 9.

23. The Vietnam Veterans Memorial, The Wall, "Names on the Wall," http://thewall-usa.com/names.asp, accessed September 7, 2006.

24. Dave Grossman, *On Killing: The Psychological Cost of Learning to Kill in War and Society* (New York: Back Bay Books, 1995), 268–70.

25. Charles C. Moskos Jr., *The American Enlisted Man: The Rank and File in Today's Military* (New York: Russell Sage, 1970), 161–62.

26. Letter from Richard E. Marks to his Mother, December 12, 1965, in Edelman, *Dear America*, 123.

27. Hiram D. Strickland to his parents, January 2006, in Bill Adler, ed., *Letters From Vietnam* (New York: Ballantine, 2003), 193.

28. Robert Tonsetic, *Warriors: An Infantryman's Memoir of Vietnam* (New York: Ballantine, 2004), x.

29. Allen Paul to Bev (unknown relation), May 8, 1968, in Edelman, *Dear America*, 48.

30. Ken Moorefield, "Company Commander and Aide-de-camp, 1st and 25th Infantry Divisions, III Corps, July 1969–July 1970," in Santoli, *To Bear Any Burden*, 191.

31. Michael Kimmel, *Manhood in America: A Cultural History* (New York: Free Press, 1996), 144.

32. Peterson, *Rites of Passage*, 3.

33. Ketwig, *. . . And a Hard Rain Fell*, 8.

34. Angel Qunitana in Harry Maurer, ed., *Strange Ground: An Oral History of Americans in Vietnam, 1945–1975* (New York: Da Capo Press, 1998), 175.

35. Jonathan Schell, *The Real War: The Classic Reporting on the Vietnam War* (New York: Pantheon, 1988), 230.

36. Reginald "Malik" Edwards, "Rifleman, 9th Regiment, U.S. Marine Corps, Danang, June 1965–March 1966," in Wallace Terry, ed., *Bloods: An Oral History of the Vietnam Veteran by Black Veterans* (New York: Random, 1984), 7–8.

37. James Simmen to Vern Simmen, undated letter, in Edelman, *Dear America*, 94.

38. Letter from George Olsen to Red (unknown person), August 31, 1969, in ibid., 118.

39. As cited in Andrew Kimbrell, *The Masculine Mystique: The Politics of Masculinity* (New York: Ballantine, 1995), 252.

40. Francis Whitebird interview in *South Dakotans in Vietnam*, 61.

41. Michael Sallah and Mitch Weiss, *Tiger Force: A True Story of Men and War* (New York: Little, Brown, 2006), 42–45.

42. Parks, *GI Diary*, 81.

43. Robert Santos, "My Men," in Santoli, *Everything We Had*, 111.

44. Grossman, *On Killing*, 141–76.

45. Parks, *GI Diary*, 75.

46. Adrian Gilbert, *Sniper: One-on-One* (London: Sigwick & Jackson, 1994), 137.

47. John J. Culbertson, *13 Cent Killers: The 5th Marine Snipers in Vietnam* (New York: Ballantine, 2003), 17.

48. Corporal Gary Heeter, 4th Battalion, 25th Infantry, in Donald L. Gilmore, with D.M. Giangreco, *Eyewitness Vietnam: Firsthand Accounts From Operation Rolling Thunder to the Fall of Saigon* (New York: Sterling, 2006), 55–56.

49. Tim O'Brien, "The Bouncing Betty Is Feared Most," in James W. Mooney and Thomas R. West, *Vietnam: A History and Anthology* (St. James, NY: Brandywine Press, 1994), 223.

50. Michael Clodfelter, *Mad Minutes and Vietnam Months: A Soldier's Memoir* (Jefferson, NC: McFarland, 1988), 4.

51. Puller, *Fortunate Son*, 115.

52. Tom Roubideaux interview in *South Dakotans in Vietnam*, 22–23.

53. Corporal Walter L. Sudol, 3d Platoon, Delta Company, 1st Battalion, 9th Marines, in Gilmore, *Eyewitness Vietnam*, 191.

54. Corporal Walter L. Sudol, 3d Platoon, Delta Company, 1st Battalion, 9th Marines, Retired, in ibid., 191–92.

55. One of the best books on the subject is Tom Mangold and John Penycate, *The Tunnels of Cu Cui* (New York: Berkley Books, 1985).

56. Sergeant Art Tejeda in Gilmore, *Eyewitness Vietnam*, 96–97.

57. Ibid., 97.

58. Ibid., 98.

59. James R. Ebert, *A Life in a Year: The American Infantryman in Vietnam, 1965–1972* (Novato, CA: Presidio Press, 1993), 1–2.

60. Kevin Macauly to his parents, January 29, 1968, in Edelman, *Dear America*, 80.

61. John A. Fosland to Carol Jackson, July 18, 1969, in Adler, *Letters From Vietnam*, 205–6.

62. Angel Quintana in Maurer, *Strange Ground,* 171.

63. Clodfelter, *Mad Minutes and Vietnam*, 3–4.

64. Caputo, *A Rumor of War*, xiv.

65. Captain Edward Allen Boardman, March 7, 1968, in Adler, *Letters From Vietnam*, 122.

66. Frederick Downs Jr. to Linda Downs, November 5, 1967, in Edelman, ed., *Dear America,* 60.

67. Jim Pew interview in *South Dakotans in Vietnam*, 45.

68. Richard Loffler, April 15, 967, in Edelman, *Dear America,* 156. A very good example of the REMF attitudes includes George M. Watson Jr., *Voices From the Rear: Vietnam, 1969–1970* (New York: Xlibris, 2001), and a novel by David A. Willson, *REMF Diary* (Seattle: Black Heron Press, 1988).

69. Tom Magedanz interview in *South Dakotans in Vietnam*, 12.

70. Parks, *GI Diary*, 104.

71. Tonsetic, *Warriors*, 129.

72. Dennis Deal, "Man, If We're Up Against This, It's Gonna Be a Long-Ass Year," in Christian G. Appy, *Patriots: The Vietnam War Remembered From All Sides* (New York: Penguin, 2003), 130, 135. For more on the battle, see Lt. Gen. Harold G. Moore and Joseph L. Galloway, *We Were Soldiers Once . . . and Young: Ia Drang, the Battle That Changed the War in Vietnam* (New York: Ballantine, 1992).

73. Interview of Neil Couch by Ron Frankum, June 16, 2000, Vietnam Archive Oral History Project, 30.

74. Telephone interview of Michael Cisco by Mark Taylor, March 21, 1990, ibid., 9.

75. Ken Korkow interview in *South Dakotans in Vietnam*, 27.

76. Interview of Paul Morgan by Sandra Gray Thacker, Lexington, Kentucky, July 12, 1990, University of Kentucky Oral History Program, 2.

77. Harry Behret in Maurer, *Strange Ground*, 181.

78. Sergeant C.W. Bowen, 4th Battalion, 9th Infantry Regiment, 25th Infantry Division, in Gilmore, *Eyewitness Vietnam*, 43.

79. Lance Corporal Gary Conner in Otto J. Lehrack, ed., *No Shining Armor: The Marines at War in Vietnam* (Lawrence: University Press of Kansas, 1992), 201.

80. Colonel Chester B. McCoid II to his wife, Dorothy, August 12, 1966, in Adler, *Letters From Vietnam*, 103.

81. Stanley Karnow, *Vietnam: A History* (New York: Penguin, 1983), 260.

82. Ibid., 262.

83. Neil Sheehan, *A Bright Shining Lie: John Paul Vann and America in Vietnam* (New York: Random, 1988), 265.

84. Ibid., 270–386.

85. Telephone interview of Michael Cisco by Mark Taylor, March 21, 1990, Vietnam Archive Oral History Project, 4–5.

86. Bobby Muller interview in Kim Willenson, ed., *The Bad War: An Oral History of the Vietnam War* (New York: NAL Books, 1987), 112.

87. Bernard Trainor, "It Turned Out the Mayor of Danang Was a Double Agent," in Appy, *Patriots*, 4.

88. Puller, *Fortunate Son*, 153.

89. Thomas Bird, "Ia Drang," in Santoli, *Everything We Had*, 43.

90. Loren Baritz, *Backfire: A History of How American Culture Led Us to Vietnam and Made Us Fight the War We Did* (Baltimore: Johns Hopkins University Press, 1998), 23; Charles J. Levy, "ARVN as Faggots: Inverted Warfare in Vietnam," *Transaction* (October 1971): 18–27.

91. Dennis Greenbaum in Maurer, *Strange Ground*, 269.

92. Frank McCarthy in Santoli, *To Bear Any Burden*, 108–9. Other positive views are related in Kregg P.J. Joregenson, *Acceptable Loss* (New York: Ballantine, 1991), 101–3.

93. For the best study of the many problems encountered in trying to create an effective fighting force among the South Vietnamese, see Robert K. Brigham, *ARVN: Life and Death in the South Vietnamese Army* (Lawrence: University Press of Kansas, 2006). Another interesting read is Andrew Wiest, *Vietnam's Forgotten Army: Heroism and Betrayal in the ARVN* (New York: New York University Press, 2007).

94. Timothy L. Cochran, "Forgotten Allies: The Republic of Korea's Involvement in South Vietnam, 1964–1965," MA thesis, Arizona State University, 2004.

95. Telephone interview of Michael Cisco by Mark Taylor, March 21, 1990, Vietnam Archive Oral History Project, 6.

96. Ediberto Rodriguez, "Ace of Spades," in Charley Trujillo, ed., *Soldados: Chicanos in Viet Nam* (San Jose: Chusma House, 1990), 55.

97. Yoshia Chee in Maurer, *Strange Ground*, 356.

98. Bob Moran interview in *South Dakotans in Vietnam*, 51.

99. Puller, *Fortunate Son*, 181.

100. Ronald Bruce Frankum Jr., *The United States and Australia in Vietnam, 1954–1968* (Lewiston, NY: Edwin Mellen Press, 2001), 229–79. For the decisions of the New Zealanders to be "dovish hawks," see Roberto Rabel, *New Zealand and the Vietnam War: Politics and Diplomacy* (Auckland, New Zealand: Auckland University Press, 2005).

101. Scott Brodie, *Titling at Dominoes: Australia and the Vietnam War* (Brookvale, Australia: Child and Associates, 1987), 38–57.

102. David H. Hackworth, with Julie Sherman, *About Face: The Odyssey of an American Warrior* (New York: Touchstone, 1989), 495.

103. Gordon L. Steinbrook, *Allies & Mates: An American Soldier With the Australians and New Zealanders in Vietnam, 1966–67* (Lincoln: University of Nebraska Press, 1995), 35, 50, 61.

104. John Dabonka to his parents, December 23, 1966, in Edelman, *Dear America*, 54.

105. Tom Magedanz interview in *South Dakotans in Vietnam*, 47.

106. Letter from Bruce McInnes to his mother, July 20, 1969, in Edelman, *Dear America*, 111.

107. Marion Lee Kempner to Marion Levy, August 12, 1966, in ibid., 113–14.

108. Bobby Muller interview in Willenson, *The Bad War*, 111–12.

109. Bird, "Ia Drang," 43.

110. Leroy TeCube, *Year in Nam: A Native American Soldier's Story* (Lincoln: University of Nebraska Press, 1999), xii.

111. Charlie B. Dickey to his wife, August 22, 1969, in Adler, *Letters From Vietnam*, 83.

112. Colonel Chester B. McCoid II to his wife, Dorothy, August 12, 1966, in ibid., 104.

113. Frederick Downs to his wife, November 5, 1967, in Edelman, *Dear America*, 60.

114. Larry Holguin, "Marine," in Trujillo, *Soldados*, 80.

115. Sharon A. Lane to her parents, June 4, 1969, in Edelman, *Dear America*, 285.

116. John Talbott in Maurer, *Strange Ground*, 275.

117. Tom Magedanz interview in *South Dakotans in Vietnam*, 15.

118. "Gilberto, U.S. Army-Corporal E4, 11th Armored Division, August 1966–January 1967," in Lea Ybarra, ed., *Vietnam Veteranos: Chicanos Recall the War* (Austin: University of Texas Press, 2004), 19–20.

119. Interview of Robert Wrinn by Wayne Johnson, May 12, 19, 1989, University of Kentucky Oral History Program, Lexington, Kentucky, 11.

120. Peterson, *Rites of Passage*, 324.

121. Ray Sarlin, "100% Alert and Then Some," Vietnam War Stories–1st Battalion, 50th Infantry Web site, www.ichiban1.0rg/html/stories/story_38.htm, accessed June 29, 2006.

122. "My Experience as Grunt Medic," 1st Cav Medic (Airmobile) Web site, www.1stcavmedic.com/experiences.html, accessed June 29, 2006.

123. Peterson, *Rites of Passage*, 324.

124. Tom Magedanz interview in *South Dakotans in Vietnam*, 15.

125. Interview of Gary Franklin by Jonathan Bernstein, November 1, 2001, Vietnam Archive Oral History Project, 6.

126. McDonough, *Platoon Leader*, 179.

127. Willie Booth in Maurer, *Strange Ground*, 213–14.

128. Martin J. Dockery, *Lost in Translation: Vietnam, a Combat Advisor's Story* (New York: Ballantine, 2003), 163.

129. Tonsetic, *Warriors*, 129.

130. Ibid., 136.

131. Eddie "Coyote" Rodriguez, "Teenage Soldier," in Trujillo, *Soldados*, 5.

132. Jim Robbennolt interview in *South Dakotans in Vietnam*, 49.

133. Pat Murphy interview in ibid., 48.

134. Steinbrook, *Allies & Mates*, 71.

135. James Simmen to Vern Simmen, May 10, 1968, in Edelman, *Dear America*, 178. Also for another on R&R in Japan, see Peterson, *Rites of Passage*, 344–49.

136. James Simmen to Vern Simmen, March 13, 1968, in Edelman, *Dear America*, 94.

137. Jim Simmen to Vern Simmen, undated letter, 1968, in ibid., 247.

138. William J. Brinker, "Seawillow Chambers: Soldier's Wife," in David L. Anderson, *The Human Tradition in the Vietnam Era* (Wilmington: Scholarly Resources, 2000), 106.

139. Walter Mack in Maurer, *Strange Ground*, 170.

140. Rick Atkinson, *The Long Gray Line: The American Journey of West Point's Class of 1966* (New York: Holt, 1999), 307.

141. Ted A. Burton, "Poor Valley Community, Hawkins County, Tennessee, Army Medic," in Wilson, *Landing Zones*, 72.

142. David Forrest to Lynne Forrest (his wife), January 29, 1969, in Edelman, *Dear America*, 236.

143. Names on the Wall section, Vietnam Veterans Memorial, The Wall-USA, http://thewall-usa.com, accessed August 17, 2006.

144. Phone interview of Gary Smith by Stephen Maxner, December 4, 2003, Vietnam Archive Oral History Project, 76.

145. Larry Gates interview in *South Dakotans in Vietnam*, 63.

146. Micki Voisard, "Civilian Airline Flight Attendant," in Walker, *A Piece of My Heart*, 233–34. For another view, see Charles Gadd, *Line Doggie: Foot Soldier in Vietnam* (Novato, CA: Presidio Press, 1987), 184–87.

Chapter 4

1. Larry Gates interview in *South Dakotans in Vietnam: Excerpts From the South Dakota Vietnam Veterans Oral History Project, Pierre Area* (Pierre: State Publishing, 1986), 8.

2. Army Officer (1969–1970), in William J. Brinker, ed., *A Time for Looking Back: Putnam County Veterans, Their Families, and the Vietnam War* (Cookeville: Tennessee Technological University, 1990), 59.

3. Don Oberdorfer, *Tet! The Turning Point in the Vietnam War* (Baltimore: Johns Hopkins University Press, 2001); Keith Nolan, *Battle for Saigon: Tet 1968* (San Francisco: Presidio Press, 2002); James R. Arnold, *Tet Offensive 1968: Turning Point in Vietnam* (Westport, CT: Praeger, 2004).

4. Edward F. Murphy, *Semper Fi Vietnam: From Da Nang to the DMZ Marine Corps Campaigns, 1965–1975* (San Francisco: Presidio Press, 1997), 149–69; Gordon Rottman, *Khe Sanh, 1967–1968: Marines Battle for Vietnam's Vital Hilltop Base* (New York: Osprey, 2005); Ronald J. Drez and Douglas Brinkley, *Voices of Courage: The Battle of Khe Sanh, Vietnam* (New York: Bulfinch, 2005); John Corbett, *West Dickens Avenue: A Marine at Khe Sanh* (New York: Ballantine, 2003).

5. Ken Korkow interview in *South Dakotans in Vietnam*, 26.

6. Ibid., 27.

7. *Arizona Republic*, July 3, 2005.

8. William U. Tant, "Memphis, Tennessee, Marine rifleman, 1967–69," in James R. Wilson, ed., *Landing Zones: Southern Veterans Remember Vietnam* (Durham, NC: Duke University Press, 1990), 125.

9. Lewis Sorley, *A Better War: The Unexamined Victories and Final Tragedy of America's Last Years in Vietnam* (New York: Harvest Books, 1999), 155.

10. William J. Duiker, *Sacred War: Nationalism and Revolution in a Divided Vietnam* (New York: McGraw-Hill, 1995), 208–18.

11. As cited in Murphy, *Semper Fi Vietnam*, 148.

12. Walter LaFeber, *The Deadly Bet: LBJ, Vietnam, and the 1968 Election* (New York: Rowman and Littlefield, 2005), 22.

13. Charles E. Neu, *America's Lost War Vietnam: 1945–1975* (Wheeling, IL: Harlan-Davidson, 2005), 134.

14. Harry Spiller, *Death Angel: A Vietnam Memoir of a Bearer of Death Messages to Families* (Jefferson, NC: McFarland, 1992), 164–66.

15. Ibid., 166–67.

16. Ibid., 167–68.

17. Ibid., 168–72.

18. Ibid.

19. Pauline Laurent, *Grief Denied: A Vietnam Widow's Story* (Santa Rosa, CA: Catalyst for Change, 1999), 9–10.

20. Ibid., 11–12.

21. Ibid., 37–38.

22. Ibid., 38–39.

23. Ellen Dale in Barthy Byrd, ed., *Home Front: Women and Vietnam* (Berkeley: Shameless Hussy Press, 1986), 16.

24. Humberto Rosario in Norman E. Berg, ed., *Regret to Inform You: Experiences of Families Who Lost a Family Member in Vietnam* (Central Point, OR: Hellgate Press, 1999), 131.

25. Ibid., 132–34.

26. Edward F. Murphy, *Vietnam Medals of Honor Heroes*, expanded and revised edition (New York: Ballantine, 2005), xi–7.

27. Murphy, *Vietnam Medals of Honor Heroes*, 70–71.

28. Ibid., 71–72.

29. Bob Kerrey, *When I Was a Young Man: A Memoir* (New York: Harvest Books, 2002), 186–87.

30. Ibid., 187–89.

31. Ibid., 190–236.

32. Ibid., 243.

33. Ibid., 252–57; Murphy, *Vietnam Medals of Honor Heroes*, 197.

34. Franklin D. Miller, with Elwood J.C. Kureth, *Reflections of a Warrior: Six Years as a Green Beret in Vietnam* (New York: Pocket Books, 2003), 189–90.

35. Ibid., 194–96.

36. Ibid., 197–99.

37. Ibid., 199–203.

38. Ibid., 204–5.

39. Ibid., 226–29.

40. Ibid., 233–40. He died after a bout with cancer in 2000. *New York Times,* July 17, 2000.

41. Melvin Small, *Antiwarriors: The Vietnam War and the Battle for America's Hearts and Minds* (Wilmington, DE: Scholarly Resources, 2002), 57–60.

42. Herman Graham III, *The Brothers' Vietnam War: Black Power, Manhood, and the Military Experience* (Gainesville: University of Florida Press, 2003), 21.

43. Paul Hathaway, "The Problem Is Back Home," *Washington Evening Star*, May 7, 1968.

44. Wayne Smith, "I Was Thanking God They Didn't Have Air Support," in Christian G. Appy, *Patriots: The Vietnam War Remembered From All Sides* (New York: Penguin, 2003), 363.

45. Interview of Larry Burke by Steve Maxner, April 21, 2001, Vietnam Archive Oral History Project, Texas Tech University, Lubbock, Texas, 21.

46. Ronald H. Spector, *After Tet: The Bloodiest Year in Vietnam* (New York: Vintage, 1993), 259.

47. Smith, "I Was Thanking God," 363.

48. Ibid., 363.

49. Ibid., 363.

50. James E. Westheider, *Fighting on Two Fronts: African Americans and the Vietnam War* (New York: New York University Press, 1997), 5.

51. Smith, "I Was Thanking God," 363.

52. Woody Wanamaker in Harry Maurer, ed., *Strange Ground: An Oral History of Americans in Vietnam, 1945–1975* (New York: Da Capo Press, 1998), 245.

53. Lorena Oropeza, *¡Raza Sí, ¡Guerra No! Chicano Protest and Patriotism During the Vietnam War Era* (Berkeley: University of California Press, 2005).

54. Charley Trujillo, "It Sure as Hell Wasn't 'English Only' in Vietnam," in Appy, *Patriots*, 367.

55. Luis Martinez, "A Puerto Rican Marine," in Al Santoli, ed., *Everything We Had: An Oral History of the Vietnam War by Thirty-Three America Soldiers Who Fought It* (New York: Random, 1981), 160.

56. "Charley, U.S. Army—Sergeant E5, Infantry/Squad Leader, First of the Forty-sixth, 196 Light Infantry Brigade, Americal Division, Base of Operations: Chu Lai, Vietnam: January 1970–July 1970," in Lea Ybarra, ed., *Vietnam Veteranos: Chicanos Recall the War* (Austin: University of Texas Press, 2004), 97.

57. "Tony, U.S. Army—Specialist E-4, Microwave Radio Equipment Operator, 442nd Signal Battalion, 114th Signal Detachment, Base of Operations: Quinon, Vietnam: April 1968–April 1969," in ibid., 51.

58. As cited in Tom Holm, *Strong Hearts, Wounded Souls: Native American Veterans of the Vietnam War* (Austin: University of Texas Press, 1996), 129.

59. Tom Roubideaux interview in *South Dakotans in Vietnam*, 61.

60. Ray Leanna interview in ibid., 61.

61. Vincent Okamoto, "Damn, I'm a Gook," in Appy, *Patriot*, 358.

62. Ernest Fujimura, email to the author, November 8, 2006.

63. Yoshia Chee in Maurer, *Strange Ground*, 352–53.

64. Donald L. Gilmore, with D.M. Giangreco, *Eyewitness Vietnam: Firsthand Accounts From Operation Rolling Thunder to the Fall of Saigon* (New York: Sterling, 2006), 154.

65. Jay Dee Ruybal, *The Drug Hazed War in Indochina* (New York: Creative Designs, 1998); Morris D. Stanton, "Drugs, Vietnam, and the Vietnam Veteran," *American Journal of Drug and Alcohol Abuse* (March 1976); Clinton R. Sanders, "Dopers Wonderland," *Journal of Drug Issues* (Winter 1973).

66. Loren Baritz, *Backfire: A History of How American Culture Led Us to Vietnam and Made Us Fight the Way We Did* (Baltimore: Johns Hopkins University Press, 1998), 315.

67. William Thomas Allison, *Military Justice in Vietnam: The Rule of Law in an American War* (Lawrence: University Press of Kansas, 2007), 122. Allison also includes numerous charts on reported drug use in the chapter on drugs and prosecution in Vietnam.

68. Bob Moran interview in *South Dakotans in Vietnam*, 55.

69. Ibid., 55.

70. "Obed, U.S. Army Medical Corpsman, Seventh/Eighth Artillery, Headquarters Battery, Base of Operations: Bien Hoa, May 1970–July 1971," in Ybarra, *Vietnam Veteranos*, 97.

71. Richard C. Ensminger, "Blowing Rock, North Carolina, Marine Forward Observer," in Wilson, *Landing Zones*, 29.

72. Juan Ramirez, *A Patriot After All: The Story of a Chicano Vet* (Albuquerque: University of New Mexico Press, 1999), 73.

73. Rodney R. Chastant to Rod Chastant, September 10, 1967, in Bernard Edelman, ed., *Dear America: Letters Home From Vietnam* (New York: Norton, 1985), 209–10.

74. Norman Summers, "A Sense of Duty," in Stanley W. Beesley, *Vietnam: The Heartland Remembers* (Norman: University of Oklahoma Press, 1987), 14.

75. Robert Tonsetic, *Warriors: An Infantryman's Memoir of Vietnam* (New York: Ballantine, 2004), 132.

76. Christian Appy, *Working Class War: American Combat Soldiers and Vietnam* (Chapel Hill: University of North Carolina Press, 1993), 43.

77. Colonel Chester B. McCoid II to his wife, Dorothy, August 21, 1966, in Bill Adler, ed., *Letters From Vietnam* (New York: Ballantine, 2003), 101.

78. Bruce Lawlor, "The Missing Ingredients," in Santoli, *Everything We Had*, 176.

79. Baritz, *Backfire*, 303.

80. Thomas Bird, "Ia Drang," in Santoli, *Everything We Had*, 43.

81. Ken Moorefield, "Company Commander and Aide-de-camp, 1st and 25th Infantry Divisions, III Corps, July 1969–July 1970," in ibid., 192.

82. Bernard Trainor, "It Turned Out the Mayor of Danang Was a Double Agent," in Appy, *Patriots*, 6.

83. Trujillo, "It Sure as Hell Wasn't 'English Only' in Vietnam," 369.

84. John S. Candler Jr., "Atlanta, Georgia, Army Platoon Leader, 1968–1969," in Wilson, *Landing Zones*, 151.

85. Baritz, *Backfire*, 315.

86. Jeff Bussiere in Otto J. Lehrack, ed., *No Shining Armor: The Marines at War in Vietnam* (Lawrence: University Press of Kansas, 1992), 326.

87. Woody Wanamaker in Maurer, *Strange Ground*, 243.

88. Ibid.

89. Ibid., 244–45.

90. Ibid., 244–48.

91. Bobby Muller interview in Kim Willenson, ed., *The Bad War: An Oral History of the Vietnam War* (New York: NAL Books, 1987), 153.

92. Ted A. Burton, "Poor Valley Community, Hawkins County, Tennessee, Army medic," in Wilson, *Landing Zones*, 77. While the majority condemned Fonda, not everyone agreed. One Mississippi veteran, a Purple Heart winner who lost a leg in combat, acknowledged, "I don't know that much about Jane Fonda, but I can understand her reasoning behind what she did. I really don't think she did that much. . . . But I think she was more or less trying to find an end to the war. She don't bother me. If that's what she believed in, fine." George D. Riels, "Sunrise Community, Forrest County, Mississippi, Marine rifleman, 1967–68," in Wilson, *Landing Zone*, 116.

93. Don Trimble interview in *South Dakotans in Vietnam*, 70.

94. Bill McCloud to his mother, September 23, 1968, in Adler, *Letters From Vietnam*, 202.

95. Tom Magedanz interview in *South Dakotans in Vietnam*, 58.

96. Joseph Morrissey to Paul Morrissey, October 1969, in Edelman, *Dear America*, 223.

97. Charles F. Hawkins, "Friendly Fire: Facts, Myths and Misperceptions," *U.S. Naval Institute Proceedings* (June 1994): 54–59; Kenneth K. Steinweg," Dealing Realistically with Fratricide," *Parameters* (Spring 1995): 4–29. Others estimate that the figure is much lower, around 2 percent; see, for example, Charles R. Shrader, *Amicicide: The Problems of Friendly Fire in Modern War*, U.S. Army Command and General Staff College Combat Studies Institute Research Study no. 1 (Washington, DC: U.S. Government Printing Office, December 1982).

98. Robert Ransom Jr. to his mother and father, April 3, 1968, in Edelman, *Dear America*, 48.

99. Ensminger, "Blowing Rock, North Carolina," 31.

100. Robert Peterson, *Rites of Passage: Odyssey of a Grunt* (New York: Ballantine, 1997), 526–28. For another example and the psychological damage done to people involved, see James D. Johnson, *Combat Chaplain: A Thirty-Year Vietnam Battle* (Denton: University of North Texas Press, 2001), 182–85.

101. C.D.B. Bryan, *Friendly Fire* (New York: G.P. Putnam's Sons, 1976), 102.

102. Ibid., 129.

103. Peg Mullen, *Unfriendly Fire: A Mother's Memoir* (Iowa City: University of Iowa Press, 1995), 72–78.

104. Ibid., 123–38.

105. *Waterloo-Cedar Falls Courier*, August 18, 2005.

106. David Cortright, *Soldiers in Revolt: GI Resistance During the Vietnam War* (Chicago: Haymarket Books, 1975).

107. *Los Angeles Times,* July 23, 1966.

108. As cited in George Mariscal, ed., *Aztlán and Viet Nam: Chicano and Chicana Experiences of War* (Berkeley: University of California Press, 1999), 29. Another good example of the conflict between family over Vietnam and military service can be found in John Douglas Marshall, *Reconciliation Road: A Family Odyssey of War and Honor* (Syracuse, NY: Syracuse University Press, 1993).

109. Lawrence M. Baskir and William Strauss, *Chance and Circumstance: The Draft, the War, and the Vietnam Generation* (New York: Knopf, 1978), 112–13.

110. G. David Curry, *Sunshine Patriots: Punishment and the Vietnam Offender* (Notre Dame, IN: University of Notre Dame Press, 1985), x–xii.

111. Dick Perrin, with Tim McCarthy, *GI Resister: The Story of How One American Soldier and His Family Fought the War in Vietnam* (Victoria, British Colombia: Trafford Press, 2001), 42.

112. Ibid., 35–59.

113. Ibid., 67–116.

114. Ibid., 140–67.

115. Baskir and Strauss, *Chance and Circumstance*, 111.

116. Riels, "Sunrise Community, Forrest County, Mississippi," 116.

117. Candler, "Atlanta, Georgia, Army Platoon leader," 155.

118. Lieutenant William L. Hauser, *America's Army in Crisis: A Study in Civil-Military Relations* (Baltimore: Johns Hopkins University Press, 1973), 99–104.

119. Stephen E. Ambrose, "Atrocities in Historical Perspective," in David L. Anderson, *Facing My Lai: Moving Beyond the Massacre* (Lawrence: University Press of Kansas, 1998), 107–20.

120. George R. Bassett to Veronica and George E. Bassett, March 28, 1966, in Adler, *Letters From Vietnam*, 28.

121. As cited in Andrew Kimbrell, *The Masculine Mystique: The Politics of Masculinity* (New York: Ballantine, 1995), 251. One Army lieutenant told a Yale professor that "if it run, it's VC; waste it. If it hides, it's VC; waste it. If it's dead, it's VC; count it and wait for your promotion." As cited in Douglas Brinkley, *Tour of Duty: John Kerry and the Vietnam War* (New York: William Morrow, 2004), 48.

122. Jonathan Schell, *The Real War: The Classic Reporting on the Vietnam War* (New York: Pantheon, 1988), 197–99.

123. Tom Roubideaux interview in *South Dakotans in Vietnam*, 51.

124. As cited in Gilmore, *Eyewitness Vietnam*, 220.

125. *New York Times,* December 28, 2003.

126. The most comprehensive examination of the massacre is found in Michael Bilton and Kevin Sim, *Four Hours at My Lai* (New York: Penguin, 1992).

127. James S. Olson and Randy Roberts, *My Lai: A Brief History With Documents* (Boston: Bedford Books, 1998), 2.

128. Ibid., 3.

129. William R. Peers, *The My Lai Inquiry* (New York: Norton, 1979); Joseph Goldstein, Burke Marshall, Jack Schwartz, *The My Lai Massacre and Its Cover-up: Beyond the Reach of Law? The Peers Commission Report* (New York: Free Press, 1976).

130. Seymour Hersh, *My Lai 4: A Report on the Massacre and Its Aftermath* (New York: Random, 1970).

131. Walter Mack in Maurer, *Strange Ground*, 171.

132. B.G. Burkett and Glenna Whitley, *Stolen Valor: How the Vietnam Generation Was Robbed of Its Heroes and Its History* (Dallas: Verity Press, 1998), 117.

133. Michael Sallah and Mitch Weiss, *Tiger Force: A True Story of Men and War* (New York: Little, Brown, 2006); Gary D. Solis, *Son Thang: An American War Crime* (Annapolis: Naval Institute Press, 1997); Gerald Nicosia, *Home to War: A History of the Vietnam Veterans' Movement* (New York: Carroll and Graf, 2001), 79–93.

134. Colonel Robert D. Heinl Jr., "The Collapse of the Armed Forces," in Marvin Gettleman, Jane Franklin, Marilyn Young, and H. Bruce Franklin, eds., *Vietnam and America: A Documented History* (New York: Grove Weidenfeld, 1985), 323–25.

135. Ibid., 325–31.

136. Hauser, *America's Army in Crisis*, 3–4.

137. Ibid., 201.

138. Tonsetic, *Warriors*, 190.

139. John Leppelman, *Blood on the Risers: An Airborne Soldier's Thirty-Five Months in Vietnam* (New York: Ballentine, 1991), 335.

Chapter 5

1. Loren Baritz, *Backfire: A History of How American Culture Led Us to Vietnam and Made Us Fight the Way We Did* (Baltimore: Johns Hopkins University Press, 1998), 319–20.

2. George Herring, *America's Longest War: The United States and Vietnam, 1950–1975*, 4th edition (New York: McGraw-Hill, 2002), 347.

3. James D. Seddon, *Morning Glories Among the Peas: A Vietnam Veteran's Story* (Ames: Iowa State University Press, 1990), 3.

4. Ibid., 3–4.

5. Mike Soliz, "The Military Shaft," in Charley Trujillo, ed., *Soldados: Chicanos in Viet Nam* (San Jose: Chusma House, 1990), 99.

6. Eddie "Coyote" Rodriguez, "Teenage Soldier," in ibid., 8.

7. "Leonel, U.S. Army—U.S. Army—First Lieutenant, Company Commander, Charlie Company, Second Battalion, 505 Infantry, Base of Operations: Phu Bai/Bien Hoa/Cambodia, Vietnam, 1968," in Lea Ybarra, ed., *Vietnam Veteranos: Chicanos Recall the War* (Austin: University of Texas Press, 2004), 97.

8. Jerry Lembcke, *The Spitting Image: Myth, Memory, and the Legacy of Vietnam* (New York: New York University Press, 1998), 71–83.

9. George S. Patton III interview in Kim Willenson, ed., *The Bad War: An Oral History of the Vietnam War* (New York: NAL Books, 1987), 264.

10. Terry Topple interview in *South Dakotans in Vietnam: Excerpts From the South Dakota Vietnam Veterans Oral History Project, Pierre Area* (Pierre: State Publishing, 1986), 64.

11. Frederick Downs, *The Killing Zone: My Life in the Vietnam War* (New York: Norton, 1978), 10.

12. Pat Murphy interview in *South Dakotans in Vietnam*, 64.

13. George D. Riels, "Sunrise Community, Forrest County, Mississippi, Marine rifleman, 1967–68," in James R. Wilson, ed., *Landing Zones: Southern Veterans Remember Vietnam* (Durham, NC: Duke University Press, 1990), 115.

14. William Jayne, "Immigrants From the Combat Zone," in A.D. Horne, ed., *The*

Wounded Generation: America After Vietnam (Englewood Cliffs, NJ: Prentice Hall, 1981), 161.

15. Nilo Reber interview in *South Dakotans in Vietnam*, 66.

16. Wayne Smith, "I Was Thanking God They Didn't Have Air Support," in Christian G. Appy, *Patriots: The Vietnam War Remembered From All Sides* (New York: Penguin, 2003), 366.

17. Adolphus Stuart, "Scout, Special Landing Force Alpha, 1st Battalion, 3rd Marines, I Corps, April 1967–March 1968," in Al Santoli, ed., *To Bear Any Burden: The Vietnam War and Its Aftermath in the Words of Americans and Southeast Asians* (Bloomington: Indiana University Press, 1999), 207.

18. Interview of David Shelly by Stephen Maxner, April 18, 2000, Vietnam Archive Oral History Project, Texas Tech University, Lubbock, Texas, 30.

19. Tim O'Brien, novelist, "Biography," www.illyria.com/tobhp.html, accessed May 28, 2005.

20. Bobby Muller interview in Willenson, *The Bad War*, 372.

21. Admiral Elmo Zumwalt Jr., and Lieutenant Elmo Zumwalt III, with John Pekkanen, *My Father, My Son* (New York: Macmillan, 1986), 126.

22. As cited in Myra MacPherson, *Long Time Passing: Vietnam and the Haunted Generation*, new edition (Bloomington: Indiana University Press, 2001), 15.

23. Ches Schneider, *From Classrooms to Claymores: A Teacher at War in Vietnam* (New York: Ivy Books, 1999), 1–3.

24. Telephone interview by the author with Novice Kniffen, August 11, 2005.

25. William J. Brinker, "Nancy Randolph: Army Nurse," in David L. Anderson, *The Human Tradition in the Vietnam Era* (Wilmington, DE: Scholarly Resources, 2000), 117.

26. Don Trimble interview in *South Dakotans in Vietnam*, 67.

27. Brinker, "Nancy Randolph: Army Nurse," 116.

28. Senator (then Lieutenant) Max Cleland, 1st Cavalry Division (Airmobile) in Donald L. Gilmore, with D.M. Giancreco, *Eyewitness Vietnam: Firsthand Accounts From Operation Rolling Thunder to the Fall of Saigon* (New York: Sterling Publishing, 2006), 163.

29. Max Cleland, *Strong at the Broken Places: A Personal Story* (Atlanta: Cherokee Publishing Company, 1986), 49–50.

30. Ibid.

31. Ibid., 77.

32. Ibid., 65–66.

33. Ibid., 82–84.

34. Ibid., 90–96.

35. Ibid., 110–13.

36. Ibid., 157.

37. Rudolph Bridges, "Black Marine," in Stanley W. Beesley, *Vietnam: The Heartland Remembers* (Norman: University of Oklahoma Press, 1987), 15.

38. Sergeant Major Edgar A. Huff, "Sergeant Major, 1st Military Police Battalion, May 1967–July 1968, III Marine Amphibious Force October 1970–April 1971, U.S. Marine Corps, Danang," in Wallace Terry, ed., *Bloods: An Oral History of the Vietnam War* (New York: Random, 1984), 147–48.

39. David L. Anderson, "Bill Henry Terry Jr., Killed in Action," in Anderson, *The Human Tradition in the Vietnam Era*, 139.

40. Ibid., 138–40.

41. Francis Whitebird interview in *South Dakotans in Vietnam*, 71.

42. For more on survivor's guilt, see Johnnie M. Clark, *Gun's Up!* (New York: Ballantine, 1984), 320; Jayne, "Immigrants From the Combat Zone," 162; "Tony, U.S.

Army—Specialist E-4, Microwave Radio Equipment Operator, 442nd Signal Battalion, 114th Signal Detachment, Base of Operations: Quinon, Vietnam: April 1968–April 1969," in Ybarra, *Vietnam Veteranos*, 97.

43. Gerald Nicosia, *Home to War: A History of the Vietnam Veterans' Movement* (New York: Carroll and Graf, 2001), 15–55.

44. Melvin Small, *Antiwarriors: The Vietnam War and the Battle for America's Hearts and Minds* (Wilmington, DE: Scholarly Resources, 2002), 139–43.

45. Ibid., 150–51.

46. Nicosia, *Home to War,* 217.

47. Douglas Brinkley, *Tour of Duty: John Kerry and the Vietnam War* (New York: William Morrow, 2004), 53–62.

48. Michael Kranish, Brian C. Mooney, and Nina Easton, *John F. Kerry: The Complete Biography of the Boston Globe Reporters Who Know Him Best* (New York: PublicAffairs, 2004), 71–109.

49. Ibid., 109.

50. Ibid., 110–23.

51. John Kerry, "How Do You Ask a Man to Be the Last Man to Die in Vietnam?" Statements made before the Senate Foreign Relations Committee, April 23, 1971, History News Network, http://hnn.us/articles/3631.html, accessed August 21, 2007.

52. Kranish, Mooney, and Easton, *John F. Kerry*, 130–36.

53. Vietnam Veterans of America, "Who We Are," www.vva.org/who.html, accessed September 24, 2007.

54. *New York Times*, May 28, 1984. The VVLP came to my attention through Charlotte Cahill's paper, "'Surely Vietnam Veterans Were Men': Public Policy and Masculinity in Reagan's America," paper presented at the Society for Historians of American Foreign Relations, Reston, Virginia, June 2007.

55. Ibid., 5.

56. James Webb, "What the Vietnam Vet Needs," *Soldier of Fortune* (May 1980): 52–53.

57. For more on the movies and other forms of popular culture related to the Vietnam War, see Milton J. Bates, *The Wars We Took to Vietnam: Cultural Conflict and Storytelling* (Berkeley: University of California Press, 1996); Jim Neilson, *Warring Factions: Cultural Politics and the Vietnam War Narrative* (Oxford: University Press of Mississippi, 1998); Jeremy M. Devine, *Vietnam at 24 Frames a Second* (Austin: University of Texas Press, 1995); Michael Anderegg, ed., *Inventing Vietnam: The War in Film and Television* (Philadelphia: Temple University Press, 1991); Katherine Kinney, *Friendly Fire: American Images of the Vietnam War* (New York: Oxford University Press, 2000); H. Bruce Franklin, *Vietnam and Other American Fantasies* (Amherst: University of Massachusetts Press, 2000); Linda Dittmar and Gene Michaud, eds., *From Hanoi to Hollywood: The Vietnam War in American Film* (New Brunswick, NJ: Rutgers University Press, 2000).

58. Cahill, "'Surely Vietnam Veterans Were Men,'" 10.

59. Michael J. Allen, "'The War's Not Over Until the Last Man Comes Home': Body Recovery and the Vietnam War," Ph.D. diss., Northwestern University, 2003; Douglas Clarke, *The Missing Man: Politics and the MIA* (Washington, DC: National Defense University Press, 1979); Robert Doyle, *Voices from Captivity: Interpreting the American POW Narrative* (Lawrence: University Press of Kansas, 1994); H. Bruce Franklin, *M.I.A., or Mythmaking in America* (New Brunswick, NJ: Rutgers University Press, 1993); Elliot Gruner, *Prisoners of Culture: Representing the Vietnam P.O.W.* (New Brunswick, NJ: Rutgers University Press, 1993); Thomas Hawley, *The Remains of War: Bodies, Politics, and the Search for American Soldiers Unaccounted for in Southeast*

Asia (Durham, NC: Duke University Press, 2005); Craig Howes, *Voices of the Vietnam POWs: Witnesses to Their Fight* (New York: Oxford University Press, 1993); John Hubbell, *P.O.W.: A Definitive History of the American Prisoner-of-War Experience in Vietnam, 1964–1973* (New York: Reader's Digest Press, 1976); Susan Keating, *Prisoners of Hope: Exploiting the POW/MIA Myth in America* (New York: Random, 1994); Jeanne M. Lesinski, *MIAs: A Reference Handbook* (Santa Barbara: ABC-CLIO, 1998); Stuart I. Rochester and Frederick Kiley, *Honor Bound: American Prisoners of War in Southeast Asia, 1961–1973* (Annapolis: Naval Institute Press, 1999); Lewis M. Stern, *Imprisoned or Missing in Vietnam: Policies of the Vietnamese Government Toward Captured and Detained United States Soldiers, 1969–1994* (Jefferson, NC: McFarland, 1995). For more on the children, see Robert S. McKelvey, *The Dust of Life: America's Children Abandoned in Vietnam* (Seattle: University of Washington Press, 1999); Trin Yarborough, *Surviving Twice: Amerasian Children of the Vietnam War* (Washington, DC: Potomac Books, 2005).

60. For more on the story, see James Kitfield, *Prodigal Soldiers: How the Generation of Officers Born of Vietnam Revolutionized the American Style of War* (Herndon, VA: Potomac Books, 1997).

61. Bernard Trainor, "It Turned Out the Mayor of Danang Was a Double Agent," in Appy, *Patriots*, 8.

62. Jonathan Shay, *Achilles in Vietnam: Combat Trauma and the Undoing of Character* (New York: Scribner, 1994), xx, 169; Ronald J. Glasser, *Wounded: Vietnam to Iraq* (New York: George Braziller, 2006), 95; Patience H.C. Mason, *Recovering From the War: A Guide for All Veterans, Family Members, Friends and Therapists* (High Springs, FL: Patience Press, 1998), 221–67. For the changing tactics of dealing with PTSD, see Ben Shephard, *A War of Nerves: Soldiers and Psychiatrists in the Twentieth Century* (Cambridge, MA: Harvard University Press, 2000), 389–96.

63. Robert D. Schulzinger, *A Time for Peace: The Legacy of the Vietnam War* (New York: Oxford University Press, 2006), 78–79. See also Robert Jay Lifton, *Home From the War: Vietnam Veterans, Neither Victims nor Executioners* (New York: Simon & Schuster, 1973).

64. William U. Tant, "Memphis, Tennessee, Marine Rifleman, 1967–69," in Wilson, *Landing Zones*, 127.

65. Angel Quintana in Harry Maurer, ed., *Strange Ground: An Oral History of Americans in Vietnam, 1945–1975* (New York: Da Capo Press, 1998), 178.

66. For the full story of Ybarra and others from the special unit, see Michael Sallah and Mitch Weiss, *Tiger Force: A True Story of Men and War* (New York: Little, Brown, 2006).

67. Ibid., 312–13.

68. Andrew Kimbrell, *The Masculine Mystique: The Politics of Masculinity* (New York: Ballantine, 1995), 256–57.

69. Ibid., 257–58. A full story appears in Doug Magee, "The Long War of Wayne Felde," *The Nation* (2–9 January 1982).

70. Kimbrell, *The Masculine Mystique*, 255.

71. Ibid.

72. Roger Willcut interview in *South Dakotans in Vietnam*, 71.

73. For more on the issue, see Allan Young, *The Harmony of Illusions: Inventing Post–Traumatic Stress Disorder* (Princeton, NJ: Princeton University Press, 1995).

74. Schulzinger, *A Time for Peace*, 81.

75. Ibid., 79–84.

76. Richard C. Ensminger, "Blowing Rock, North Carolina, Marine Forward Observer," in Wilson, *Landing Zones*, 33.

77. Aphrodite Matsakis, *Vietnam Wives: Facing the Challenges with Veterans Suffering Post–Traumatic Stress*, 2nd edition (Baltimore: Sidran Press, 1996), 9.

78. Ibid.

79. Ibid.

80. Ibid., 10.

81. Ibid., 228.

82. Ibid., 229.

83. Ibid.

84. For other books on the impact of the war on the families, even those without the trauma of PTSD, see Karen Spears Zacharias, *Hero Mama: A Daughter Remembers the Father She Lost in Vietnam—and the Mother Who Held Her Family Together* (New York: William Morrow, 2004); Jedwin Smith, *Our Brother's Keeper: My Family's Journey Through Vietnam to Hell and Back* (New York: Wiley, 2005); Danielle Trussoni, *Falling Through the Earth: A Memoir* (New York: Holt, 2006).

85. Jack Doyle, *Trespass Against Us: Dow Chemical and the Toxic Century* (Monroe, ME: Common Courage Press, 2004), 54–55.

86. Paul Frederick Cecil, *Herbicidal Warfare: The RANCH HAND Project in Vietnam* (Westport, CT: Praeger, 1996), 231.

87. "Ray, U.S. Army—Specialist E-5, Helicopter Door Gunner, 116th Assault Helicopter Company, Twenty-Fifth Infantry, Base of Operations, Cu Chi, Vietnam: July 1968–January 1970," in Ybarra, *Vietnam Veteranos*, 127–28.

88. Michael Ryan, Maureen Ryan, and Clifford Linedecker, *Kerry: Agent Orange and an American Family* (New York: Dell, 1982).

89. Zumwalt and Zumwalt, *My Father, My Son*, 162.

90. Ibid., 69.

91. Ibid., 158–59.

92. Ibid., 163.

93. Doyle, *Trespass Against Us*, 72–78; Fred A. Wilcox, *Waiting for an Army to Die* (Washington, DC: Seven Locks Press, 1989), xi–xxiii.

94. Michael Kammen, *Mystic Chords of Memory: The Transformation of Tradition in American Culture* (New York: Knopf, 1991); David Waldstreicher, *In the Midst of Perpetual Fetes: The Making of American Nationalism, 1776–1820* (Chapel Hill: University of North Carolina Press, 1997); James Mayo, *War Memorials as Political Landscape: The American Experience and Beyond* (New York: Praeger, 1988); John E. Bodnar, *Remaking America: Public Memory, Commemoration, and Patriotism* (Princeton, NJ: Princeton University Press, 1992).

95. Jayne, "Immigrants From the Combat Zone," 163.

96. Victor Westphall, *David's Story: A Casualty of Vietnam* (Springer, NM: Center for the Advancement of Human Dignity, 1981), 1–151.

97. David Westphal Veterans Foundation, "A History of the Vietnam Veterans National Memorial," www.angelfirememorial.com/history/index.html, accessed August 15, 2007.

98. Schulzinger, *A Time for Peace*, 104.

99. David Westphal Veterans Foundation, "A History of the Vietnam Veterans National Memorial," www.angelfirememorial.com/history/index.html.

100. Jan C. Scruggs and Joel L. Swerdlow, *To Heal a Nation: The Vietnam Veterans Memorial* (New York: Harper and Row, 1985), 7.

101. Schulzinger, *A Time for Peace*, 96.

102. Ibid., 98.

103. Ibid., 99.

104. Kristin Ann Hass, *Carried to the Wall: American Memory and the Vietnam Veterans Memorial* (Berkeley: University of California Press, 1998), 15–16.

105. Susan Jeffords, *The Remasculization of America: Gender and the Vietnam War* (Bloomington: Indiana University Press, 1989).

106. Hass, *Carried to the Wall*, 18.

107. Scruggs and Swerdlow, *To Heal a Nation*, 24.

108. Hass, *Carried to the Wall*, 20–21.

109. Tom Magedanz interview in *South Dakotans in Vietnam*, 72.

110. As cited in Christian Appy, *Working Class War: American Combat Soldiers and Vietnam* (Chapel Hill: University of North Carolina Press, 1993), 9.

111. Elizabeth Weber, "In My Brother's Name: The Life and Death of Spec. 4 Bill Weber," in Anderson, *The Human Tradition in the Vietnam Era*, 94.

112. Hass, *Carried to the Wall*, 21.

113. Veterans of Foreign Wars, "An Era in Vietnam Veterans Benefits Ends . . . and Begins," www.vfw.org/index.cfm?fa=news.magDtl&dtl=3&mid=2513, accessed September 4, 2006.

114. The best example is John O'Neill, *Unfit for Command: Swift Boat Veterans Speak Out Against John Kerry* (Washington, DC: Regnery Press, 2004).

Epilogue

1. *Tucson Citizen*, April 26, 2005; *Washington Post*, April 29, 2005.

2. *San Francisco Chronicle*, March 25, 2007.

3. Ibid.

4. Ibid.

Bibliography

Interviews

Interview by the author with Leroy Cisneros, August 19, 2001, Yuma, Arizona.
Interview by the author with Mike Cranford, May 23, 2003, Duncan, Arizona.
Interview by the author with Steve Guzzo, May 23, 2003, Clifton, Arizona.
Telephone interview by the author with Novice Kniffen, August 11, 2005.
Interview by the author with Joe Sorrelman, July 20, 2003, Glendale, Arizona.
Interview by the author with Oscar Urrea, January 30, 2004, Mesa, Arizona.
Interview by the author with George Vasquez, April 23, 2004, Morenci, Arizona.

Letters

Adler, Bill. *Letters From Vietnam.* New York: Ballantine, 2003.
      George R. Bassett
      Edward Allen Boardman
      Charlie B. Dickey
      John A. Fosland
      Bill McCloud
      Chester B. McCoid II
      Hiram D. Strickland
Garcia, Clive, Jr. Personal letters, 1966–69. Personal collection of Garcia family, Safford, Arizona.
Edelman, Bernard. *Dear America: Letters Home From Vietnam.* New York: Norton, 1985.
      Rodney R. Chastant
      John Dabonka
      Frederick Downs Jr.

David Forrest
Marion Lee Kempner
Sharon A. Lane
Richard Loffler
Kevin Macauly
William A. Maguire
Richard E. Marks
Bruce McInnes
Joseph Morrissey
George Olsen
Allen Paul
Robert Ransom Jr.
James Simmen
George Williams

Marks, Richard E. *The Letters of Pfc. Richard E. Marks, USMC.* Philadelphia: Lippincott, 1967.

Memoirs

Ball, Phil. *Ghosts and Shadows: A Marine in Vietnam, 1968–1969.* Jefferson, NC: McFarland, 1998.

Brown, John M.G. *Rice Paddy Grunt: Unfading Memories of the Vietnam Generation.* Lake Bluff, IL: Regnery Books, 1986.

Callaway, Joseph W., Jr. *Mekong First Light.* New York: Ballantine, 2004.

Caputo, Philip. *A Rumor of War.* New York: Holt, 1977.

Carroll, James. *American Requiem: God, My Father, and the War That Came Between Us.* Boston: Houghton Mifflin, 1996.

Clark, Johnnie M. *Gun's Up!* New York: Ballantine, 1984.

Cleland, Max. *Strong at the Broken Places: A Personal Story.* Atlanta: Cherokee Publishing, 1986.

Clodfelter, Michael. *Mad Minutes and Vietnam Months: A Soldier's Memoir.* Jefferson, NC: McFarland, 1988.

Corbett, John. *West Dickens Avenue: A Marine at Khe Sanh.* New York: Ballantine, 2003.

Dockery, Martin J. *Lost in Translation: Vietnam, a Combat Advisor's Story.* New York: Ballantine, 2003.

Downs, Frederick. *The Killing Zone: My Life in the Vietnam War.* New York: Norton, 1978.

Ehrhart, W.D. *Vietnam-Perkasie: A Combat Marine Memoir.* Jefferson, NC: McFarland, 1983.

Gadd, Charles. *Line Doggie: Foot Soldier in Vietnam.* Novato, CA: Presidio Press, 1987.

Hackworth, Colonel David H., with Julie Sherman. *About Face: The Odyssey of an American Warrior.* New York: Touchstone, 1989.

Johnson, James D. *Combat Chaplain: A Thirty-Year Vietnam Battle.* Denton: University of North Texas Press, 2001.

Joregenson, Kregg P.J. *Acceptable Loss.* New York: Ballantine, 1991.

Kerrey, Bob. *When I Was a Young Man: A Memoir.* New York: Harcourt, 2002.

Ketwig, John. . . . *And a Hard Rain Fell: A GI's True Story of the War in Vietnam.* Naperville, IL: Sourcebooks, 2002.

Kovic, Ron. *Born on the Fourth of July.* New York: Pocket Books, 1976.

Marshall, John Douglas. *Reconciliation Road: A Family Odyssey of War and Honor.* Syracuse, NY: Syracuse University Press, 1993.

McDonough, James R. *Platoon Leader: A Memoir of Command in Combat.* New York: Ballantine, 1985.

Merritt, William E. *Where the Rivers Ran Backward.* Athens: University of Georgia Press, 1989.

Miller, Franklin, with Elwood J.C. Kureth. *Reflections of a Warrior: Six Years as a Green Beret in Vietnam.* New York: Pocket Books, 1991.

Miller, Rad, Jr. *Whattaya Mean I Can't Kill 'Em.* New York: Ivy Books, 1998.

Moore, Lt. Gen. Harold G., and Joseph L. Galloway. *We Were Soldiers Once . . . and Young: Ia Drang, the Battle That Changed the War in Vietnam.* New York: Ballantine, 1992.

Morton, Jerry. *Reluctant Lieutenant: From Basic to OCS in the Sixties.* College Station: Texas A&M Press, 2004.

Mullen, Peg. *Unfriendly Fire: A Mother's Memoir.* Iowa City: University of Iowa Press, 1995.

O'Brien, Tim. *If I Die in a Combat Zone: Box Me Up and Ship Me Home.* New York: Laurel Books, 1987.

Parks, David. *GI Diary.* Washington, DC: Howard University Press, 1984.

Perrin, Dick, with Tim McCarthy. *GI Resister: The Story of How One American Soldier and His Family Fought the War in Vietnam.* Victoria, British Colombia: Trafford Press, 2001.

Peterson, Robert. *Rites of Passage: Odyssey of a Grunt.* New York: Ballantine, 1997.

Powell, Colin, with Joseph Perisco. *My American Journey.* New York: Random, 1995.

Puller, Lewis B., Jr. *Fortunate Son: The Autobiography of Lewis B. Puller, Jr.* New York: Bantam, 1991.

Ramirez, Juan. *A Patriot After All: The Story of a Chicano Vet.* Albuquerque: University of New Mexico Press, 1999.

Schneider, Ches. *From Classrooms to Claymores: A Teacher at War in Vietnam.* New York: Ivy Books, 1999.

Seddon, James D. *Morning Glories Among the Peas: A Vietnam Veteran's Story.* Ames: Iowa State University Press, 1990.

Smith, Jedwin. *Our Brother's Keeper: My Family's Journey Through Vietnam to Hell and Back.* New York: Wiley, 2005.

Spiller, Harry. *Death Angel: A Vietnam Memoir of a Bearer of Death Messages to Families.* Jefferson, NC: McFarland, 1992.

Steinbrook, Gordon L. *Allies & Mates: An American Soldier with the Australians and New Zealanders in Vietnam, 1966–67.* Lincoln: University of Nebraska Press, 1995.

TeCube, Leroy. *Year in Nam: A Native American Soldier's Story.* Lincoln: University of Nebraska Press, 1999.

Tonsetic, Robert. *Warriors: An Infantryman's Memoir of Vietnam.* New York: Ballantine, 2004.

Trussoni, Danielle. *Falling Through the Earth: A Memoir.* New York: Holt, 2006.

Van Devanter, Lynda. *Home Before Morning: The Story of an Army Nurse in Vietnam.* New York: Time Warner Books, 1983.

Watson, George M., Jr. *Voices From the Rear: Vietnam, 1969–1970.* New York: Xlibris, 2001.

Willson, David A. *REMF Diary.* Seattle: Black Heron Press, 1988.

Zacharias, Karen Spears. *Hero Mama: A Daughter Remembers the Father She Lost in Vietnam—and the Mother Who Held Her Family Together.* New York: William Morrow, 2004.

Zumwalt, Admiral Elmo, Jr., and Lieutenant Elmo Zumwalt III, with John Pekkanen. *My Father, My Son.* New York: Macmillan, 1986.

Oral History Collections

Appy, Christian G. *Patriots: The Vietnam War Remembered From All Sides.* New York: Penguin, 2003.
> Dennis Deal
> Vincent Okamoto
> Wayne Smith
> Bernard Trainor
> Charley Trujillo

Baker, Mark. *Nam: The Vietnam War in the Words of the Men and Women Who Fought There.* New York: Quill Books, 1982.

Beesley, Stanley W. *Vietnam: The Heartland Remembers.* Norman: University of Oklahoma Press, 1987.
> Rudolph Bridges
> Kathryn Fanning
> Norman Summers

Berg, Norman E., ed. *Regret to Inform You: Experiences of Families Who Lost a Family Member in Vietnam.* Central Point, OR: Hellgate Press, 1999.
> Humberto Rosario

Brinker, William J., ed. *A Time for Looking Back: Putnam County Veterans, Their Families, and the Vietnam War.* Cookeville: Tennessee Technological University, 1990.

Byrd, Barthy, ed. *Home Front: Women and Vietnam.* Berkeley: Shameless Hussy Press, 1986.
> Ellen Dale

Drez, Ronald J., and Douglas Brinkley. *Voices of Courage: The Battle of Khe Sanh, Vietnam.* New York: Bulfinch, 2005.

Gettleman, Marvin, Jane Franklin, Marilyn Young, and H. Bruce Franlkin, eds. *Vietnam and America: A Documented History.* New York: Grove Weidenfeld, 1985.
> Colonel Robert D. Heinl Jr.

Gilmore, Donald L., with D.M. Giangreco. *Eyewitness Vietnam: Firsthand Accounts From Operation Rolling Thunder to the Fall of Saigon.* New York: Sterling, 2006.
> C.W. Bowen

Max Cleland
Gary Heeter
Walter L. Sudol
Art Tejada

Goldman, Peter, and Tony Fuller. *Charlie Company: What Vietnam Did To Us.* New York: William Morrow, 1983.

Bert Kennish
David and Michel Rioux

Horne, A.D., ed. *The Wounded Generation: America After Vietnam.* Englewood Cliffs, NJ: Prentice Hall, 1981.

William Jayne
Tim O'Brien

Lehrack, Otto J., ed. *No Shining Armor: The Marines at War in Vietnam.* Lawrence: University Press of Kansas, 1992.

Jeff Bussiere
Gary Conner
Ray Wilmer

Mariscal, George, ed. *Aztlán and Vietnam: Chicano and Chicana Experiences of the War.* Berkeley: University of California Press, 1999.

Marshall, Kathryn. *In the Combat Zone: An Oral History of American Women in Vietnam, 1966–1975.* Boston: Little, Brown, 1987.

Becky Pietz
Cherie Rankin

Maurer, Harry, ed. *Strange Ground: An Oral History of Americans in Vietnam, 1945–1975.* New York: Da Capo Press, 1998.

Harry Behret
Willie Booth
Yoshia Chee
Dennis Greenbaum
Walter Mack
Angel Quintana
John Talbott
Woody Wanamaker

Mooney, James W., and Thomas R. West. *Vietnam: A History and Anthology.* St. James, NY: Brandywine Press, 1994.

Tim O'Brien

Rosario, Carina A. del, ed. *A Different Battle: Stories of Asian Pacific American Veterans.* Seattle: University of Washington Press, 1999.

Santoli, Al, ed. *Everything We Had: An Oral History of the Vietnam War by Thirty-Three American Soldiers Who Fought It.* New York: Random, 1981.

Thomas Bird
Bruce Lawlor
Luis Martinez
Jonathan Polansky
Robert Santos
Gayle Smith

———. *To Bear Any Burden: The Vietnam War and Its Aftermath in the Words of Americans and Southeast Asians.* New York: Dutton, 1985.

    Frank McCarthy

    Ken Moorefield

    Aldophus Stuart

South Dakotans in Vietnam: Excerpts from the South Dakota Vietnam Veterans Oral History Project, Pierre Area. Pierre: State Publishing, 1986.

    Tom Birhanzel

    Martin Brady

    Larry Gates

    Ken Korkow

    Ray Leanna

    Tom Magedanz

    Bob Moran

    Pat Murphy

    Jim Pew

    Jim Raysor

    Nilo Reber

    Dennis Rickley

    Jim Robbennolt

    Tom Roubideaux

    Terry Topple

    Don Trimble

    Francis Whitebird

    Roger Willcut

Steinman, Ron, ed. *Women in Vietnam*. New York: TV Books, 2000.

    Lily Jean Adams

    Judy Hartline Elbring

Terry, Wallace, ed. *Bloods: An Oral History of the Vietnam War*. New York: Random, 1984.

    Reginald "Malik" Edwards

    Edgar A. Huff

    Haywood T. Kirkland

Texas Tech University, the Vietnam Center, the Vietnam Archive Oral History Project, Lubbock, Texas.

    Gonzalo Baltazar

    Michael Bradbury

    Martin Brady

    Thomas Brown

    Larry Burke

    Michael Cisco

    Ted Cook

    Neil Couch

    David Crawley

    Alfred DeMailo

    Keith Erdman

    Gary Franklin

    David Shelly

Trujillo, Charley, ed. *Soldados: Chicanos in Vietnam*. San Jose: Chusma House, 1990.

Larry Holguin
Manuel "Peanuts" Marin
Eddie "Coyote" Rodriguez
Mike Soliz
University of Kentucky, University of Kentucky Oral History Program, Lexington, Kentucky.
David Brown
William Terry Ginter
Paul Morgan
V. Dean Quillet
Robert Wrinn
Walker, Keith, ed. *A Piece of My Heart: The Stories of 26 American Women Who Served in Vietnam.* San Francisco: Presidio Press, 1985.
Christine McGinley Schneider
Micki Voisard
Willenson, Kim, ed. *The Bad War: An Oral History of the Vietnam War.* New York: NAL Books, 1987.
Bobby Muller
George S. Patton III
Wilson, James R., ed. *Landing Zones: Southern Veterans Remember Vietnam.* Durham, NC: Duke University Press, 1990.
Ted A. Burton
John S. Candler Jr.
Brenda Sue Castro
Richard C. Ensminger
Allen C. LoBean
Rev. J. Houston Matthews
George D. Riels
William U. Tant
Manuel T. Valdez
Ybarra, Lea. *Vietnam Veteranos: Chicanos Recall the War.* Austin: University of Texas Press, 2004.
Charley
Gilberto
Leonel
Obed
Ray
Tony

Books

Allen, Michael J. "'The War's Not Over Until the Last Man Comes Home': Body Recovery and the Vietnam War." PhD diss., Northwestern University, 2003.
Allison, William Thomas. *Military Justice in Vietnam: The Rule of Law in an American War.* Lawrence: University Press of Kansas, 2007.
Anderegg, Michael, ed. *Inventing Vietnam: The War in Film and Television.* Philadelphia: Temple University Press, 1991.

Anderson, Charles R. *The Grunts*. New York: Berkley Books, 1984.

Appy, Christian. *Working Class War: American Combat Soldiers and Vietnam*. Chapel Hill: University of North Carolina Press, 1993.

Arnold, James R. *Tet Offensive 1968: Turning Point in Vietnam*. Westport, CT: Praeger, 2004.

Atkinson, Rick. *The Long Gray Line: The American Journey of West Point's Class of 1966*. New York: Owl Books, 1989.

Baritz, Loren. *Backfire: A History of How American Culture Led Us Into Vietnam and Made Us Fight the Way We Did*. 2nd edition. Baltimore: Johns Hopkins University Press, 1998.

Barnes, Peter. *Pawns: The Plight of the Citizen-Soldier*. New York: Knopf, 1972.

Baskir, Lawrence M., and William A. Strauss. *Chance and Circumstance: The Draft, the War, and the Vietnam Generation*. New York: Knopf, 1978.

Bates, Milton J. *The Wars We Took to Vietnam: Cultural Conflict and Storytelling*. Berkeley: University of California Press, 1996.

Bilton, Michael, and Kevin Sim. *Four Hours at My Lai*. New York: Penguin, 1992.

Bingham, Howard, and Max Wallace. *Muhammad Ali's Greatest Fight: Cassius Clay vs. the United States of America*. New York: M. Evans, 2000.

Bodnar, John E. *Remaking America: Public Memory, Commemoration, and Patriotism*. Princeton, NJ: Princeton University Press, 1992.

Brigham, Robert K. *ARVN: Life and Death in the South Vietnamese Army*. Lawrence: University Press of Kansas, 2006.

Brinkley, Douglas. *Tour of Duty: John Kerry and the Vietnam War*. New York: Morrow, 2004.

Brodie, Scott. *Titling at Dominoes: Australia and the Vietnam* War. Brookvale, Australia: Child and Associates, 1987.

Bryan, C.D.B. *Friendly Fire*. New York: G.P. Putnam's Sons, 1976.

Burkett, B.G., and Glenna Whitley. *Stolen Valor: How the Vietnam Generation Was Robbed of Its Heroes and Its History*. Dallas: Verity Press, 1998.

Cecil, Paul Frederick. *Herbicidal Warfare: The Ranch Hand Project in Vietnam*. Westport, CT: Praeger, 1996.

Cincinnatus. *Self-Destruction: The Disintegration and Decay of the United States Army During the Vietnam Era*. New York: Norton, 1981.

Clarke, Douglas. *The Missing Man: Politics and the MIA*. Washington: DC: National Defense University Press, 1979.

Cochran, Timothy L. "Forgotten Allies: The Republic of Korea's Involvement in South Vietnam, 1964–1965." MA thesis, Arizona State University, 2004.

Corkin, Stanley. *Cowboys as Cold Warriors: The Western and U.S. History*. Philadelphia: Temple University Press, 2004.

Cortright, David. *Soldiers in Revolt: GI Resistance During the Vietnam War*. Chicago: Haymarket Books, 1975.

Culbertson, John J. *13 Cent Killers: The 5th Marine Snipers in Vietnam*. New York: Ballantine, 2003.

Curry, G. David. *Sunshine Patriots: Punishment and the Vietnam Offender*. Notre Dame, IN: University of Notre Dame Press, 1985.

Davis, James W., Jr., and Kenneth M. Dolbeare. *Little Groups of Neighbors: The Selective Service System*. Chicago: Markham, 1968.

Dawson, Graham. *Soldier Heroes: British Adventure, Empire and the Imaging of Masculinities.* New York: Routledge, 1994.

Dean, Robert D. *Imperial Brotherhood: Gender and the Making of Cold War Foreign Policy.* Amherst: University of Massachusetts Press, 2001.

Devine, Jeremy M. *Vietnam at 24 Frames a Second.* Austin: University of Texas Press, 1995.

Dittmar, Linda, and Gene Michaud, eds. *From Hanoi to Hollywood: The Vietnam War in American Film.* New Brunswick, NJ: Rutgers University Press, 2000.

Dower, John. *War Without Mercy: Race and Power in the Pacific War.* New York: Pantheon, 1987.

Doyle, Jack. *Trespass Against Us: Dow Chemical & the Toxic Century.* Monroe, ME: Common Courage Press, 2004.

Doyle, Robert. *Voices From Captivity: Interpreting the American POW Narrative.* Lawrence: University Press of Kansas, 1994.

Duiker, William J. *Sacred War: Nationalism and Revolution in a Divided Vietnam.* New York: McGraw-Hill, 1995.

Dyer, Gwynne. *War.* New York: Crown, 1985.

Ebert, James R. *A Life in a Year: The American Infantryman in Vietnam, 1965–1972.* Novato, CA: Presidio Press, 1993.

Enloe, Cynthia H. *Ethnic Soldiers: State Security in Divided Societies.* Athens: University of Georgia Press, 1980.

Fasteau, Marc Feigen. *The Male Machine.* New York: McGraw-Hill: 1974.

Flynn, George Q. *The Draft, 1940–1973.* Lawrence: University Press of Kansas, 1993.

Franco, Jere Bishop. *Crossing the Pond: The Native American Effort in World War II.* Denton: University of North Texas Press, 1999.

Franklin, H. Bruce. *M.I.A., or Mythmaking in America.* New Brunswick, NJ: Rutgers University Press, 1993.

———. *Vietnam and Other American Fantasies.* Amherst: University of Massachusetts Press, 2000.

Franks, Lucinda. *Waiting Out a War: The Exile of Private John Picciano.* New York: Coward, McCann, and Geoghegan, 1974.

Frankum, Ronald Bruce, Jr. *The United States and Australia in Vietnam, 1954–1968.* Lewiston, NY: Edwin Mellen Press, 2001.

Fry, Joseph A. *Dixie Looks Abroad: The South and U.S. Foreign Relations, 1789–1973.* Baton Rouge: Louisiana State University Press, 2002.

Gilbert, Adrian. *Sniper: One-on-One.* London: Sigwick & Jackson, 1994.

Glasser, Ronald J. *Wounded: Vietnam to Iraq.* New York: George Braziller, 2006.

Goldstein, Joseph, Burke Marshall, and Jack Schwartz. *The My Lai Massacre and Its Cover-up: Beyond the Reach of Law? The Peers Commission Report.* New York: Free Press, 1976.

Graham, Herman, III. *The Brothers' Vietnam War: Black Power, Manhood, and the Military Experience.* Gainesville: University of Florida Press, 2003.

Grossman, Dave. *On Killing: The Psychological Cost of Learning to Kill in War and Society.* New York: Back Bay Books, 1995.

Gruner, Elliot. *Prisoners of Culture: Representing the Vietnam P.O.W.* New Brunswick, NJ: Rutgers University Press, 1993.

Halloran, Richard. *My Names Is . . . Shinseki . . . and I am a Soldier.* Honolulu: Hawaii Army Museum Society, 2004.

Hass, Kristin Ann. *Carried to the Wall: American Memory and the Vietnam Veterans Memorial.* Berkeley: University of California Press, 1998.

Hauser, Lieutenant William L. *America's Army in Crisis: A Study in Civil-Military Relations.* Baltimore: Johns Hopkins University Press, 1973.

Hawley, Thomas. *The Remains of War: Bodies, Politics, and the Search for American Soldiers Unaccounted for in Southeast Asia.* Durham, NC: Duke University Press, 2005.

Herring, George. *America's Longest War: The United States and Vietnam, 1950–1975.* 4th edition, New York: McGraw-Hill, 2002.

Hersh, Seymour. *My Lai 4: A Report on the Massacre and Its Aftermath.* New York: Random, 1970.

Holm, Tom. *Strong Hearts, Wounded Souls: Native American Veterans of the Vietnam War.* Austin: University of Texas Press, 1996.

Howes, Craig. *Voices of the Vietnam POWs: Witnesses to Their Fight.* New York: Oxford University Press, 1993.

Hubbell, John. *P.O.W.: A Definitive History of the American Prisoner-of-War Experience in Vietnam, 1964–1973.* New York: Reader's Digest Press, 1976.

Jeffords, Susan. *The Remasculization of America: Gender and the Vietnam War.* Bloomington: Indiana University Press, 1989.

Kammen, Michael. *Mystic Chords of Memory: The Transformation of Tradition in American Culture.* New York: Knopf, 1991.

Karnow, Stanley. *Vietnam: A History.* New York: Penguin, 1983.

Keating, Susan. *Prisoners of Hope: Exploiting the POW/MIA Myth in America.* New York: Random, 1994.

Kimbrell, Andrew. *The Masculine Mystique: The Politics of Masculinity.* New York: Ballantine, 1995.

Kimmel, Michael. *Manhood in America: A Cultural History.* New York: Free Press, 1996.

Kindsvatter, Peter S. *American Soldiers: Ground Combat in the World Wars, Korea, and Vietnam.* Lawrence: University Press of Kansas, 2003.

Kinney, Katherine. *Friendly Fire: American Images of the Vietnam War.* New York: Oxford University Press, 2000.

Kitfield, James. *Prodigal Soldiers: How the Generation of Officers Born of Vietnam Revolutionized the American Style of War.* Herndon, VA: Potomac Books, 1997.

Kranish, Michael, Brian C. Mooney, and Nina J. Easton. *John F. Kerry: The Complete Biography by the Boston Globe Reporters Who Know Him Best.* New York: PublicAffairs, 2004.

Krepinevich, Andrew F., Jr. *The Army and Vietnam.* Baltimore: Johns Hopkins University Press, 1986.

LaFeber, Walter. *The Deadly Bet: LBJ, Vietnam, and the 1968 Election.* New York: Rowman and Littlefield, 2005.

Laffin, John. *Americans in Battle.* New York: Crown, 1973.

Lembcke, Jerry. *The Spitting Image: Myth, Memory, and the Legacy of Vietnam.* New York: New York University Press, 1998.

Leppelman, John. *Blood on the Risers: An Airborne Soldier's Thirty-Five Months in Vietnam.* New York: Ballantine, 1991.

Lesinski, Jeanne M. *MIAs: A Reference Handbook.* Santa Barbara: ABC-CLIO, 1998.

Lifton, Robert Jay. *Home From the War: Vietnam Veterans, Neither Victims nor Executioners.* New York: Simon & Schuster, 1973.

Loveland, Anne C. *American Evangelicals and the U.S. Military, 1942–1993.* Baton Rouge: Louisiana State University Press, 1996.

MacPherson, Myra. *Long Time Passing: Vietnam and the Haunted Generation.* New edition. Bloomington: Indiana University Press, 2001.

McKelvey, Robert S. *The Dust of Life: America's Children Abandoned in Vietnam.* Seattle: University of Washington Press, 1999.

Mangold, Tom, and John Penycate. *The Tunnels of Cu Cui.* New York: Berkley Books, 1985.

Mason, Patience H.C. *Recovering From the War: A Guide for All Veterans, Family Members, Friends and Therapists.* High Springs, FL: Patience Press, 1998.

Matsakis, Aphrodite. *Vietnam Wives: Facing the Challenges With Veterans Suffering Post–Traumatic Stress.* 2nd edition. Baltimore: Sidran Press, 1996.

Mayo, James. *War Memorials as Political Landscape: The American Experience and Beyond.* New York: Praeger, 1988.

Meadows, William C. *Kiowa, Apache, and Comanche Military Societies: Enduring Veterans, 1800 to the Present.* Austin: University of Texas Press, 1999.

Mechling, Jay. *On My Honor: Boy Scouts and the Making of American Youth.* Chicago: University of Chicago Press, 2001.

Moreau, Donna. *Waiting Wives: The Story of Schilling Manor, Home Front to the Vietnam War.* New York: Atria Books, 2005.

Moskos, Charles C., Jr. *The American Enlisted Man: The Rank and File in Today's Military.* New York: Russell Sage Foundation, 1970.

Murphy, Edward F. *Semper Fi Vietnam: From Da Nang to the DMZ Marine Corps Campaigns, 1965–1975.* San Francisco: Presidio Press, 1997.

―――. *Vietnam Medals of Honor Heroes.* Expanded and revised edition. New York: Ballantine, 2005.

Neilson, Jim. *Warring Factions: Cultural Politics and the Vietnam War Narrative.* Oxford: University Press of Mississippi, 1998.

Neu, Charles E. *America's Lost War Vietnam: 1945–1975.* Wheeling, IL: Harlan-Davidson, 2005.

Nicosia, Gerald. *Home to War: A History of the Vietnam Veterans' Movement.* New York: Carroll and Graf, 2001.

Nolan, Keith. *Battle for Saigon: Tet 1968.* San Francisco: Presidio Press, 2002.

Oberdorfer, Don. *Tet! The Turning Point in the Vietnam War.* Baltimore: Johns Hopkins University Press, 2001.

Olson, James S., and Randy Roberts. *My Lai: A Brief History with Documents.* Boston: Bedford Books, 1998.

O'Neill, John. *Unfit for Command: Swift Boat Veterans Speak Out Against John Kerry.* Washington, DC: Regnery Press, 2004.

Oropeza, Lorena. *¡Raza si! ¡Guerra no! Chicano Protest and Patriotism During the Viet Nam War Era.* Berkeley: University of California Press, 2005.

Peers, William R. *The My Lai Inquiry.* New York: Norton, 1979.

Perone, James. *Songs of the Vietnam Conflict.* Westport, CT: Greenwood Press, 2001.

Peterson, Robert. *The Boy Scouts: An American Adventure*. New York: American Heritage, 1984.

Rabel, Roberto. *New Zealand and the Vietnam War: Politics and Diplomacy*. Auckland, New Zealand: Auckland University Press, 2005.

Raphael, Ray. *The Men from the Boys: Rites of Passage in Male America*. Lincoln: University of Nebraska Press, 1988.

Rochester, Stuart I., and Frederick Kiley. *Honor Bound: American Prisoners of War in Southeast Asia, 1961–1973*. Annapolis: Naval Institute Press, 1999.

Rottman, Gordon. *Khe Sanh, 1967–1968: Marines Battle for Vietnam's Vital Hilltop Base*. New York: Osprey, 2005.

Rotundo, E. Anthony. *American Manhood: Transformations in Masculinity from the Revolution to the Modern Era*. New York: Basic Books, 1993.

Ruybal, Jay Dee. *The Drug Hazed War in Indochina*. New York: Creative Designs, 1998.

Ryan, Michael, Maureen Ryan, and Clifford Linedecker. *Kerry: Agent Orange and an American Family*. New York: Dell, 1982.

Sallah, Michael, and Mitch Weiss. *Tiger Force: A True Story of Men and War*. New York: Little, Brown, 2006.

Schell, Jonathan. *The Real War: The Classic Reporting on the Vietnam War*. New York: Pantheon, 1988.

Schulzinger, Robert D. *A Time for Peace: The Legacy of the Vietnam War*. New York: Oxford University Press, 2006.

Scruggs, Jan C., and Joel L. Swerdlow. *To Heal a Nation: The Vietnam Veterans Memorial*. New York: Harper and Row, 1985.

Shay, Jonathan. *Achilles in Vietnam: Combat Trauma and the Undoing of Character*. New York: Scribner, 1994.

Sheehan, Neil. *A Bright Shining Lie: John Paul Vann and America in Vietnam*. New York: Random, 1988.

Shephard, Ben. *A War of Nerves: Soldiers and Psychiatrists in the Twentieth Century*. Cambridge, MA: Harvard University Press, 2000.

Shrader, Charles R. *Amicicide: The Problems of Friendly Fire in Modern War*. U.S. Army Command and General Staff College Combat Studies Institute Research Study no. 1. Washington, DC: U.S. Government Printing Office, December 1982.

Small, Melvin. *Antiwarriors: The Vietnam War and the Battle for America's Hearts and Minds*. Wilmington, DE: Scholarly Resources, 2002.

Solis, Gary D. *Son Thang: An American War Crime*. Annapolis: Naval Institute Press, 1997.

Sorley, Lewis. *A Better War: The Unexamined Victories and Final Tragedy of America's Last Years in Vietnam*. New York: Harvest Books, 1999.

Spector, Ronald H. *After Tet: The Bloodiest Year in Vietnam*. New York: Vintage Books, 1993.

Stern, Lewis M. *Imprisoned or Missing in Vietnam: Policies of the Vietnamese Government Toward Captured and Detained United States Soldiers, 1969–1994*. Jefferson, NC: McFarland, 1995.

Sticht, Thomas G., William B. Armstrong, Daniel T. Hickey, and John S. Caylor. *Cast-off Youth: Policy and Training Methods from the Military Experience*. New York: Praeger, 1987.

Suid, Lawrence H. *Guts and Glory: The Making of the American Military Image in Film.* Revised and expanded edition. Lexington: University of Kentucky Press, 2002.

Townsend, Kenneth W. *World War II and the American Indian.* Albuquerque: University of New Mexico Press, 2000.

Waldstreicher, David. *In the Midst of Perpetual Fetes: The Making of American Nationalism, 1776–1820.* Chapel Hill: University of North Carolina Press, 1997.

Westheider, James E. *Fighting on Two Fronts: African Americans and the Vietnam War.* New York: New York University Press, 1997.

Westphall, Victor. *David's Story: A Casualty of Vietnam.* Springer, NM: Center for the Advancement of Human Dignity, 1981.

Wetta, Frank J., and Stephen J. Curley. *Celluloid Wars: A Guide to Film and the American Experience of War.* Westport, CT: Greenwood Press, 1992.

Wiest, Andrew. *Vietnam's Forgotten Army: Heroism and Betrayal in the ARVN.* New York: New York University Press, 2007.

Wilcox, Fred A. *Waiting for an Army to Die.* Washington, DC: Seven Locks Press, 1989.

Wright, Bradford W. *Comic Book Nation: The Transformation of Youth Culture in America.* Baltimore: Johns Hopkins University Press, 2001.

Yarborough, Trin. *Surviving Twice: Amerasian Children of the Vietnam War.* Washington, DC: Potomac Books, 2005.

Young, Allan. *The Harmony of Illusions: Inventing Post–Traumatic Stress Disorder.* Princeton, NJ: Princeton University Press, 1995.

Articles and Essays

Ambrose, Stephen E. "Atrocities in Historical Perspective." In David L. Anderson, *Facing My Lai: Moving Beyond the Massacre.* Lawrence: University Press of Kansas, 1998, 107–20.

Anderson, David L. "Bill Henry Terry Jr., Killed in Action." In David L. Anderson, *The Human Tradition in the Vietnam Era.* Wilmington, DE: Scholarly Resources, 2000.

Brinker, William J. "Nancy Randolph: Army Nurse." In David L. Anderson, *The Human Tradition in the Vietnam Era.* Wilmington, DE: Scholarly Resources, 2000.

———. "Seawillow Chambers: Soldier's Wife." In David L. Anderson, *The Human Tradition in the Vietnam Era.* Wilmington, DE: Scholarly Resources, 2000.

Cahill, Charlotte. "'Surely Vietnam Veterans Were Men': Public Policy and Masculinity in Reagan's America." Paper presented at the Society for Historians of American Foreign Relations, Reston, Virginia, June 2007.

"*Combat!* Storms back into action with 24-hour memorial day marathon and new original special." www.jodavidsmeyer.com/combat/episodes/encore-action-special.htm.

Danziger Borchert, Susan. "Masculinity and the Vietnam War." *Michigan Academician* (Winter 1983): 195–208.

David Westphal Veterans Foundation. "A History of the Vietnam Veterans National Memorial." www.angelfirememorial.com/history/index.html.

Eisenhart, R. Wayne. "You Can't Hack It Little Girl: A Discussion of the Covert Psychological Agenda of Modern Combat Training." *Journal of Social Issues* 31 (Fall 1975): 13–24.

Hawkins, Charles F. "Friendly Fire: Facts, Myths and Misperceptions." *U.S. Naval Institute Proceedings* (June 1994): 54–59.

Kerry, John. "How Do You Ask a Man to Be the Last Man to Die in Vietnam?" Statements made before the Senate Foreign Relations Committee, April 23, 1971, History News Network, http://hnn.us/articles/3631.html.

Levy, Charles J. "ARVN as Faggots: Inverted Warfare in Vietnam." *Transaction* (October 1971): 18–27.

Magee, Doug. "The Long War of Wayne Felde." *The Nation* (January 2–9, 1982).

"My Experience as Grunt Medic," 1st Cav Medic (Airmobile) Web site, www.1stcavmedic.com/experiences.html.

Patrick, Bethanne Kelly. "Lt. Gen. Lewis Berwell Puller: The Legendary 'Chesty' Puller Was a True 'Marine's Marine' Who Never Forgot His Noncom Days." Military.com, www.military.com/Content/MoreContent?file=ML_puller_bkp.

Sanders, Clinton R. "Dopers Wonderland." *Journal of Drug Issues* (Winter 1973).

Sarlin, Ray. "100% Alert and Then Some." Vietnam War Stories–1st Battalion, 50th Infantry Web site, www.ichiban1.0rg/html/stories/story_38.htm.

Stanton, Morris D. "Drugs, Vietnam, and the Vietnam Veteran." *American Journal of Drug and Alcohol Abuse* (March 1976).

Steinweg, Kenneth K. "Dealing Realistically with Fratricide." *Parameters* (Spring 1995): 4–29.

"Tim O'Brien, Novelist," Biography, www.illyria.com/tobhp.html.

Treviso, Ruben. "Hispanics and the Vietnam War." In Harrison E. Salisbury, ed., *Vietnam Reconsidered: Lessons From a War.* New York: Harper and Row, 1984.

Veterans of Foreign Wars. "An Era in Vietnam Veterans Benefits Ends . . . And Begins." www.vfw.org/index.cfm?fa=news.magDtl&dtl=3&mid=2513.

Vietnam Veterans of America. "Who We Are." www.vva.org/who.html.

Webb, James. "What the Vietnam Vet Needs." *Soldier of Fortune* (May 1980): 52–53.

Weber, Elizabeth. "In My Brother's Name: The Life and Death of Spec. 4 Bill Weber." In David L. Anderson, *The Human Tradition in the Vietnam Era.* Wilmington, DE: Scholarly Resources, 2000.

Newspapers

Arizona Republic
Los Angeles Times
Mesa Tribune
New York Times
Washington Evening Star
Waterloo-Cedar Falls Courier

Index

A

accidents, 56–57, 145
Advanced Infantry Training (AIT), 39,
    56, 61–65
    critiques of, 65–68
African Americans, 28–30, 38, 49, 63–64
    and burden of sacrifice, 128
    and community support, 29, 128
    death rates among, 30, 128
    and discrimination, 29, 170
    dissent among, 29
    and draft, 8
    and military service, 29, 128
    radicalism of, 129–130
    reintegration of, 169–170
    and Project 100,000, 8
    volunteerism among, 29, 128
Agent Orange, 181–185
Agent Orange Victims International, 182
Air Medal, 127
Albanese, Lewis (Pvt.), 123–124, 127
alcohol. *See* drugs and alcohol
Ali, Muhammad, 6
Allgood, Jim, 55
allies, 98–101
    Australians, 100–101
    South Koreans, 98–100

allies *(continued)*
    South Vietnamese, 95–98
    See also ARVN; ROK
Americal Division, 152
American Indian Movement (AIM), 170
American Institute of Architects, 187
American Legion, 20, 174
amputees, 167
An Khe, 77
antiwar activists, 113, 144, 160–161
    Iraq War, 145
    in France, 147
    and "spitting image," 160
    veterans as, 53, 170–175
Ap Bac, Battle of, 96
Arizona Territory, 185
Armed Forces Qualification Test, 7
Article 32 investigator, 55
ARVN (Army of the Republic of
    Vietnam), 45, 93, 95–98, 101,
    117–118, 138
    Rangers, 98, 117
A Shau Valley, 85
Ashford, Walter, 139–140
Asian Americans, 34–35, 63, 132–133
athletes, professional, and draft
    avoidance, 10–11

atrocities, 101, 149–151, 176
  NVA, 150
  See also My Lai
Australians, 100–101
AWOL (Absent Without Leave), 10,
    54–55, 57, 115
  See also UA (Unauthorized Absence);
    desertion

B
Bailey, F. Lee, 153
Ball, Phil, 12
Baltazar, Gonzalo, 45
Bangkok, 110
Barker, Frank (Col.), 152
Barry, Jan, 171
basic training (Army), xiv, 38, 41,
    42–43
  accidents, 56–57
  church attendance, 58
  and (social) class, 50–51
  classes during, 44
  and failure, 52, 58
  and individualism, 47, 58
  and indoctrination, 44
  movies, 44–45, 53
  physical abuse in, 41, 43, 46
  and physical training, 44
  psychological stress in, 42, 46
  and racism, 49–50
  and sexuality, 47–49, 54
  and suicide, 55–56
  See also boot camp
Bien Hoa, 100, 113
Binh Dinh Province, 123
black market, 109
bonding, personal. *See* comradeship
booby traps, xvii, 63, 66, 67, 82–84, 86,
    90
boot camp (Marines), xiv, 38, 42, 50, 60
  See also basic training
boredom, 79, 89–91
"bouncing Betty," 83, 84
Boyles, Chuck, 20
Boy Scouts, 20–22
Branch Officer Basic Course (Army), 41

bravery, 16
  See also heroism
Bronze Star, 123, 127, 169
Brown, John, 16
Brown, Thomas, 7
"Bulletstoppers," xv, 61
Bush, George W., 10

C
Calley, William F. (Lt.), 151–152, 153
Cambodia, 118, 125, 137, 142
Cam Lo, 102
Cam Ranh Bay, 124, 129
Can Tho, 117
Caputo, Phil, 23, 57, 69, 156, 177
Carhart, Tom, 187
Carmichael, Stokley, 147
Carter, Jimmy (President), 148, 168
Chamber, Ron, 111
Chamber, Seawillow, 111
Charlie Company, 1st Battalion, 20th
    Infantry, 151, 152, 153
chemical weapons, 181–185
children, 101
China Beach, 109
Chu Lai, 106
CIA, 97
Cisneros, Leroy, xiii, xv, xvi, xviii
  See also Morenci Nine
Citadel, 118
civilians, 63, 80, 82, 149, 150
Cleland, Max (Capt.), 166–168, 179, 189
climate, 75, 104, 106
Cobra (gun), 118, 125
Colson, Charles, 172
Combat Infantry Badge (CIB), 46
combat soldier. *See* grunt
comradeship, 20, 78–79, 87, 128–129,
    130
Congressional Medal of Honor, 77
Con Thien, 185
Correctional Custody, 53
Cranford, Mike, xiii, xvi, xviii
  See also Morenci Nine
Cranston, Alan (Sen.), 178
Cronkite, Walter, 119

D

Da Nang, xv, 74, 108
Datel, William E. (Lt. Col.), 61
Davison, Phillip (Lt. Gen.), 151
Deal, Dennis, 93
death
  of friends, 87–89
  notification visit, 119–123
  and wounded, 166
dehumanization
  of civilians, 150
  of recruits, 42
  of Vietnamese, 63–64, 80–81, 132, 150
Denver, U.S.S., 156
DEROS (Date Eligible for Return from
  Overseas), 72
desertion, 54–56, 145, 146–147
"Dewey Canyon III," Operation, 171
DI. *See* drill instructor
Dien Bien Phu, 117
Disabled American Veterans (DAV), 174,
  186
discipline
  in basic training, 52
  breakdown of, 136, 148
  and dissent, 145
  and drug use, 133, 135
discrimination. *See* racial discrimination;
  religious discrimination
disease, 103–104, 106–107, 123
Distinguished Service Cross, 34, 123,
  126
DMZ (Demilitarized Zone), 106, 117
Dogpatch, 108
Dong Ha, 128
Doubek, Robert, 187
Dow Chemical, 184
draft, 4–5
  appeals, 6
  arbitrariness of, 7
  avoidance, 10–11
  deferment, 7, 9
  as enlistment factor, 4–5, 11
  evasion, 6
    clemency for, 148
  exemptions, 9

draft *(continued)*
  inequities, 7, 9–11
  opposition to, 7
  and racial discrimination, 9
draft boards, 5–6, 7, 9
Draper, Bobby Dale, xiv, xv, xvi, xviii
  See also Morenci Nine
drill instructors (DI), xiv, 45–47, 49–50,
  58, 59, 60
  in advanced training, 64–65
  and combat experience, 46
  and corruption, 45
  and discipline, 52
  physical abuse by, 41, 43
  and racism, 50
drugs and alcohol, 90, 133–135, 139,
  177, 178

E

Eckhard, G.S. (Maj. Gen.), 137
economic pressures, 13
education
  and basic training, 50–51
  draft exemptions, 9
  as social consensus, 19
Ehrhart, W.D., 58
11th Infantry Brigade, 152
enemy, respect for, 93–95
  See also Viet Cong; NVA

F

families, separation from, 40–41, 70–71
Fanning, Kathryn, 71
fathers, as influence to service, 15–18,
  70
fear, coping with, 79–80
Felde, Wayne, 177
5th Marines, 138
Fire Base Polly Ann, 177
1st Cavalry, 78, 93
first impressions, of Vietnam, 75–76
First Persian Gulf War, 185
FNGs (fucking new guys), 76–77, 88
Fonda, Jane, 147
Ford, Gerald (President), 147
Form 1049, 78

442nd Regimental Combat Team, 34–35
fraggings, 135, 139–140
freedom birds, 111–113
French, 117, 132, 137
friendly fire, 67, 123, 142–145
Friendly Fire (book/movie), 144–145
Fulbright, J. William (Senator), 152
funerals, xvii–xviii, 120, 121–22

G

General Gaffey, U.S.S., xv
Garcia, Clive Jr., xvii, xviii
    See also Morenci Nine
Gelson, George Jr., 10
GI Bill, 33
Gilman, Mark, 147
Green, Kenneth, 176
Green Berets. *See* Special Forces
Green Berets (movie), 27, 133
grunts
    and ARVN, 97–98, 138
    and atrocities, 151
    and boredom, 89–91
    and burden of fighting, 91, 142
    and civilians, 101–103
    and FNGs, 76–77
    frustrations, 136–139
    perspectives, 73, 92, 136–137, 138,
        139, 150
    and protestors, 141–142
    as protestors, 145–149
    and REMFs, 91–93
    and South Vietnamese children,
        101–102
Gruver, Charles (Pfc.), 152
guerilla warfare, 63, 82–83, 91, 101,
    103–104, 149
Guzzo, Steve, 16

H

Hackworth, David H. (Col.), 67
Hagel, Chuck, 164
Halberstam, David, 96, 153
Hart, Frederick, 187
Hawaii, 110
hazing, 76–77

Heeter, Gary (Corp.), 83
Heim, Bruce (Lt.), 66
Heinl, Robert D. (Col.), 154
Helms, Jack, 9
Henderson, Oran K. (Col.), 152, 153
heroism, 16, 26, 34, 117, 123–127
    See also bravery
Herrera, Douglas MacArthur, 146
Hersh, Seymour, 152–153
Hershey, Lewis, 5
Hibbard, Susie, xvii
Hightower, John M. (Maj. Gen.), 146
Highway 15, 73
Hill 881, 185
Hill 1044, 85
hot zones, 85–87
Hue (city), 116 (photo), 118–119
Hueys, 125, 126
Huff, Edgar (Sgt. Maj.), 169–170

I

Ia Drang Valley, 94
idealism, 78, 136
indoctrination, 44, 47, 64, 81
induction, 6, 39–40
infantry. *See* grunts; MOS 0311
influences. *See* motivations
integration, military, 28, 127
Iron Triangle, 86

J

Jackson State, 142
Jayne, William, 162
Johnson, James, 146
Johnson, Lyndon B. (President), 18, 98,
    116 119, 128
Joslyn, William C. (Col.), 53
Judge, Clark, 138
jungle rot, 106–107

K

K-Bar knife, 86, 117
Kennedy, John F., 22–24, 36, 172
Kent State, 142
Kerrey, Bob (Senator), xx, 124–25, 127,
    168

Kerry, John Forbes, 23, 171–173, 186, 189

Ketwig, John, 19, 47

Khe Sanh, xvi, 116, 117, 166, 186

KIA (killed in action), 57, 119
  Australian, 100
  Korean, 99

killing, 80–82
  training for, 62–64
  views of, 81–82

King, Martin Luther Jr. (Rev.), 128, 129

King, Stan, xiii, xiv, xvi
  See also Morenci Nine

Korkow, Ken, 117

Koster, Samuel (Maj. Gen.), 152, 153

Koupman, Gillian, 40

Kovic, Ron, 25

L

Laird, Melvin, 152

Laos, xvii, 118, 125, 137

Latinos, 30–32, 130–131

Lawton, Jack (Capt.), 167

leeches, 104, 105

Letgers, Llewellyn J. (Lt. Col.), 61

Lin, Maya, 187

Long Binh, 76

losing a friend, 87–89

Luna, Ted, 186

M

malaria, 104–105

manhood, 14–15, 27–28, 58, 60, 61, 79, 84, 131, 178
  and basic training, 42, 48
  and Boy Scouts, 20, 22
  and class and race, 14
  and movies, 24
  influences on, 15
  role models, 14
  social construction of, 14–15, 20

Marines, 12, 27, 38

masculinity. *See* manhood

McCain, John, 189

McCarthy, Eugene, 116, 152

McDonough, James, 71

medals. *See* individual awards

Medal of Honor, 27, 53, 124, 125, 126, 127

media influences, 24–27

Medina, Ernest (Capt.), 152–153

memorials, xix, 20, 185–186, 189
  "Three Soliders, The" (statue), 184 (photo), 187
  Vietnam Veterans (national), 123, 185–189
  Vietnam Veterans Peace and Brotherhood Chapel, 186

Merritt, William, 39–40

Meskill, Thomas (Congressman), 56

Mexican Americans, 30–32, 45, 49–50, 63

MIA (missing in action), 71, 122–123, 174

military
  adaptation by, 155
  challenges of, in Vietnam, 154–156
  integration, 28, 127
  justice, 151
  reform, 61, 154, 155, 174
  role models, 16–17

Miller, Franklin, 77, 125–127

Moncayo, Robert, xvi, xvii, xviii
  See also Morenci Nine

Moniyhan, Daniel Patrick (Sen.), 7

Montagnards, 98, 125, 126, 151

Mora, Dennis, 146

morale, 135, 145, 154

Morenci (AZ), xiii, xv

Morenci Nine, xv–xviii, xix, 59 (photo)
  recruitment of, xiv
  See also Cisneros; Cranford; Draper; Garcia; King; Moncavo; Sorrelman; West; Whitmer

Morton, Jerry, 43

MOS (Military Occupational Specialty) 0311 (Marines), xv, 61

MOS (Military Occupational Specialty) 11-B (Army), 61

mosquitoes, 104

motivations, 3–4, 19–20
  among Asian Americans, 35
  in basic training, 57
  for enlistment, xiv, 11, 20
    from media, xiv, 24–27
    World War II, 16
  for fighting, 77–79
  for draft evasion, 6
  among Native Americans, 33–34
  religious, 22–23
  social pressure as, 13–14
  for women, 35–37
mourning, 88–89
Mullen, Gene, 144–145
Mullen, Michael, 143–145
Mullen, Peg, 144–145
Muller, Bobby, 173
Murphy, Audie, 24–25, 123, 175–176
My Lai Incident, 151–154, 172

N

National Guard and Reserves, 10–11, 51
National Vietnam Resources Project
    (NVRP), 176, 178
Native Americans, 32–34, 41, 81, 131
  and community support, 33, 41, 170
  influences on, 33
  and PTSD, 176–177
  recognition of, 32–33
  reintegration, 170
  role models for, 33–34
  and volunteerism, 32
Navy Cross, 117
New Zealanders, 100–101
Nha Trang Island, 124
Night of the Dragon (film), 44–45
9th Marine Regiment, 160
Nixon, Richard (President), 18, 116, 125,
    126, 144, 152, 153
Nui Dat, 100
NVA (North Vietnamese Army), 93–95,
    117–118
  See also enemy; Viet Cong

O

O'Brien, Tim, 3, 48, 158–159, 163

O'Neill, John, 173, 189
101st Airborne, 22, 67, 88
173rd Airborne Brigade, 100
Operation Ranch Hand, 182

P

parades, 160, 165 (photo), 174
Paralyzed Veterans of America, 169
Paris Peace Accords, 122
Park, Chung Hee Park (President), 99
Parks, David, 72
Patch, U.S.S., 72
patriotism, 28, 32
Patton, George S., III, 160
PD. *See* Phelps Dodge Company
Peers, William (Lt. Gen.), 152
Peregrine Group, 132
Perot, Ross, 187
Perrin, Dick, 146–147
Peterson, Earl (Sgt.), xiv
Peterson, Robert, 75, 143
Phelps Dodge Company (PD), xiii, xvi
Phu Muu, 123
Phuoc Tuy Province, 100
Platoon 1055 (Marine), xv, 59 (photo)
Pleiku, 126
post–traumatic stress disorder. *See* PTSD
POW (prisoner of war), 71, 122
Powell, Colin, 11, 155
pressures, to serve, 13–14, 16–18
prisoners, 150
Project 100,000, 7–8, 31
prostitution, 108–109
protestors, 39, 141–142
  military, 145–149
  See also antiwar activists
psychological stress, 4, 39, 113
  of basic training, 41–43
  on communities, xvii–xviii
  of death and loss, 72, 87
  and drugs, 135
  of jungle environment, 103–107
  on marriages, 70–71, 179–181
  on families, xvi, 4, 40–41, 70–71,
    179–181
  of guerilla warfare, 83–84

psychological stress *(continued)*
  of killing, 82
  PTSD, 175–179
  short time syndrome, 112
  of wounds (during recovery), 167–169
PTSD (post–traumatic stress disorder),
    xviii, 175–179, 180
  and Latinos, 30
  and Veterans Administration, 179
Puerto Ricans, 30–31, 49
Puller, Lewis (Chesty), 17–18, 70
Puller, Lewis B. Jr., 17–18, 70
Purple Heart, 46, 84, 87, 123, 127, 172

Q
Quayle, Dan, 10
Querry, Howard E. (Sgt.), 121
Querry, Pauline, 121

R
racial discrimination, 9, 11, 29, 130–133
  by draft boards, 9–10
  and the military, 28, 132
  and reintegration, 169–170
  and Vietnamese, 96–98
racial tension, 127–133, 135, 139
racism, 28, 63, 81, 127–133, 176
  and Asian Americans, 132–133
  and civilians, 150
  and reintegration, 169–170
  in training, 49–50, 63–64
  and Vietnamese, 50, 81, 98
R&R (rest and relaxation), 54, 92, 107
    (photo), 108–111
Ransom, Robert (2nd Lt.), 143
readjustment. *See* reintegration
Reagan, Ronald (President), 173
rear echelon troops, 146
  See also REMFs
reception of veterans, 142, 159–161,
    162–163
reform, of military, 61, 154, 155, 174
rehabilitation, 124, 166–169, 178–179
reintegration, 142, 159–161, 163–166,
    169–170
religious discrimination, 53

REMFs (Rear Echelon Mother Fuckers),
    91–93, 134
replacements, 65, 72
Resistance In the Armed Forces (RITA),
    147
Reutershan, Paul, 182
reservists, 51
Ridenhour, Ron, 152
Riley, John, 86–87
rite of passage, 20, 41, 60, 75, 114
Rivera-Toledo, Carlos, 31
ROK (Republic of Korea) army, 99–100
role models, 16, 22–24
  actors, 24–26
  Boy Scouts, 21
  fathers, 15–18
  Kennedy, John F., 22–24, 36, 172
  military, 16
  teachers and coaches, 18–20
Rosario, Alberto, 122–123
Rosario, Humberto (Cpl.), 122–123
rotation system, 77, 137–138
ROTC, 41, 155
Roubideaux, Tom, 85

S
Saigon, 92, 109, 116, 156
Samas, David, 146
Schilling Manor, 71
Schwarzkopf, Norman, Jr. (Gen.), 144,
    145
Scruggs, Jan, 186
SEALS, 12, 15, 68, 124
Seddon, James, 159
Selective Service System, 5, 12
  See also draft; draft boards
Sheehan, Casey, 145
Sheehan, Cindy, 145
short timers, 111–112
"Silent Majority," 144
Silver Star, 123, 125, 127, 172
Simms, James (Lt.), 85
Slovik, Eddie (Pvt.), 146
snakes, 105–106
snipers, 82–83, 90, 138–139
Son Thang, 154

Sorrelman, Joe, xiii, xiv, xv, xvi, xviii
    See also Morenci Nine
South Koreans, as allies, 98–100
South Vietnamese, as allies, 95–98
Special Forces (Green Berets), 15, 23,
    27, 85, 98, 127, 170, 178
Spiller, Harry, 119–120
spitting incidents, 160
stress. *See* psychological stress
Sudol, Walter, 85–86
suicide, 55–56, 179
survival instinct, 65, 78, 80, 116, 136,
    139
survivors' guilt, xviii
Swanson, David, 55
Swift boats, 23, 124, 163, 172, 173,
    183

T
Tan Son Nhut, 91
Teague, Olin "Tiger" (Cong.), 178
technology, effects of, 80, 145, 149, 166
Tejeda, Art, 86–87
*Terry, Margaret Faye, etc., et al. v. the
    Elmwood Cemetery, et al.*, 170
Tet Offensive, xvi, 85, 91, 114, 115,
    116–118, 127, 139
Texas League of United Latin American
    Citizens (LULAC), 146
Thailand, 110
Thais, 101
Thanh Phong, 124
The Basic School (TBS) (Marines), 41,
    57
3rd Battalion, 39th Regiment, 9th
    Infantry Division, 121
Thompson, Hugh, Jr., 152, 153
"Three Soldiers, The" (statue), 184
    (photo), 187
Thuy, Hoa, 167
Tiger Force, 82, 153, 176
Training. *See* advanced infantry training
    (AIT); basic training; weapons
    training
Trainor, Bernard, 97, 138, 175
travel, to Vietnam, 72–74

tunnel rats, 86–87
tunnels, 86
25th Infantry Division, 83, 95

U
Udall, Morris (Sen.), 152
Unauthorized absence (UA) (Marine
    Corps), 10, 54
    See also Absent Without Leave
    (AWOL)
"unsat," 57, 59
Urrea, Oscar, 16
UUUU, 137

V
VA. *See* Veterans Administration
Valdez, Manuel, 31
Van Devanter, Linda, 36
Vann, John Paul (Lt. Col.), 96
VC. *See* Viet Cong
venereal disease, 108–109
Veterans Administration (VA), 168, 169,
    178
    and Agent Orange, 184
    and PTSD, xviii, 179
Veterans of Foreign Wars (VFW), 20,
    162, 174
Viem Dong, 100
Viet Cong (VC), 93–95, 117–118
    See also enemy
Vietnam Veterans Against the War
    (VVAW), 171–173
Vietnam Veterans Leadership Program
    (VVLP), 173–174
Vietnam Veterans Memorial, 174, 184
    (photo), 185–189
Vietnam Veterans Memorial Fund
    (VVMF), 186
Vietnam Veterans of America (VVA),
    173
Vietnam Veterans Peace and Brotherhood
    Chapel, 186
Viet Nam Veterans II (painting), 175
    (photo)
Vietnamese allies. *See* allies; ARVN
Vietnamization, 138, 139

Vinh-Son Orphanage, 102
volunteerism, 4
  and African Americans, 29, 128
  and coercion, 12
  and Marines, 12
  and Native Americans, 32
  among women, 35
Vung Tau, 100, 109

W
Wannamaker, Woody, 139–140
Watt, James, 187
Wayne, John, 24–25
weapons training, 58–59, 62
Webb, James, 174, 187
Westphall, Jeanne, 186
Westphall, Victor, 186
Westphall, Victor, II, 186
West, Larry, xv, xvi, xviii
  See also Morenci Nine
Westmoreland, William (Gen.), 118, 127, 137
Wheeler, John, 173, 174

Whitmer, Van, xv, xvi
  See also Morenci Nine
Williams, John W., 119–120
"Winter Soldier" hearings, 154, 172
women, 24, 35–37, 48
  as caregivers, 36–37
  and dissent, 36
  roles for, 35
  motivations of, 35
  and prostitution, 108
  as snipers, 83
Wood, Donald (Lt.), 82
wounded, care of, 166, 179

Y
Ybarra, Sam, 176–177
Young, George (Brig. Gen.), 153

Z
Zulu (base camp), 73
Zumwalt, Elmo, Jr. (Adm.), 182–184
Zumwalt, Elmo, III, 183–184
Zumwalt, Russell, 183–184

About the Author

Kyle Longley is the Snell Family Dean's Distinguished Professor and professor of history at Arizona State University. He is the author of *The Sparrow and the Hawk: Costa Rica and the United States During the Rise of José Figueres* (1997), which received the A.B. Thomas Book Prize for outstanding book published in Latin American Studies from the Southeastern Council on Latin American Studies; *In the Eagle's Shadow: The United States and Latin America* (2002); *Senator Albert Gore, Sr.: Tennessee Maverick*; and editor of *Deconstructing Reagan: Conservative Mythology and America's Fortieth President* (M.E. Sharpe 2007). Professor Longley has also published numerous journal articles and essays, encyclopedia entries, and book reviews.